WITH STIRLING'S
SAS
IN THE DESERT

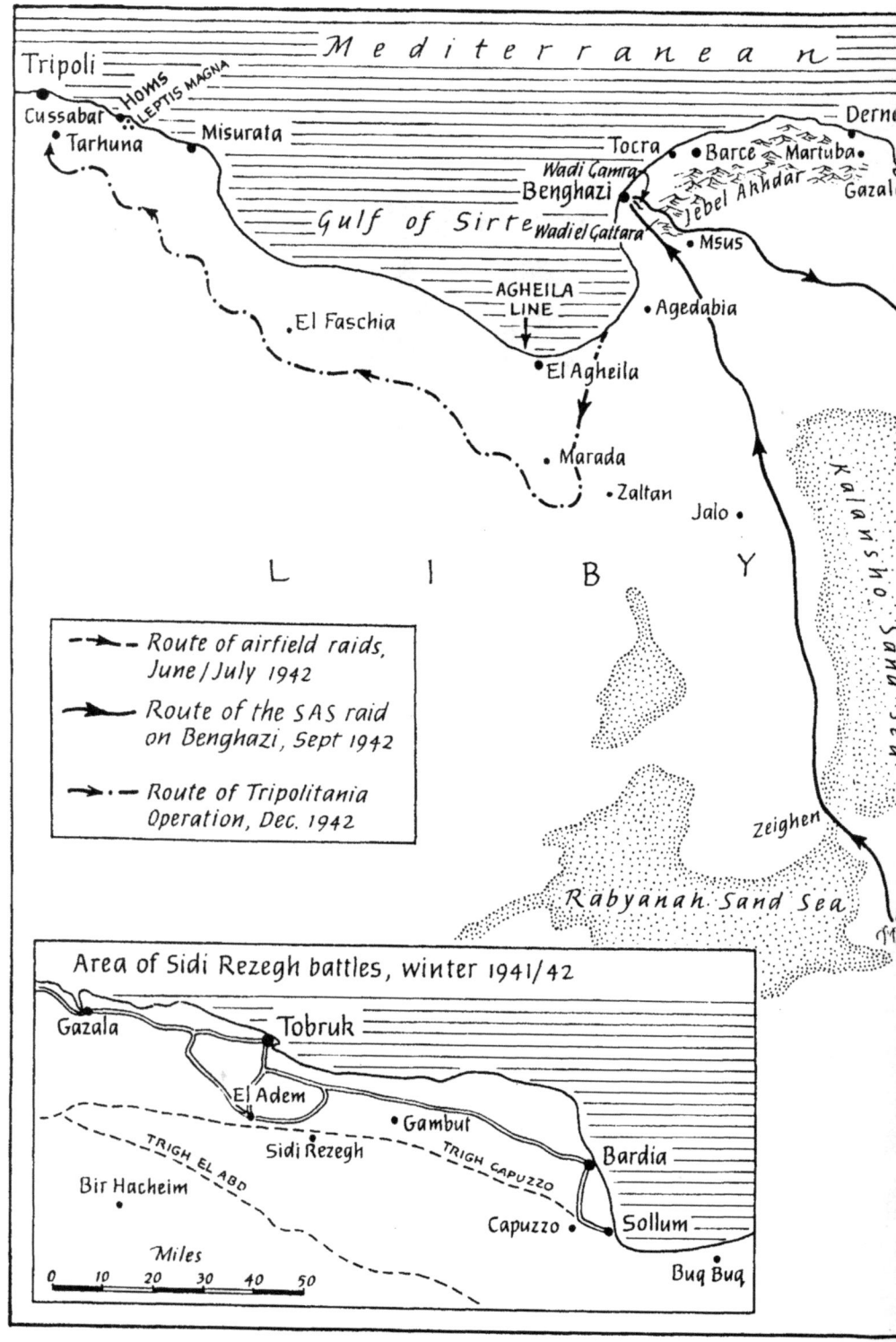

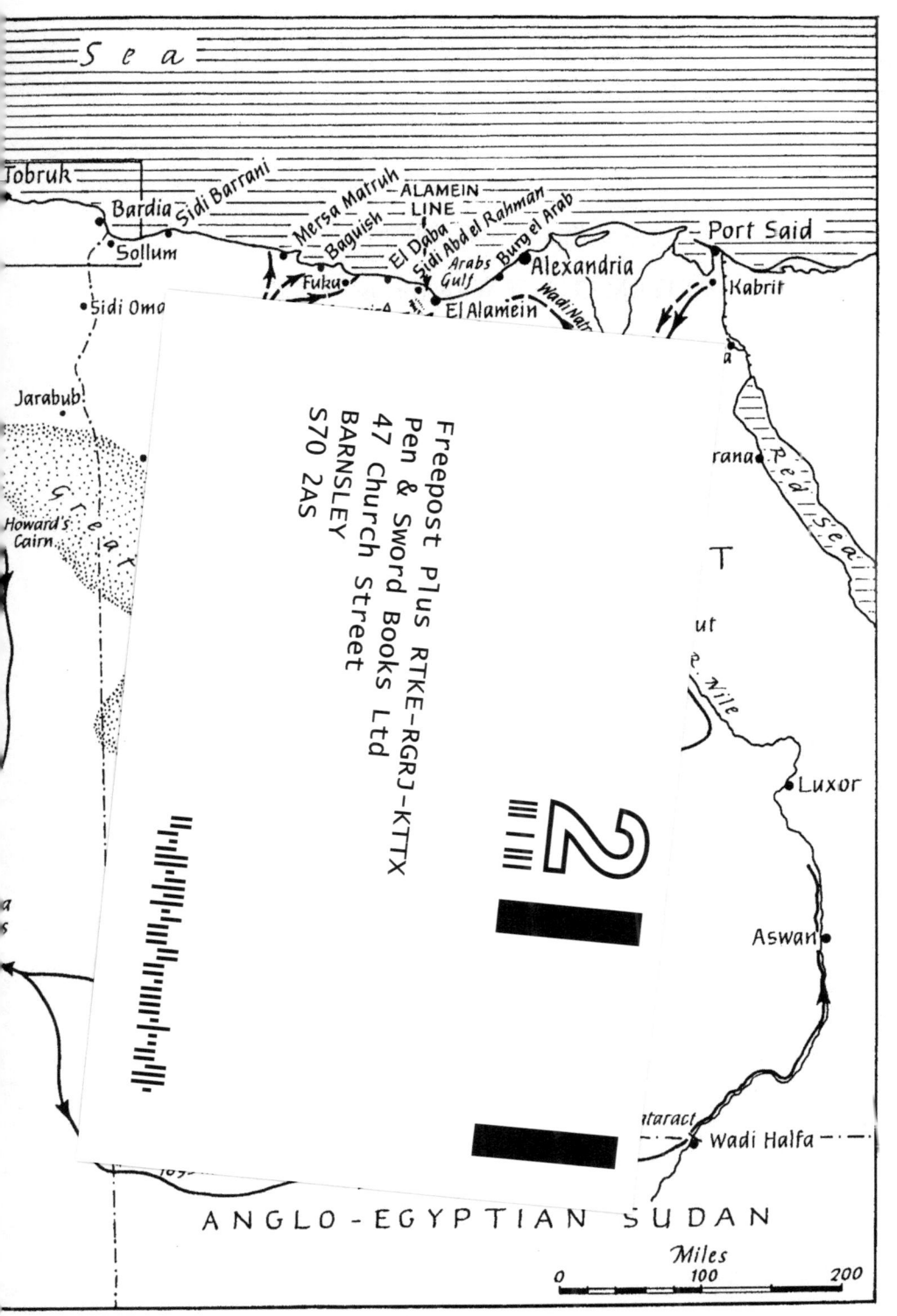

By the same author:

AFTERMATH OF WAR (Brassey's, 1992)

WITH STIRLING'S SAS IN THE DESERT

WHEN THE GRASS STOPS GROWING

by

Carol Mather MC

Pen & Sword
MILITARY

Originally published in 1997 as *When the Grass Stops Growing* and reprinted in 1999 by Leo Cooper

Reprinted in 2006 and republished in this format in 2021 by
Pen & Sword Military
An imprint of
Pen & Sword Books Ltd
Yorkshire – Philadelphia

Copyright © The Estate of Carol Mather, 1997, 1999, 2006, 2021

ISBN 978 1 52679 650 9

The right of Carol Mather to be identified as Author of this work has been asserted by him in accordance with the Copyright, Designs and Patents Act 1988.

A CIP catalogue record for this book is
available from the British Library

All rights reserved. No part of this book may be reproduced or transmitted in any form or by any means, electronic or mechanical including photocopying, recording or by any information storage and retrieval system, without permission from the Publisher in writing.

Printed in the UK by CPI Group (UK) Ltd, Croydon, CR0 4YY

Pen & Sword Books Limited incorporates the imprints of Atlas, Archaeology, Aviation, Discovery, Family History, Fiction, History, Maritime, Military, Military Classics, Politics, Select, Transport, True Crime, Air World, Frontline Publishing, Leo Cooper, Remember When, Seaforth Publishing, The Praetorian Press, Wharncliffe Local History, Wharncliffe Transport, Wharncliffe True Crime and White Owl.

For a complete list of Pen & Sword titles please contact

PEN & SWORD BOOKS LIMITED
47 Church Street, Barnsley, South Yorkshire, S70 2AS, England
E-mail: enquiries@pen-and-sword.co.uk
Website: www.pen-and-sword.co.uk

Or

PEN AND SWORD BOOKS
1950 Lawrence Rd, Havertown, PA 19083, USA
E-mail: Uspen-and-sword@casematepublishers.com
Website: www.penandswordbooks.com

TO PHILIPPA
Who shared the beginning and end of the story

CONTENTS

Introduction   xi
Part I – The Winter War

Chapter 1	Finland Overrun	3
Chapter 2	A Wild Goose Chase	9
Chapter 3	The Phoney War at Sandown Park	13

Part II – Commando Days

Chapter 4	The Steam-Operated Bren Gun	27
Chapter 5	'Ship Me Somewhere East of Suez'	33
Chapter 6	The Voyage of the *Aphis*	41
Chapter 7	The Seige of Tobruk	44
Chapter 8	Death of a Commando	49

Part III – The Western Desert War

Chapter 9	Phantom Patrol	57
Chapter 10	Sidi Rezegh – Baptism of Fire	62
Chapter 11	Forty Days On	68
Chapter 12	Out of the Line	74

Part IV – Desert Journeys I

Behind the Lines with the SAS

Chapter 13	Escarpment Rendezvous – The Airfield Raids	82
Chapter 14	The Mass Attack	90
Chapter 15	Crossing the Qattara Depression	98

Part V – Desert Journeys II

The Deep South

Chapter 16	Benghazi – 'Mission Impossible'	107
Chapter 17	Near Disaster in the Gilf Kebir	120
Chapter 18	Kufra Oasis and the Approach March	130

| Chapter 19 | Ambush! Death Wadi and Escape | 140 |
| Chapter 20 | South Across the Great Sand Sea | 153 |

Part VI – With Montgomery at Alamein

Chapter 21	Flashback	165
Chapter 22	'The Killing Grounds'	169
Chapter 23	Alamein Diary	175
Chapter 24	The Breakout	185
Chapter 25	A Fateful Decision	191

Part VII – Capture and Escape

Chapter 26	Journey's End	199
Chapter 27	Capture	204
Chapter 28	The Italian Submarine	209
Chapter 29	Life as a Prisoner of War	214
Chapter 30	Escape – The Long Walk Home	223
Chapter 31	Escape – Crossing the Lines	229
Chapter 32	End of Story	238

Part VIII – The Second Front – I Rejoin Montgomery

Chapter 33	Preparing for D-Day	243
Chapter 34	Normandy Landings	251
Chapter 35	Bizarre Encounters	257
Chapter 36	Visit of De Gaulle	263
Chapter 37	Motorbikes and Snipers	269
Chapter 38	Knocking at the Door	273
Chapter 39	The Arnhem Operation	279
Chapter 40	The Ardennes	284
Chapter 41	Ardennes Aftermath	292

Epilogue	298
Notes	300
Index	317

ACKNOWLEDGEMENTS

In the first place I would like to thank several of my wartime friends who have allowed me to quote from diaries or written accounts of the events described in this memoir.

In particular Toby Wake (Sir Hereward Wake Bt) who gave me access to his diary of the elusive ski battalion which never got to Finland. To Christopher Thursby-Pelham (Brigadier MC) and Johnny Retallack, joint editors of the monograph of Colonel 'Chicot' Leatham, and to Regimental Headquarters Welsh Guards. To the Scots Guards Regimental Headquarters for access to their archive on the 5th Battalion, including diaries and a unique collection of photographs, some of which I have permisssion to include. To David (Sir David) Hunt who gave me invaluable advice concerning the Benghazi raid and intelligence matters generally.

To Morgan Giles (Rear Admiral Sir Morgan) who provided a number of stories about our time in Tobruk. To Sandy Fletcher for research on quotations. To my brother Bill (Sir William) Mather for his recollections of the Battle of Alamein seen from General Lumsden's HQ. To Annette Street for assistance in describing her husband's escape.

To J.R. (Johnny) Henderson, former ADC to Montgomery, for reading and commenting upon the Ardennes chapters and for the photograph following my escape in Italy. To Claire Woodruffe for the photograph on the back cover. To Dorothy Thompson, executor of the late Frank Thomson. And to G.T. Clarke of Photocare, who restored some very old film.

I must acknowledge a debt to various authors whose works I have either quoted or used as factual background. Notably Nigel Hamilton, whose book *Monty The Field Marshal* gives a unique account of the

Ardennes affair. To Alastair Horne and David Montgomery, for their recent book *The Lonely Leader*; to Barrie Pitt whose book on the desert campaign, *The Crucible of War*, gave me the first intelligible insight into the battles in which I took part. I have also quoted from the works of Evelyn Waugh, a former comrade-at-arms, and from the description of the life of a young Guards Officer by Sir Osbert Sitwell in *Great Morning*. The late Tom Bingland's *War Letters 1941–1945* (he was British Liaison Officer to General Omar Bradley, commanding the American Armies in the Ardennes) has shed new light on an experience we both shared. To Dick Harden, fellow Liaison Officer, without whose skill this book might never have appeared!

To this long list of people to whom I am indebted I must add Christopher Dowling of the Imperial War Museum who read the manuscript and who gave me invaluable advice; and to Philip Dutton of the Imperial War Museum photographic library. I am also grateful to the Royal Geographical Society for allowing me to reprint extracts fom the RGS Journal. The Public Record Office at Kew has been an invaluable source of information, as has Her Majesty's Stationery Office's official War Histories, material from which has been reproduced by permission of the Controller. The Ministry of Defence has allowed me to describe certain military operations that took place in the Middle East.

Anita Rogers typed the manuscript throughout, and prepared the index, and I am very grateful to her for taking on this task in her spare time.

Lastly I must express my warmest thanks to Tom Hartman, who edited the work, and to Leo Cooper, my publisher, for a most agreeable and harmonious partnership.

INTRODUCTION

The pattern of life endlessly repeats itself. Cambridge 1939! Dreaming spires – the smack-smack of water lapping round the punts on the Backs. Trouble in some faraway country, of which we know nothing. Czechoslovakia! Poland!

Cambridge 1914! Ethereal buildings. The splosh of oars on the Cam. Trouble in some far away country. Serbia! Sarajevo!

The rhythm of the oars is the rhythm of life. We create a beautiful whirlpool as we sink the oar in the river. The boat speeds on, our imprint lingers for a moment, and fades as if it had never been.

It sounds depressing that we leave no human mark. But some, by chance, are destined to live through cataclysmic times, which leave a mark on the pages of history. This book is about one of those times in which I was fated to take part. It should not be read merely as an adventure story, but will, I hope, give an impression of the times in which we lived.

The notorious debate at the Oxford Union in 1933 sent the clear message to the country (and to some parts of the outside world) that the gilded youth of the country were effete and were not prepared to fight for 'King and Country'. This pathetic motion had a profound effect, triggering off a sharp reaction at Cambridge University. Here a group of undergraduates invited Winston Churchill, then in the political wilderness, to Cambridge to denounce this shameful declaration. At a packed meeting in the Corn Exchange a few years earlier, Churchill did just that with great effect – a foretaste of his wartime speeches. Those of us involved in this invitation were not active members of the Cambridge Union, but we had an uneasy feeling that the Oxford message might give a misleading signal to the outside world, exemplified by the power-hungry Adolf Hitler. My job was to let out a crate of pigeons after the speech was over but in my anxiety to get the timing right I let them out too soon and they invaded the platform with all too embarrassing results! However, the meeting was a rousing success and was well reported in the newspapers. For it seemed now as though war was well-nigh inevitable.

In a year's time I was to make up my mind what to do in life. In those days the world was one's oyster with the vast terrains of the British Empire to be ruled and administered. I favoured this course rather than staying at home. Generations of public schoolboys, and honours graduates, emerged from their studies well equipped to run all these far-flung territories. For such elite Services as the Sudan Political or Indian Civil Service a double first and a double blue were considered desirable qualifications. I hardly aspired to this, but perhaps I could find a rôle in some romantic frontier region.

Past generations had been able to use this inheritance as a vast playground, where adventurers, sportsmen, plant-collectors and climbers could follow their pursuits. But it was also a playground for the British idea of good government and administration, for health and the eradication of endemic disease, and for basic education, in continents that had only known tribal warfare since time immemorial. It was also synonymous with justice and decency and the now outmoded concept of 'fair play'.

The easy answer was to join the family firm. But I still had some wild oats to sow, and in the 'long vac' from Cambridge in the summer of 1939 (my second year) I departed on a journey of exploration to the Yukon and Alaska to visit the Klondike where there was still gold to be found.[1]*

The outbreak of war found me on my way back home, at Chicago. I had to wait for a boat, for the U-Boat menace had already started, and a long and circuitous Atlantic crossing had to be made.

But on landing in Britain after our Atlantic crossing it was not all doom and gloom. Admittedly there was the blackout, and the long banshee wail of the first air-raid sirens. But there was an overwhelming feeling of relief. At last we had taken a decision. People were steeled for a different life. And there were no regrets!

---

* See p 300 for reference notes.

PART I
THE WINTER WAR

The Winter War arose out of the notorious 'secret protocol' of the German-Soviet Pact, signed by the two foreign ministers, Ribbentrop and Molotov, on 23 August, 1939. This was a bare week before Poland was invaded. The secret provisions of the non-aggression pact allowed Germany and the Soviet Union to divide not only Poland but the Baltic States into 'spheres of influence'. On 1 September Hitler invaded Poland from the west. On 3 September Britain declared war. On 17 September Stalin drove in from the east. The Red Army was then in a position to march into the Baltic States which it lost no time in doing, and Stalin's ambition to win back the territories lost to Russia in 1918 was thereby gratified. The most important of these territories was Finland.

Stalin demanded land bases in Finnish territory. The appropriate 'diplomatic negotiations' were carried out with the Finns rejecting the Soviet proposals. Stalin then decided to strike. The **casus belli** *were a series of Soviet contrived explosions, 'the Manila Rounds', within Russian territory, purported to come from Finnish guns. On 1 January, 1940, the Soviet Army launched their attack. The Finns under Field Marshal Mannerheim were prepared and deployed in considerable strength across the Karelian Isthmus, the landbridge between Lake Ladoga and the Baltic Sea. Despite the overwhelming strength of the Soviet forces, in men and materials, the Finns inflicted upon them enormous losses.*

Although Britain was fully committed on the Western Front in Belgium and France, she yet deemed it necessary to give some help to Finland. On 3 January 1940, the Cabinet, under Prime Minister Chamberlain, agreed that 'our best point of attack on the whole structure of the enemies defences' might be Finland, given the supposed impregnability of Germany's Siegfried Line. The main problem was how to get our forces into Finland.

Scandinavia, it must be said, was of significance in that Sweden produced strategic raw materials essential for the war effort of either combatant.

And so it was that before the fighting on the Western Front had barely begun the scene was set for the opening of a second theatre of war.

1

FINLAND OVER-RUN – SEND IN THE CADETS!

In November, 1939, the Royal Military Academy at Sandhurst was in the process of a transition from peace to war. The last company of 'gentlemen cadets' was still in place, and the first company of wartime 'officer cadets' had been formed, but there was no uniform immediately available; instead, officer cadets wore chocolate-coloured fatigues. Until almost the end of the course some were without military headdress and wore tweed caps on parade. But these difficulties were made up for by the superb standard of officer and warrant officer instructors, all pre-war guardsmen.

Christmas, 1939, was a bitterly cold one. As an officer cadet on night patrol in the grounds of the Royal Military Academy, among the pine trees and the snow, I felt very close to the 'winter war'. News of the fighting dominated the newspapers. The gallant Finnish army were faced with overwhelming Russian odds, but they were fighting back and giving a very good account of themselves. Finnish ski troops in action and the corpses of Russian soldiers frozen into grotesque attitudes stared at one out of the pages of the daily newspapers. Field Marshal Mannerheim, the Finnish Commander-in-Chief, we all knew, was the hero of the day.[1]

Suddenly, out of the blue, there came a call for 'volunteers', for a secret assignment, destination unknown. Experienced ski-ers only need apply. Naturally those of us who were qualified leapt at the opportunity. A dozen or so cadets then left the Royal Military Academy, confident that the destination was Finland. Being a skier and knowing Finland as I did, I decided to volunteer.

What followed is one of the more bizarre episodes of the entire war. In retrospect it can be seen as a foolhardy venture, for the campaign was taking place in the depths of the arctic winter in one of the most inhospitable terrains in the world. It was not as if Britain was yet at war with Russia, or had even declared its intentions, apart from the fact that at that time the Ribbentrop-Molotov non-aggression pact was in operation, a marriage of convenience which only lasted a short time, but made the USSR and the German Reich allies in all but name.

The reason that officers and cadets were recruited in such large numbers into this battalion and volunteered to fight as private soldiers was for the simple reason that this was to be a ski-battalion and skiing at that time was a sport indulged in by only a select few.

The first thing I had heard was one morning when Captain Johnny Goschen, my Company Commander, announced in the Anteroom that 'a special unit was to be formed to operate in countries where snow conditions prevail'.

I told my platoon commander, John Harvey, that I should like to do it, and he advised me 'to sleep on it'. As I wrote,

> 'Everyone at once thought it was for Finland, which was then in the thick of a bloody war, and it was *very* cold! Very few people at Sandhurst thought it a good thing, all saying "it was crazy, and a wild goose chase – much better to get one's Commission in the Brigade where one was certain of a good place and security. And at any rate one was fighting for England and not for Finland. What was that war miles away in the north to do with us?"'

I had actually suggested to Johnny Goschen and one or two other officers at an earlier stage the idea of a ski battalion and they had pooh-poohed it. Soon it all died down and, as no one in authority seemed to know anything about it, and said that in any case nothing would happen till the end of the course, I went back to the dull routine.

Two days later a fellow cadet, Rupert Clarke, who had put his name down, got orders to move to Bordon Camp. This shook me out of my torpor and I rushed round to see the Adjutant, Company and Platoon commanders again. They all said 'too late'. In the meantime, fellow cadets Eric Hopton and Alastair Timpson and I had frantic discussions as to whether we should go or not.

> 'Eric dashed up to London and saw the Finnish Minister [at the Legation], who he reported as saying "My country needs you!", and promised him a castle at the end of the war! We all went

round seeing different people, until one evening out of the blue we were told we could go.'

It was a great moment. We were overcome with the thrill of it all.

'Great excitement. We were to leave by lunch-time the next day, hand in all our kit, draw webbing, new rifles and bayonets. It was wonderful to be leaving Sandhurst, but I also felt a little sorry to be leaving such a pleasant crowd of people, and not finish my course. My new bayonet had been sharpened, I discovered.'

Arriving at Bordon Camp we were interviewed by the second-in-command of the new battalion, Brian Mayfield. He asked how much ski-ing we had done.

'I opened up truthfully with "nine seasons", so of course the others had to follow suit. He seemed most impressed, and told us that we would be under fighting conditions in a very few weeks. Got organized, saw doctor. Scenes of immense activity; of an expeditionary force being got together in a very short time. Dinner at the Royal Anchor, Liphook, and to bed for the first time in a freezing barrack room, sleeping on three biscuits [the military mattress].'

Thus was formed the 5th (Special Reserve) Battalion of the Scots Guards, at Quebec Barracks, Bordon Camp near Aldershot. We assembled on 5 February, 1940. For us cadets it was no hardship to become guardsmen. But as all the rank and file had to be ski-ers the majority of officer volunteers had agreed to drop their rank and become private soldiers. When the call went out in January one thousand volunteers responded to the appeal, of whom 600 were serving officers and 180 civilians, some to wear uniform for the first time. As the Regimental Diary of the 5th Battalion explains:

'The Roll, as cosmopolitan a list of names as could readily be compiled, contained men from all parts of the British Empire, possessed of every imaginable form of human experience, Regulars, Territorials, veterans of the Spanish war, soldiers of fortune, undergraduates and all varying in age between twenty and forty.'[2]

For some, dropping rank was not so easy, as one former officer remarked, with some astonishment:

> 'I went rather scared into the men's dining hall and sat down. But there were a hundred faces I knew and I can honestly say that I had never seen such a marvellous collection of tough athletes. I don't suppose there has ever been a Bn. of such material.'[3]

So, the Scots Guards was the host regiment to an extraordinary polyglot and talented collection of individuals. All the pre-war generation of young explorers had joined. Arctic expertise was much in evidence. Officer Cadet J.M. Scott had been with Gino Watkins (whose younger brother was now in the battalion) in Labrador and Greenland. Martin Lindsay (in charge of sledging) and Quinton Riley had been members of the Gino Watkins British Arctic Air Route Expedition to Greenland in 1930–31, as had F. Spencer Chapman, his sledging assistant,[4] while Captain J.M.L. Gavin was a member of the 1936 Everest Expedition, as was Lieutenant E.H.L. Wigram, coming from the Royal Army Medical Corps. Another aspiring Everest man was Sergeant David Stirling, later to raise and command the SAS. Naval officers were also included. The veteran ski-er Bill Bracken represented an older ski-ing generation. The roll-call was a distinguished one. The sole criteria for this exclusive unit were the ability to cross country and fight on skis. The Commanding Officer was a Coldstreamer, Jimmy (J.S.) Coats, a distinguished skier and exponent of the famous Cresta Run, a fine leader we all thought.[5]

Apart from drawing kit and rifles the routine was as follows. Early morning PT with strenuous exercises for ski-ing muscles. Drill on the Square followed by a route march in the afternoon.

> 'The route march was very funny, two people in the newfangled battledress, and the rest officers without their pips. Two in kilts, three in field boots carrying canes, and others carrying walking sticks. Two Scots Guards sergeants brought up the rear.'

The regular sergeants did not know quite what to make of us. Instead of 'fall in sharp gentlemen and get a move on!', as it had been at Sandhurst, it was now, addressing the rank and file, a polite request, 'Would you mind taking your place, sir, the parade is about to commence!' However, I noted that the RMA contingent 'was by far the smartest, most of the others had no idea at all, including the officers'.

More and more friends and acquaintances kept on arriving: George Jellicoe, David Russell and Brodie Knight from Sandhurst, Brian Kent, an ensign from the Welsh Guards training battalion. It was becoming more and more fun, all these old friends whom one had last seen on the peaceful slopes of Davos or Klosters.

One evening Alastair Timpson and I returned to Sandhurst to collect our kit and say goodbye.

'I sat next to John Harvey at dinner and got slightly tight. After dinner we had a heated discussion in the passage about the whole thing. John Harvey couldn't have been more against it. A waste of good officers he thought; and that this was nothing to do with us.'

As the evening went on we became more and more merry. Alastair and I climbed onto the roof, 'it was a lovely night and we could see for miles,' and from this vantage point, astride the roof ridge of the RMA, we felt on top of the world.

Back at Bordon Camp the great moment then arrived when the Regimental Lieutenant Colonel Commanding the Scots Guards and the Major General Commanding the Brigade of Guards[6] came down to visit us. These dignitaries struck a rather incongruous note given the nature of the battalion now under their command. It was therefore with some speculation on both sides that we paraded in the gym.

Squatting on the floor before them were Arctic explorers, Everest men, lean-faced men from the colonies, officers from all arms and services, and the *jeunesse dorée* of the ski-ing world in their unaccustomed uniform.

Jimmy Coats addressed us first and announced that the French Government had agreed to our doing a fortnight's ski-training with the Chasseurs Alpins at Chamonix in Haute Savoie. Cheers all round! Hats in the air!

The Colonel then told us that we must not let down the reputation of the Regiment. And we thought of the motto on our cap badges: *nemo me impune lacessit*, 'no one strikes me with impunity'. And it is true that we were immensely proud and somewhat overawed to be members of such a famous regiment, and to share with them the adventures and hardships which lay ahead. In his final words the Major General bade the troops 'God speed and a victorious return'. 'Luckily at the time no one realized how ironical this blessing would prove to be.' [SG]

> 'Simultaneously with the order for formation Colonel Coats received the date, March 1st, by which he was expected to have his Battalion ready and equipped for service overseas. Thus, from the outset, no more than twenty-three days were available for the assembly, organization, military training, equipment, inoculation and general preparation of a force of men collected at the shortest of notice not only from all ranks and branches of the Army throughout the world, but also from civil life as well. Already saddled with the sufficient problem of commanding a battalion (inadequately equipped without one wireless set), altogether unique in conception and unparalleled in content he was evidently expected to perform the miraculous in addition.' [SG]

Meantime we were not confined to camp. Wives and girlfriends collected at the Spread Eagle Hotel at Liphook. There was excitement and speculation in the air as well as tender farewells. At last we were going to do something. Perhaps we would fire the first real shots of the war.

But the official account highlights one alarming deficiency.

> 'It was only in the last few days of the month that their [the men's] sole armament, the new No. 4 Lee Enfield rifle, arrived, and it was then and then only, that the alarming fact was discovered that a considerable number of the rank and file had never before in all their lives handled, let alone fired, a service rifle.' [SG]

2

A WILD GOOSE CHASE

Just before departure, and much to our chagrin, four of our 'X' Company men, Eric Hopton, David Russell, John Cripps and myself had been posted to 1st Reinforcements. This annoyed us a lot as we thought we might be left behind. Eric believed we might have blotted our copybooks with Captain Ryder, our company commander, a very dour gentleman, who was probably not amused by our nightly trips to London for farewell parties, arriving back in barracks barely in time for first parade. On one of these occasions Guardsman B. Kent (in reality Ensign Brian Kent of the Welsh Guards) arrived on parade in a dark blue suit, bowler hat and umbrella. However, we were all four good skiers and we figured that they needed us perhaps more than we needed them! Sergeant John Cripps (formerly Captain Cripps of the 60th Rifles KRRC), had become Platoon Sergeant of 1st Reinforcements. No more incongruous appointment could be imagined, for although he was no doubt a good officer he was not a good sergeant, his main inability being to get the right number of men on parade!

As we marched from the Camp to the station it was not 'Hielan' Laddie' that we sang, like good Scots Guardsmen, but an irreverent version of 'The Keelrow'. We had already had our share of 'order, counter-order and disorder'!

'The mug tied to the haversack. No, the mug to be tied to the outside of the pack. No – the mug to be put inside the haversack.'

And so it went on! And the refrain went something like this:

'The whole thing's a balls-up, a balls-up, a balls-up! The whole thing's a balls-up – the 5th Scots Guards!'

Followed by a series of impromptu verses, one of which I recall.

'Colonel Coats has burnt his boats, and left his skis behind!'

We were not all amateur private soldiers. We had with us a regular company of Scots Guardsmen, Y Company, led by a magnificent-looking pre-war Guards Officer, Captain R.D.M. Gurowski, of Polish extraction I believe, whose figure and bearing would have adorned any *Spy* cartoon. These men were put in as a stiffener and to do the jobs we were not trained to do.

As the train drew out of the station a hundred heads were craning out of the windows, and this time it was the sentimental refrain of 'Goodbye Sally, I'm saying Goodbye,' only in this case it was 'Goodbye Bordon!'

> '6 privates in great coats, with 6 kit bags, 6 rifles, 6 packs, gas masks, gas capes and equipment in a 3rd class compartment was quite a new experience for me, but everyone was so witty and it was so exciting not having the vaguest idea where we were heading for.... How could any of us have a care or worry in the world?' (HW)

As to our final destination, speculation was rife.

> 'We were almost certainly going up the Dardanelles into the Black Sea, land in the Caucasus and make our way across to Baku on the Caspian to smash up the Russian oil wells and pipe line.
>
> 'Some still thought we were going to Finland by making a forced landing at Petsamo, already captured by the Russians, or even forcing our way up the Baltic.
>
> 'Others thought we might land in Norway or Sweden to cut across to Finland while even wilder people thought we were going to capture the Swedish iron ore districts to prevent export to North Russia and cut the Murmansk Railway: apparently the whole expedition is Ironside's pet at the War Office and isn't he the very man who knows all about Murmansk.'[1] (HW)

Happily speculating about our future movements, we reached Southampton. Here we boarded the 'grey and shabby' *Ulster Prince*. Our first duty was boat drill, as the Channel was a prey to enemy submarines, but our destroyer escort raised our morale, also our sense of self-esteem. To think that we were really worth a destroyer escort! Landing at Dieppe, and weighed down with heavy equipment, we marched towards our train, as I recalled,

> 'John as usual lost half of us and I had to struggle off with full equipment to look for them all. Eric and I had hysterics, for whilst I was doing up his shoulder buttons, the order "Advance!" was given, and everyone marched straight through us, and we were left a struggling heap on the floor.
>
> 'By a brilliant piece of initiative we obtained a compartment on the train, eight of us with full equipment crammed into a six-seater. David Gavin (known as 'Davers'), an old friend, occupied the place next to me. His teddy bear caused a big stir about 2 a.m. by getting lost, and again at 4 a.m. by sitting with his back to the engine and feeling sick!' (CM)

We were finally awakened by the cry of 'Arrest those Frenchmen!' They had apparently boarded the train by mistake. We were dreadfully hush-hush and no one was allowed to know who we were or where we were going. Passing soldiers took an inordinate interest in our Mk 4 Lee Enfield rifles, the like of which had apparently never been seen before.

But after an all-night journey, next morning we arrived at the little town of St Gervais-les-Bains-le-Fayet. Where are we? We can smell the mountain air! We are miles away from the British Expeditionary Force and see nothing of them.

> 'What fun it was to be the focus of so much attention. One wondered whether British troops had ever been seen in this part of France before and as we went along we were cheered and women rushed to the windows and hurriedly opened them to watch "Les Tommies" go by.' (HW)

We transfer to a mountain train and at 1.30 p.m. arrive at the *Chasseurs Alpins* base at Chamonix, under the massive Mont Blanc, where we are accorded a civic reception. Needless to say our arrival at Chamonix was announced to the world by the English traitor Lord Haw-Haw, broadcasting from Berlin. He failed to mention the fact that we had arrived without our skis, for the heavy baggage did not come for a further three days, as French Railways evidently thought that British equipment should go to the Western Front. However, this was time enough to discover another little difficulty. 'Armies have always marched on their stomachs and so also must ski-battalions. However, natural and willing cooks are hardly to be found from amongst a party of volunteer skiers!' (SG)

I wrote this description of our arrival at Chamonix.

> 'Generals met us, and a band marched us through the main streets, with people cheering *"Bravo les Anglais!"* This was more like it! The sun was shining and we were terribly hot in our greatcoats and equipment. When we came to a patch of ice in the road, we all fell down, which was very funny.'

John Cripps's twenty-seven men of the 1st Reinforcements were billeted in the *Patinoire*, the changing room of the ice hockey club. It was freezing cold, and the straw palliasses were as hard as iron. To open the windows was to freeze to death; to close them meant the room stank unbearably.

Very shortly after we arrived a great do was prepared for us by the Chasseurs at the Casino. We were most hospitably entertained, but some of the regular guardsmen who were present proceeded to take over the mike on the stage and gave drunken renderings of *Roll Out the Barrel*, *Kiss Me Goodnight Sergeant Major*, and *We'll Hang Out the Washing on the Siegfried Line* 'which the Chasseurs did not appreciate'. In fact they never understood how some of the 'guardsmen' spoke excellent French, drank wine and remained sober, whilst others knew not a word of French, drank beer and became roaring drunk.

During our stay at Chamonix companies were left to their own devices and we organized treks across country on skis and hauling sledges. The NCOs went to see a demonstration of sledging. A captain, turned NCO, explains,

> 'The sledge fully loaded weighs the devil of a lot. It takes 5 men to pull and one to push. What we want to know is what happens when a burst of M.G. fire kills one and wounds two out of the eight men in the section. Presumably you leave them, or the sledge, or both, and run. However, if your scouts work well you should never be surprised. . . . There are heaps of problems to be solved.
>
> 'There are no automatic weapons in the bn. so our job will be

never to get committed if we can help it. Tip and run like the cavalry and "see without being seen". Reconnaissance and Protection will be our duties.' (HW)

One day we were breakfasting at *La Poste*. The Italian Alps looked down on Chamonix. Italy was not yet in the war, but the papers were full of the fact that we had sunk an Italian coal ship, and rumour had it that Italy had already declared war on us.

'We all rushed out onto the street holding half-eaten rolls to see if we could see their ski-troops ski-ing down Mont Blanc.'

But, despite our warm reception, the *119e Bataillion des Chasseurs de Haute Montaigne* was not very keen on accompanying us to those high mountains, for their Colonel had confined them to the valley for fear of avalanches. Our brief time at Chamonix was a glorious escape from wartime England. Some camp followers from the Spread Eagle Hotel were even ensconced in the local hotels, but it was not war nor training for war. With the deterioration of things in Finland, (for this, it was now clear, was to be our destination), it was no surprise to receive orders 'to pack up and proceed to a port from which we would embark'.

'This had been preceded by a most mysterious message from London which asked if we had a Hindustani speaker. More wild rumours – it was to be Tibet! In the absence of a pre-arranged code it was evidently considered that this language would confuse the enemy. However, Lord Haw-Haw got it right again and predicted our departure time as "seven o'clock on the morning of Monday 11th March". He was only ten minutes out and that was the fault of the French train.' (SG)

The definitive message when it came was passed to us by the Chasseurs:

'Paris 8 Mars
Guerre à Commandant d'Armes Chamonix.
Pour remettre à 5e Garde Ecossaise à Chamonix
Expediteur brassard par Madelon.
Preparez vous à embarquer par train onze mars pour un port d'où vous partierez le 12.'

The formalities were completed with this reply from our CO:

> *'Je regrette que le grippe m'oblige me garder mon lit, et que je n'ai pas pu vois écrire moimême . . . la première rencontre du magnifique 199e Bataillon de Chasseurs de Haute Montaigne, que vous avez l'honneur de Commander, et le 5e Bataillon des Gardes Ecossaises serent pour moi, à jamais, de très precieux souvenirs.'* (SG)

The day before departure Brodie Knight and I, with desperate cunning, managed to hire a guide for a ski tour up the Brévan to Les Aiguillettes. Unfortunately we are apprehended near the *Gare* and ordered by an officious officer to join in a loading party. We appeal to the Adjutant, Digby Raeburn, who is charming and lets us go, followed by the muttered oaths of the officious loading officer who calls after us 'Shirkers! Slackers!' We congratulate ourselves, for we are the only ones to take the initiative, and should have been commended instead of insulted. The day turns out to be a huge success. That evening we go to a *Boîte de Nuit*

> 'where tremendous celebrations are going on. A Radio-Gram is blaring out *Tristesse* and that other haunting song of the day, *J'Attendrai*, and lots of very attractive French girls whose presence we have only just become aware of, but rather late in the day.'

We parade at the HQ Hotel at 4.30 a.m. There is no sign of John, our platoon sergeant. Just as the train is about to depart he comes rushing up with his kit half on and half off, perspiring heavily and murmering, 'Just made it old boy – God what a night!'

Last night there was an unseemly incident in *Le Patinoire*. Many of the Reinforcements came in late and very drunk. No one volunteered to turn out the lights. Eventually Eric, who is on the next palliasse to me, erupts, stumps down the gangway and crashes straight through a plate glass door which he fails to see. He is covered in blood, collapses onto the floor. Davers, who is adept at this kind of thing, staunches the blood and bandages him up. So impressed is Eric by this treatment that he offers David Gavin 5/- a day to stay with him and be his bodyguard in Finland!

> 'We rattled down the valley in our mountain train, our hearts heavy as we leant out of the windows and watched the last

familiar peaks disappear. John continues to lean out to get the last glimpse of Chamonix.'

He is humming *J'Attendrai*. Goodbye the mountains, the bars, the camp-followers, the little French girls. Goodbye the floppy berets and pencil-bearded comrades of the Chasseurs. Goodbye the place where the chamois live, we are at last off to war, untrained, unprepared, but bound for a glorious adventure!

Once again we change trains at St Gervais-les-Baines-le-Fayet. Then the awful scramble to bag a compartment with friends, with kit-bags, equipment, rifles, loaves of bread, bottles of wine all being thrown through the windows.

> 'It was very pleasant going through Haute Savoie with its delightful forests, hills and châteaux. We slept and read and talked about ski-ing and other pleasant things, and at every *Gare* there was a terrific rush for food, wine and cigarettes, as there was none supplied.'

Rumours crept round the whole time, that we were going to be disbanded, going to Finland, the Caucasus or Scotland.

> 'And then we slept and woke up with vines growing, and sloping red-roofed houses. So we knew we were bound for Marseilles and the Caucausus. But then the sun was in the wrong place! None of the stations had names, which made it more difficult.'

Then Le Havre . . . boarded SS *Ben-my-Chree* . . . fog in Channel. Crossing the Channel we were signalled from ashore 'You are urgently required in Southampton,' and then repeated.

> 'What could have been more exciting than that,' writes one of our men, 'the train was already waiting to take us up to Scotland when without a minute to waste we would be put on board a boat for Scandinavia. Probably another two divisions were waiting for us . . . the Airforce and Navy are waiting to protect us. . . . My God, this looks like a good show. Excitement reached fever pitch as we recklessly steamed through the fog. At last, boys, we're going to be in a show; we're going to get our teeth into something and the war's going to begin.' (HW)

Southampton . . . issue of tea at Birmingham . . . George V dock at Glasgow . . . embark on the Polish Motor Vessel *Baretry*. Is this a 'ghost-ship'? There are other troops on board identically equipped as ourselves.

Early next morning we are due to sail for passage through Scandinavia to Finland. But the Swedes, however, absolutely refuse to give any help to Finland! But next morning brings doleful news. The Finns and Russians have signed an Armistice! The war is off! How could they have done so? There is no rôle for a ski-battalion! We are to be disbanded! Morale collapses. This is a complete let-down. Our newly-bonded fellowship devoted to the common purpose of sport and war is at an end. And then the crude chorus, to the jogging of the Keelrow is heard again. This is taken up on all sides of the ship, and I am sure could be heard throughout the King George V Dock. (How this lusty singing would have heartened the Finnish ski-troops had they heard it before their collapse!)

In point of fact we have had a lucky reprieve, for in no way could we have survived the rigours of the campaign, as the following post-mortem report makes clear.

> 'The conclusion reached from the experience of the British Ski-Battalion is how unfit this battalion was to fight under the special conditions for which it was formed.'

No study had been made of this type of warfare, and therefore no tactics or proper equipment had been evolved. Having been formed in such a hurry, the Battalion was quite untrained in the tactics of arctic warfare. Only 25 per cent of its potential efficiency could be expected in the early stages of a campaign! About one fifth had only 3 days on skis, and therefore could not ski. About one sixth had no military experience or were specialists, and therefore could not shoot. Only about one in five knew how to use a primus stove or how to fit skins on skis. Only one man in fifty had used snowshoes or knew how to haul a sledge. A high degree of frostbite and snow blindness was expected.[2]

There were over 600 officer volunteers from all arms which made up all ranks of the battalion. One of the consequences was piquantly expressed as follows:

> 'Perhaps the greatest difficulty which faced companies was cooking. The scale required was one cook per platoon, and hardly a single man in the ranks had ever been near a kitchen in his life.'

Colonel E.W.S. Balfour, then commanding the Regiment, had the last word. Apart from the 'astonishing personnel' that was collected he was satisfied that the spirit and organization was up to standard. And one can hear his heartfelt sigh of relief as he ends his letter:

> 'The Battalion is now being wound up . . . and I hope that this most extraordinary episode in the history of the Regiment will be finished by the middle of the month.'

The military authorities having made one bad mistake in creating us, then made another in disbanding us, for with a few months' hard training, and weeding out the weaker elements, we could have played a useful part in the Norwegian campaign in May, which followed hard upon the evacuation of the BEF at Dunkirk.

Perhaps I should say, before ending on too lugubrious a note, that the 'cadets' were mostly in their early twenties, had not a care in the world, were probably more capable of looking after themselves than most of the 'de-gazetted' officers, could probably ski better, were much much fitter and, consequently, could run faster!

Indeed 'this extraordinary episode' contains a mystery which has never been properly solved. Where were we actually going?

Churchill's Private Secretary at the time, the late Jock Colville, has one solution to the problem. In his *Downing Street Diaries*, published in 1985, he says that the passage of the 'volunteers', by way of Narvik through Norway and Sweden was 'a cover plan' for the seizure of the Swedish iron-ore fields at Gallivare, then thought so essential for the German prosecution of the war. An alternative was for the ski-battalion to land at Petsamo. Discussions were taking place with the French at this time (the PM visited Paris on 5 February) with a view to joint Anglo-French landings at Narvik and Petsamo. There was also planning for a major allied landing at Murmansk as soon as the spring thaw had set in, with a view to opening up a Second Front against the Russo-German alliance.

With such amateur and enthusiastic enterprises did we begin the war. It would be many a year before the British Army turned into true professionals, as the following pages will recall. But among the rank and file of this unit there lurked some extraordinarily adventurous characters who were to make their mark in a big way, as the war progressed.

However, the story would be incomplete without the following tailpiece. For our disembarkation leave John Cripps asked me to join him climbing in North Wales.

This was an unnerving experience, for although I had climbed before I had never been led by such a climber as John Cripps. The 'leader' on a rock face, where two men are roped together, is supposed to 'belay' himself to a prominent anchorage, round which he can pass the rope. He then keeps the rope taut, as the No. 2 climbs up to join him, thus lessening his partner's fall should he slip.

'Take in the slack,' I call up to John as I begin my climb.

'I can't,' he calls back. 'You might pull me off!'

However, it all ended happily ever after, for on return to John's home at Ampney Park, Cirencester, I met the girl I was later going to marry. This was Philippa, then aged 13, John Cripps's niece.

3

THE PHONEY WAR AT SANDOWN PARK

The phoney war, strictly speaking, came to an end once the Germans had launched the *Blitzkrieg* in the west. But shortly after the remains of the British Expeditionary Force (BEF) had extracted itself from France, a second period of stalemate began.

After the abortive Finnish Expedition I was posted to the Welsh Guards Training Battalion at Roman Way Camp near Colchester. Miraculously I found myself commissioned as an ensign, although I had missed the last six weeks of my Sandhurst course and the usual passing-out procedures.

Surprisingly I cannot remember anything remarkable about my interview with the Regimental Lieutenant Colonel, Chicot Leatham, about whom so many legendary tales are told, but I can remember the *ambience* of the sacred grove where I attended him.

This consisted of a series of miniature Doric temples on the very edge of Birdcage Walk, now sadly disappeared. There was one for each regiment of Footguards, their classic outline by then dulled by battleship grey paint.

There had been scarcely any change in the proceedings since this description of the summons of a newly-joined ensign just before the First World War.

'Ushered almost at once into the august presence, he would be obliged to salute . . . as smartly as he could the idol seated at a desk, behind the cloud of incense composed of his own cigarette smoke. Directly the ensign beheld the old image, who would be puffing at a substantial but delicately aromatic Turkish or Egyptian cigarette, he would realize that here before him was the improbable realization of an ideal . . . cherished by a considerable number of contemporaries . . . including all the best tailors and haberdashers, hosiers, shoemakers and barbers in London.'

But the idol had another rôle,

> 'Besides being so important a military mandarin, the Lieutenant-Colonel was, as well, an institution comparable to that of an Elder in the monasteries of the Russian Orthodox Church, healing and bestowing advice or reprimands.'[1]

A typical story of an interview with Chicot Leatham is told by a fellow officer Christopher Thursby-Pelham.

> 'Arthur Evans went in ahead of me. He had a characteristically brisk way of marching and halting. On this occasion he was unlucky. From outside we heard Arthur come to a crashing halt, followed by a prolonged scraping noise. . . . He had marched up to the table behind which the Lieutenant-Colonel was sitting. When he halted, his feet shot away from beneath him and he finished up underneath the table with his legs on each side of a pair of highly polished field boots. Before he could scramble to his feet, the Great Man spoke "Where has the fellow gone to now?"'[2]

Chicot Leatham, for all his seemingly blimpish remarks, was no fool. He was as shrewd a judge of men as any. Every inch a Guardsman, tall and imposing, he was a magnificent sight in blue forage cap, blue-grey greatcoat (with a touch of red lining showing), hawkish nose and upturned moustache. In a way he lampooned himself, having behind the mask a well-developed sense of humour.

Our time at Roman Way Camp happened to coincide with the collapse of British and French Forces in France and Belgium and the evacuation from Dunkirk. At this stage in our new career as officers, we were indoctrinated into the meticulous details of dress and deportment. If the adjutant was dissatisfied with the appearance of a young ensign and he spotted some irregularity in his dress he was wont to exclaim 'Dirty buttons! Put your servant in the Book'. The ensign, so embarrassed by many aspects of this new world, would then be obliged to report his hapless soldier-servant to the Company Commander before whom he would be marched and given one or two extra drills for idleness, or, if he were lucky, admonished. The matter of dress was part of the mystique of the Brigade of Guards. It was the antidote to idleness, sloppiness and lack of self-respect.

So when the remains of the BEF escaped from France, and the stragglers aboard the little ships made their way across the Channel, some arrived at the port of Harwich, where we met them at the dockside. No more incongruous sight can be imagined than the tender young officers in their new service dress uniform, blue forage caps laced with gold, ash-plant (the ubiquitous walking stick) in gloved hand, organizing the disembarkation of this battered remnant. Battle-stained, faces black, with torn uniform, many without their personal weapons. Some walking-wounded, others on stretchers. They presented an alarming and heart-rending sight, as with typical British humour they made light of their ordeal. It was a defeated army. I had never seen one before, and it bit deep into my subconscious. Hard upon this came the invasion scare. Officers and men from the training battalion were out manning the church towers as lookout posts, and in defensive position along the coastline armed only with rifles, and no other aids to modern warfare. The invasion scare came and went (for the first time), and very soon we transferred to Sandown Park, the racecourse at Esher, in Surrey, which became a permanent home.

A former officer writes,

'In spite of the Fall of France, the ejection of the British Expeditionary Force from the Continent, the failure to resist the Germans in Norway and the heavy nightly bombing of London during the winter of 1940/41, morale was high. . . . Young officers, clear of duty, made for London as soon as the last parade of the day was over, spent most of their time in the night clubs and returned to Sandown Park in time for Breakfast Parade.'[3]

Following one of these excursions I found myself up before the Adjutant, Captain the Lord Delamere. 'Are you a mad officer!' he enquired as I stood before his desk. The mildness of his expression concealing an undercurrent of menace. What had got into me? How had I got into this jam, I wondered?

I had been late for breakfast parade two mornings running and had now failed to be on time even when ordered to attend his morning memorandum to explain my behaviour. The correct answer to the question he had posed was 'Sir!' No more and no less. It was a regimental tradition. It really meant, 'I have heard and understood', the ambiguity of it being quite useful. Tom Delamere was a little chap with rather a red face. He exploded. I was dealt with summarily and awarded the exemplary punishment of 14 days' extra picquets.[4]

This effectively meant that I was gated and could not leave the camp. Many of my brother officers thought this was rather harsh. However, good can come out of evil, or rather one should seize the opportunities that arise from a downturn in fortune. This black mark facilitated my departure a few weeks later for active service, whilst so many others languished in the UK for the greater part of the war.

But now I was confined to camp. In a way I was a universal benefactor, for I had relieved fourteen officers of an irksome daily task, and for future beneficiaries I compiled a book which became the Picquet Officer's manual containing everything the aspiring young officer would wish to know.

Sandown Park racecourse was a most unsuitable place for a training camp. Apart from a wooded knoll there was no green grass at all except that of the racecourse itself which was as flat as a pancake. The 'lines' were a long row of loose boxes, occupied by the men (four to a box) with the company office in another. The officers' quarters in the grandstand were almost as disagreeable as those of the men. The mess hall in which the battalion ate was the former Tote building constructed of wood and corrugated iron. Here the daily ritual took place of the Picquet Officer's inspection of the men's dinners. The Master Cook clad in white jacket and trousers would call the men up. They would sit to attention. The Picquet Officer accompanied by a suitable escort would cry,

'Any complaints?'
'Come on lads, let's hear it!'

shouts the Master Cook, and as if with one voice the reply would come:
'Nooo – Sir!'.

Any variation of this routine might have been the subject of a classic cartoon in the 'guardsman who dropped it' tradition.

Peacetime habits were dying hard, and officers were still parading 'on the square' (the cinder-track car park) in service dress or in field service order, khaki plus-fours, boots and puttees. But the drab battledress had already made its appearance, and with it came a minute but important change. The bootlace, instead of being brown cord as for officers boots, was now for both officers and men the black ammunition boot, laced with a leather thong. It was the job of the officer's servant to be present to dress his officer, taking care that no lace was twisted. If the Adjutant espied a twisted lace upon an officer's boot then the hapless servant would be 'put in the book'.

Now, this must be thought a harsh and unjust system quite out of keeping with the 20th century and notions of modern war. But everyone knew the rules of the game and a feeling of mutual understanding and respect soon grew up between the officer and his servant, as perhaps between the knight and his esquire in days gone by, whence this system had no doubt derived. And, laughable as it may seem today, the idea of personal service was a compelling ideal, sometimes leading to lifelong friendships. What class-conscious arrogance, some may say, that one man owes personal service to another. But be not so hasty in judgement. Wait till active service comes along and the relationship is fired and consolidated in battle. For the officer must at all times set an example to the men, in turnout as well as in bearing, and he must be relieved of mundane chores to achieve this end if he is to concentrate upon the real business of leadership, where men's lives may be saved as well as lost.

The honourable duty of 'officer's servant', a role that probably no longer exists in recognizable form, played a not ignoble part in all this turmoil of fifty years ago.

Chicot's selection of officers for the regiment was cast on liberal lines and represented many different professions or occupations in civilian life. There were writers and artists, notable amongst whom was the eminent society portrait painter Simon Elwes, and the artist, muralist and stage designer Rex Whistler. There was a charming wooden stand which Rex had adapted as his studio, and I remember watching enthralled, as with great rapidity he painted a portrait, with the rolling (as it was then) Surrey landscape as background.

Bill Glanusk was commanding officer of the training battalion. He had served in the Great War, and with his tall spare figure was an imposing presence. Like Chicot Leatham he was a former Grenadier who had helped to form the Welsh Guards in 1915. He wore a flat cap at a slightly jaunty angle, more like a bus conductor's.

I am indebted to a brother officer for yet another story concerning these eminent characters.

'When Francis Egerton[5] . . . was commissioned and joined the training battalion, he took with him a smallish black French poodle called "Louis", who quickly became popular with all ranks. Louis was a clever little dog with a number of tricks, such as jumping over an outstretched arm and so on. Soon Chicot came to visit the battalion and quickly espied Louis.

'"Good heavens what's that?" he exclaimed and then demanded to see his owner. Francis appeared and saluted, and then. . . . Bill Glanusk, rather mischievously suggested that Louis be put through his full repertoire of tricks. This was done to the astonishment of the Lieutenant Colonel, who finally said, not unkindly, "Foot Guards Officers normally have Labrador retrievers".'[6]

But life at Sandown Park, however diverting, was not war and at this stage in the affair the last thing I wanted was to be stuck in England. Fortune now dealt me a better card. Unexpectedly, volunteers were called for to form a mysterious unit called 'a commando' whose function, it was hinted, was to carry out raids against enemy territory. I immediately applied and was allowed to go. Perhaps my brush with Tom Delamere had done the trick.

At the beginning of August, Jock Lewis, a fellow ensign, and myself led a party of about twenty Welsh Guardsmen from Sandown Park to Woking, where we were billeted in a Victorian boathouse on the River Wey, but this was only a staging post, for very soon we were off to our rallying point 'somewhere in England'.

PART II
COMMANDO DAYS

4

THE STEAM-OPERATED BREN GUN

About six weeks later, it must have been early October, a small party of officers was proceeding to the west coast of Scotland, bound for the commando training school at Lochailort. This was set in that romantic and intractable country where Bonnie Prince Charlie had lain hidden in the heather following his defeat at Culloden, awaiting escape in a boat for France. These events were less than two hundred years earlier and were closely involved with my own family history, so by the end of our time at Lochailort, thanks to the rigours of the terrain, one could really sympathize with this unlucky prince.[1]

The train was taking us through some of the grandest scenery in those parts. The rain was lashing down, but we could catch occasional glimpses of bog, moor and mountain, and far below a river in spate as we crossed an 'eyrie' viaduct. The first-class compartment which had seen better days, for its overpoweringly musty smell told of a long retirement on some remote siding, still retained some of its original aura: faded sepia photographs of once famous watering places, button seats, broad leather straps to hitch up the windows, knotted string luggage racks wide enough for a man to sleep upon.

The four occupants of this compartment were having a heated argument about the war. Who was responsible for Dunkirk? Had we sustained the last invasion scare? What were our chances of raiding the enemy coast? What was the latest score of German planes bagged in the air battle which was then raging? These were some of the questions uppermost in our minds. There were two very young officers present, 'Kelpie' Buchanan, a Grenadier, myself and Basil Fordham, a Coldstreamer whose balding pate betrayed his youthful looks. The fourth member of our entourage was a large shambling figure who did most of the talking and who smoked a large cigar. He wore a tailor-made battledress with the insignia of the 4th Hussars, his eyes were pale grey but looked through you in a disconcerting way. This figure was none other than Randolph Churchill, the son of the then Prime Minister. Not of a particularly athletic build, as I have said, nonetheless he longed for action just as his father had, hence his membership of our commando group.

No 8 Commando had been formed at Burnham-on-Crouch in Essex a few weeks earlier. The Welsh Guards contingent was too small to form a separate troop of its own. Jock Lewis and the men were therefore posted to the Irish Guards to make up their numbers, and I was posted to the Scots Guards troop to complete their complement of officers, presumably because I had already worn their cap badge, although now I wore my own insignia.

I could not have landed in better or more friendly company. Major Dermot Daly was our commander, a Scots Guards officer of considerable experience and of pugilistic mien, an army boxer and amateur steeplechase jockey whose appearance disguised a man of considerable charm. Captain Frank Usher, our second-in-command, was a shrewd and canny Scot with whom I soon established close relations. Much older than myself, he was another amateur rider who had broken most of the bones in his body. Dear Frank was an essential stabilizer in this disparate group. My fellow subaltern, David Stirling, was a tall gangling fellow, who had also been on the Finnish expedition. His expertise was mountaineering. Before the war he had designs for an ascent of Mount Everest and, knowing him, he might have brought it off. He was brilliant at charming people into doing something they did not want to do. There was a thin border line between this and being 'hotted', as the expression went, into some chore that was really his. Frank kept a wary eye on these manoeuvres. David had a penchant for big idealistic ideas, otherwise he was considered 'rather an idle officer'. Less than one year later he was to bring off the biggest coup of all.

Frank had some memorable expressions, one was being 'hotted' or 'carted' by David. Another was the state of Dermot's health. 'Dermot's making no sense today,' he used to say lugubriously. Frank liked to use diminutives for those around him. One night he declared in the vast expanses of the Libyan Desert, 'I can't possibly go to bed. Ethel hasn't brought my hot-water bottle!' Ethel was his nickname for his soldier-servant, a tall imposing guardsman turned commando. Favourite of all, when things went wrong, was 'If you tried to run a business like this – it would be broke in a week!'

My first sight of my future companions was at the Duke of York's Headquarters at Chelsea. There we paraded at 7.30 one morning in September, to meet together and perform the inevitable and ritualistic P.T. The guardsmen wore brown gym shoes and long baggy blue shorts, an unattractive garment known by them as 'gym nicks'. But this was no chore for there was excitement in the air, the very beginning of a mysterious adventure. All volunteers, they had been specially selected by the officers, and these raw lads contained some very interesting material.

At Burnham-on-Crouch we had to unlearn all our guardsmenlike ways. No barracks, we were billeted on the local population; we were never to move in a formed body; we were to learn the stealth and cunning of the cat-burglar (indeed we had one in our ranks who could pick any lock); but despite this change of rôle innate discipline held up.

Above our heads in the clear blue September skies what we now know as the 'Battle of Britain' was being fought. Pieces of equipment and planes dropped out of the sky. On one occasion eighty-four German bombers passed overhead, no doubt bound for London. Burnham even had its own air raid, with six civilians killed and twenty-seven injured, for which the Commando provided the rescue teams. During these days the sky was criss-crossed with white vapour trails inscribing on a canvas of deep blue the progress of the battle. And up there were the real heroes.

The Royal Burnham Yacht Club was home to the officers' mess. The mess bore a resemblance to the effortless ease and nonchalance of a London Club. But we were all conscious of the subliminal drum-beats marking out our days. Jock Lewis, the wiry Australian, surveying his companions knocking back their pink gins muttered into his beer that after the war, 'all this would change', meaning that society would change and us with it, that our blameless privileged lives might be cruelly shattered. Such disturbing prophesies were not the order of the day. We had little time to dream about the future; survival for the present was enough. At least one invasion scare took place whilst we were at Burnham, and the operation order was remarkably succinct, but its aims rather vague:-

Information
Enemy: Invasion possible.
Own Troops: all standing to.

Our Colonel, Bob Laycock, was an officer in the Royal Horse Guards (Blues). He had a pug-like face and was a tough nut. Not long before he had forsaken his mount and sailed before the mast, no doubt rounding the Horn. Those pre-war Guards officers were a remarkably fine lot.

Some of our officers equipped themselves with extra weaponry, such as the long-barrelled Mauser pistol that was then in vogue, First World War pattern, carried in a wooden holster. Sword-sticks cunningly concealed in an officer's ash-plant were popular; special light-weight *papier mâché* 'steel' helmets could be obtained from Messrs Lock & Co in St James's Street; the Minox camera, the size of a cigarette lighter, which could be had from Sinclair's in Trafalgar Square was another 'must'; I remember carrying a sketch of a dagger to Wilkinson's, the swordmakers in Pall Mall, which afterwards became the standard pattern for the commando knife.

But we were not entirely land-lubbers. We were hybrids. All our later moves between Inverary, Brodick on the Isle of Arran, Largs and Greenock bear the unmistakable tang of the salt sea.

But I have digressed from the real point of this chapter, and must now rejoin the train chugging up the glens. On the afternoon of the second day we reached our destination. We were to be camped in bell tents on the lawn of Inverailort House. Lochailort, a sea-loch reached up to the edge of the policies, and the whole was surrounded by hills of the 2,500 ft mark, most of them invisible in the mist, which at sea level felt like a wet blanket. In this climate our bell tents looked particularly uninviting. The owners of the house were still in residence, but had made over most of it for our purposes.

Shimi Lovat was our chief instructor. He was also chief of the Fraser Clan, and his NCO instructors, from the Lovat Scouts, a territorial regiment raised by the then Lord Lovat at the time of the Boer War, were his former ghillies and stalkers. Their fieldcraft and marksmanship were of course beyond compare, and their soft West Highland accents were at one with the landscape. It was the kind of climate which evoked the oft-repeated phrase 'Ah wheel, it's a grand soft day', as the rain came pelting down. But we did get one or two really grand days when the green fingers of land could be seen stretching out into the deep blue sea, and at one's back a mass of heather and tumbling rock. We learnt observation, stalking and fieldcraft, live firing and the use of explosives. Two former Hong Kong police officers taught us the new sport of 'unarmed combat'. On one exercise I remember foolishly taking a short cut through a railway tunnel and our flattening ourselves against the inner walls as the train thundered by, missing us by a whisker.

At Lochailort had been gathered together the Independent Companies – 'stay-behind' bodies in case of invasion – and from them had been formed the Commandos, the name of which had been borrowed from Boer raiding-parties. There was a scintillating rumour about a submarine lying in wait to take on board a raiding party bound to blow up something on the coast of Norway. Most of these expeditions were pure private enterprise, some bright spirit knew a submarine commander who thought it would be a useful exercise, a target was selected by a friend at the War Office, and the operation was finally presented to 'the powers that be' as a *fait accompli*. Needless to say very few came off.

However, the course had not been going for more than a few days before a most unfortunate incident occurred. Randolph Churchill got into an argument with a sergeant-instructor who was teaching the operation of the Bren gun. This was, at that time, a revolutionary light machine gun, all the mechanism of which was driven by the exhaust gases from the bullet's explosion, of course under high compression. Randolph knew this, as did most of us. The sergeant-instructor, however, who had no doubt been trained at the School of Musketry at Hythe, made the mistake of simplifying the process for us unmechanically-minded officers by telling us that the Bren gun was driven by steam! Randolph of course pounced upon him and a most unseemly wrangle ensued. Randolph was enraged by this assault upon his intelligence, and the argument went on and on. Of course he should have left it, or reported it to higher authority when things had calmed down. However, the sergeant, who by this time was justifiably aggrieved, reported the officer to the Chief Instructor, Colonel Lovat. This devastatingly good-looking highland laird had a touch of arrogance about him, we must admit, and the combination of Randolph's outrage and Shimi's fury led to another explosion, and Randolph was sent home – in ignominy. Those of us who were present actually sided with Randolph, and we gave him a good send-off at Lochailort railway station. Randolph was to lead a chequered career in No 8 Commando. Truth to tell he was no good with the men, and Bob Laycock moved him from one position to another and nothing seemed to gell: from troop officer to a previously non-existent 'administrative officer', from that to intelligence officer. He loved and admired his father, but they could not get on together either. But there was something lovable about this rumbustious, outrageous, over-grown schoolboy, who, whilst excelling at nothing, added lustre to our lives.

The steam-operated Bren gun was a short-lived weapon. The Germans never suffered from it. Neither were our own troops obliged to 'get up steam' for the thing to work – Randolph saw to that! Indeed it could be said that this was his one solid contribution to the early stages of the war.

5

'SHIP ME SOMEWHERE EAST OF SUEZ'

There was little hope for anyone who remained in England seeing much of the war, for by this time the whole of the Continent and most of Scandinavia had fallen into the hands of the enemy. It was going to be years before Britain could regain a foothold in Europe, and this would depend on major powers, such as the United States, joining Britain in her lonely fight.

A small armada, consisting of three converted merchantmen, had now gathered off the west coast of Scotland. They were under sealed orders. No one knew where we were going, but our recent training on the Island of Arran had shown us that the capture of an island might be involved.

It was now December, 1940, and the Commando was camped out in numerous crofts on the flanks of Goat Fell, the highest summit on Arran. It was wintry weather and David demonstrated how the accomplished climber should approach a mountain, in this case Goat Fell. Equipped with a balaclava helmet and an Havana cigar, he advised, 'a slow steady pace, using the flat of the foot on the ground. Never use the toe'. It was a useful lesson. But how he maintained his equilibrium I do not know. For the croft which we three shared was thick with the smoke of expensive cigars, and copious drams of whisky were consumed to keep the cold out. The crofter's family managed to squeeze into one room. But they seemed to take it in good part. There was a war on!

For Christmas we were once more afloat, this time on board a steamship used on the India run. It was manned by an Indian crew and the standards of service were those of the Raj. An all-pervading spicy smell of curry enveloped the ship. We lay off Brodick and how incongruous the snow-clad skyline seemed from this oriental vantage point. Soon we cross-shipped into HMS *Glenroy*, a lightly armed 'commando' ship (one of the converted merchantmen), which lay at anchor in the roads off Arran.

Speculation was rife about our intended destination, but various signs and portents suggested that we were sailing out 'East'. On 31 January the whole commando paraded on deck. The shrill bosun's pipe announced the arrival on board of Admiral Sir Roger Keyes (hero of Zeebrugge, and now in charge of combined operations), who addressed us in stirring words, but he omitted to tell us our exact rôle or destination, in the interests of no doubt security, presumably if one of us got picked up by an enemy submarine the intended operation would be compromised. We set sail the next day and our voyage to Suez round the Cape was to last six weeks, pursuing a circuitous route because of the submarine menace.

No 8 Commando was a special unit. It was drawn from some of the finest regiments of the British Army. All five Footguard regiments were represented, each forming 'a Troop' of fifty men and three officers. The Household Cavalry (dismounted) formed another one. Then there were 'infantry of the line' and 'cavalry of the line' troops. The Royal Marines made up the complement. All were volunteers and specially selected. But apart from this we were like any other collection of human beings. We had our good ones and we had our bad ones, and our six weeks' confinement on HMS *Glenroy* was quite a test. Only once did we step ashore, at Cape Town, where we received unstinted hospitality. And through all the years of South Africa's vilification I have remained faithful to that memory, for the settlers were faithful to us in our hour of need.

The same team, Usher, Stirling and myself, were crammed into a tiny cabin on deck built for the emergency wartime accommodation of two. The younger ones gradually became aware that our senior partner was using the minute basin for improper purposes during the night. Preventing Frank from defiling our living space became a major pre-occupation of the voyage. One would have thought that the man who was shortly to mastermind the SAS would have devised a means of catching the culprit in the act, but he never did! But David spent more and more time sleeping as the voyage went on, and we became seriously worried about it. It is true that he had the curious knack of being able to disassociate himself from anything that did not interest him. This, one might say, was the gift of 'Napoleon', who could take a nap at any time. True, he was not entirely a fit man and suffered from headaches, but the sleeping sickness became so endemic that he became known among fellow officers as 'the great sloth', and one wondered whether he would last the pace.

The most bizarre couple who shipped to Suez with us were Randolph Churchill, whom I have already mentioned, and Evelyn Waugh, the writer. It was said that Evelyn had been turned down for a Guards Regiment, but he did not seem to realize that it was the unsuitable 'suede shoes' which he wore for the interview that failed him, as I heard many years later. He had now obtained a commission in the Royal Marines, and his failure to join a more 'socially acceptable' regiment wrankled with him. In a way No 8 Commando answered this need and he was now more or less in his element. By this time rather a tubby figure, short-tempered, and at times with a biting tongue, he used to argue endlessly with Randolph – they were birds of a feather. But he was ever loyal to his mentor, Bob Laycock, whom he later accompanied to Crete on that ill-fated expedition. At the time I was not aware of his acute, but not unsympathetic powers of observation which led to the famous trilogy of novels,[1] which describe so evocatively the commando days. But curiously enough the characters which in his novels are drawn closely from life do not match up to the living models in their richness, flamboyance or idiosyncratic life-styles.

One such was Eddie Fitzclarence, a swash-buckling 'Mick'[2] with a roving eye and devil-may-care looks, who made a habit of referring to the Captain on the bridge as 'the old bugger on the roof'. The Navy objected to the soldiers on board, even though the ship had been built for them, and got very touchy about criticisms of their seamanship, which became increasingly erratic. At these moments one had a nostalgic flash-back to the heroic young Laycock, swinging from a yardarm whilst reefing in the top-gallants in a blustering nor'wester coming round the Horn. Which put the matter into proper perspective!

So long did it take to reach our destination that gambling, drinking and endless speculation became the harmless pastimes of the voyage, but these brother-officers, many of whom were married, had more to lose than most, and this represented the reckless spirit of the time. For we were all gamblers, taking not only our own lives but the lives of others into our hands.

As for the men, they were housed 'tween decks and slept in hammocks in very cramped quarters. The lengthy procedure of getting out of and stowing hammocks, converting the space to a mess deck, eating and swabbing out, then converting the space back into sleeping quarters took up the greater part of the day. There was PT on deck, endless cleaning of weapons and an occasional rum ration; otherwise there was no alcohol for the men. They took it all in good part. After all we were at war. Soon we were to share all the discomforts and privations of that condition.

'When are we going to get into action, Sir?' was always the question. What a simple faith they had in their officers! And in censoring their letters what a touching simplicity was revealed. By the end of the voyage one knew them like a brother. These Scots never took advantage of my wearing a strange cap badge (a leak amongst thistles), although I learnt many years later that I was known as the 'Mountain Goat', for being able to get up and down a mountain quicker than they could.

My platoon sergeant was known as 'Daddy' Ward, an uncompromising Englishman with a northern bluntness and common sense. I could always rely on him for good advice when I needed it.

Among the younger officers was George Jellicoe, a resilient extrovert, with a well developed sense of Rabelaisian fun, but a great friend with whom I had many adventures: Billy McGowan, a brother-in-law of Dermot Daly, (wearing the bonnet of the Scottish Horse); 'Tubby' Langton, an Oxford Rowing Blue, (another *Mick*) who was later to have an astounding adventure; Gavin Astor and Julian Berry, great friends (the one a Life Guard, the other a Blues officer). Jock Lewis was the very opposite to many in our party. He was not really an Aussie, but had been partly brought up there, and looked the part. Striking in appearance, with auburn hair and a moustache to match, he had an inventive and creative mind. If he had been spared he would have found his way into the ranks of the more individualistic war leaders. It was the combination of single-mindedness, inventive skill, improvisation, combined with leadership qualities that marked him as a man apart. He was tragically to lose his life on one of the early SAS raids.[3]

The Coldstream were perhaps the most talented lot. Apart from Jellicoe, their leader was Mervyn Griffith-Jones. He became a distinguished QC, and later prosecutor at the Nuremburg War Crimes Trials and was later responsible for the famous boob at the *Lady Chatterley's Lover* case 'Would you allow your servant to read this book?' No doubt with his tongue in his cheek, but reported as a classic *faux pas* by the press. The third member of this troop was Ian Collins, shrewd publisher and Wimbledon tennis star.

Then there was Philip Dunne (The Blues and former MP), and Peter Milton (a Grenadier) – so many hard-riding horsemen seem to have joined the ranks of these dedicated foot-soldiers. In reality Bob

Laycock had had the brilliant idea of recruiting his friends, on the same grounds as the old army adage that 'any fool can be uncomfortable', so why not go to war with your friends, and what was easier than to find them in White's Club, a ready-made recruiting ground.

On our long sea voyage we were fortunate in having these two competent scribes to enter up the War Diary, as seen by the following entry, from HMS *Glenroy* at sea:

'21 Feb 1941. Lt. E. Waugh, on his appointment to Lt. Col. Laycock's staff handed over the War Diary to 2/Lt. R.S. Churchill.'[4]

But the modern historian will search the record in vain for any mark left by these two giants among scribblers. The laconic entries simply record warships joining and leaving the convoy.

On 7 March, 1941, we were steaming up the Suez Canal towards the Great Bitter Lake, where we dropped anchor. On 10 March, still afloat, we were addressed by General Evetts, under whose command we were to come. He told us that 7, 8 and 11 Commandos were to be brigaded into Layforce (under command of Bob Laycock) for 'an important and hazardous operation against the Germans, for which one month's hard training would be required'[4]. It later became apparent that this was to be the island of Rhodes, then occupied by the Italians. Wearing our newly issued Wolseley Helmets we disembarked and made our way to an arid plot named Geneifa Camp.

Meanwhile a laborious and not very professional rehearsal took place for the impending operation. We marked out the supposed coastline of the unknown island in the sand, hard up against a rocky outcrop in the desert. Strenuous route marches took place. There were other distractions. Ismailia and Suez offered the semi-colonial pleasures of the French Canal Company, and its attractive daughters. Dermot was now commanding the battalion in place of Bob Laycock who was often away in Cairo negotiating about our rôle. Geneifa Camp was an awful dump. It was difficult keeping the men's morale up for there seemed to be deafening silence about our future operation. The whole thing had become a bit of a charade.

The scene inside our tent resembled a Maugham-like tragedy on a colonial theme. It was the siesta hour. On a camp table stood a half-empty whisky bottle with two dirty glasses. Scurries of sand blew in through the flapping tent wall leaving a thin film of dust over all. The sun beat down mercilessly. Bets were laid on the progress of a scorpion across the sandy floor. On a safari camp bed lay David Stirling wearing dark glasses. His jowl was blue with a healthy growth of stubble.

It was during our time at this unpromising spot that things began to happen. We began to think furiously about our own future, each keeping his thoughts to himself. For David, comatose as he appeared to be, it was the beginning of a big idea, and of great things to come.

By 1941 we had been thrust out of Cyrenaica, the scene of Wavell's victorious advance only months earlier. Western Desert Force, Desforce as it was called, had left behind a pocket of resistance, the encircled garrison of Tobruk. Tobruk and its harbour and hinterland was now under seige, and Wavell's relief attempt 'Operation Battleaxe' (15–17 June) had been a costly failure with a disastrous loss of men and equipment.

Meantime, before April was out, the British had to evacuate their Expeditionary Force from Greece in face of irresistible German pressure from the north. On 21 May, 1941, the Germans, albeit with heavy losses, had carried out a massive airborne landing on the island of Crete whence Wavell had withdrawn his forces, from where he had decided to make a final stand.

In the evacuation of British Forces from Greece the Army had to abandon 8,000 lorries. The Royal Air Force lost 209 aircraft, whilst the heaviest price was paid by the Royal Navy. Naval losses included the warships HMS Diamond *and* Wryneck, *the transports* Ulster Prince, Pennland, *and* Slamat *and* Costa Rica. *The Landing Ship* Glencairn, *one of our sister ships, was badly damaged.*

On 1 June, 1941, after ten days' bitter fighting, during which the Germans paid a heavy penalty, the decision was taken, much against Churchill's wishes, to pull out of Crete.

The official History of the Second World War gives the total number of British (including Australians and New Zealanders), then in Crete, as 32,000. The total number of British killed was nearly 1,800 with about 12,000 taken prisoner. Estimates for German killed were 1,990. For Crete alone, 'The loss in warships was very heavy; one aircraft carrier and three battleships damaged . . . three cruisers and six destroyers sunk, six cruisers and seven destroyers damaged.'[1]

No sooner had we arrived in Egypt when this disastrous scenario began to unfold. It was to dash the high hopes of exercising our commando skills so painfully learnt. But it was not quite the end of the story. No 8 Commando would not lie down quite yet.

6

THE VOYAGE OF THE *APHIS*

At short notice we were moved to Alexandria, where we occupied a camp outside the city, Sidi Baguish. From here we were warned for embarkation in a former river gunboat, HMS *Aphis*, (Capt Campbell, RN) now lying in Alexandria Harbour. Here grand British naval vessels lay at anchor, including the submarine depot ship HMS *Medway* which we were to get to know very well later. Their grey shapes spoke of British power and might, calm but full of menace.

HMS *Aphis* was a little river gunboat.[2] She and her sister ships had been brought all the way from the China Sea to take part in raiding operations in the Mediterranean. She carried one main 6-inch gun for bombardment purposes, and for anti-aircraft defence a few pom-poms and Breda guns.

By this time Tobruk had been cut off. We were to mount a raid on the inlet of Ain el Gazala, an enemy base 20 miles west and causing trouble to the Tobruk garrison. In fact it was the main base for the seige of that port.

On 20 May, 1941, eleven officers and ninety-nine other ranks from our commando boarded the river gunboat at Mersa Matruh. Unwittingly we were to take part in an extraordinary battle at sea.

During the course of the operation we spent seven days on the deck of this little vessel (there was no room below) under spasmodic and then continuous attack by enemy dive-bombers. One hundred and seventy-two bombs (according to the ship's log) were aimed at the *Aphis*, not one of which made a direct hit. But the near misses deluged us in spray and played ducks and drakes around the ship, landing on one side of the ship and exploding on the other. We returned a hot fire at the enemy aircraft with our puny weapons, Bredas, pom-poms and anything we could lay our hands on, LMGs, Tommy guns and rifles, downing several aircraft. One entry in the log reads, 'One seen down, several hard hit,'[1] reminiscent of palmier days! The ship's log records the following incidents on 22 May: 'Thirty-two bombs were dropped by seven Savoia 79 aircraft from a height of about 5,000 ft,' These were medium-sized bombs believed to be 250–500 pounders. They fell all round the ship. But the aircraft were out of range of small arms fire. A heavy swell was breaking over the deck, so the landing had to be temporarily abandoned. After sheltering in the little harbour of Mersa Matruh again, on 25 May the *Aphis* weighed anchor for a second attempt to reach our objective. The ship's log described it as follows:

'On 26 May the ship was sighted by enemy aircraft at 1100 hours and shadowed continuously till nightfall. At 1530 hours attacks were sustained from all quarters. Twenty-seven JU 87's and 88's took part in this attack, the Stuka dive-bombers coming as low as 100ft. Fifty bombs were dropped and the ship was badly shaken aft. We sustained two minor injuries. The JU 87s were approaching at 100ft from two miles out, dropping 1,000 lb bombs, four of which were seen to hit the water on the port beam about 50 to 100 yards off and to bounce over the ship and land on the starboard beam. One 1,000 pounder passed between the deck and the forestay. Meantime a desultory fire was kept up from the ship using every conceivable weapon. The decks were awash with spray, and empty cartridge cases rolling this way and that with the movement of the ship. Captain Campbell was taking such evasive action as he could with such an unwieldy vessel.

'At 1840 hours, travelling at our top speed of 12 knots, we were attacked by thirty-three JU 88s and Savoia bombers. The ship was badly shaken again aft. The wind was 6 points on bow, and Captain Campbell put the helm over first one way and then the other way to avoid the bombs. On this attack we were luckier and brought down one enemy aircraft in the sea, and saw one with its tail shot away.

'At 1900 hours we were attacked from both quarters and ahead, by some twenty JU 88s dropping forty bombs. No direct hits had been sustained by the *Aphis* but the ship was again badly shaken. Still we knocked down another aircraft with several hard hits.'[1]

By now the game was up, the after-part of our vessel was so badly shaken that the steering gear was out of action, reducing us to steaming round and round in a circle in the eerie silence before our attackers returned. As darkness fell both engines stopped. If there had been a clear moon we would have been a sitting duck, for we could still see the enemy aircraft by their navigation lights searching overhead. But the gallant crew of the *Aphis* somehow managed to rig up a jury system to steer the ship by, and under cover of darkness and several hair-raising daylight hours we were able to limp back to port. This was the end of our abortive raid to help Tobruk.

This story is not complete without recording that on board was a 71-year-old admiral who had been on the retired list for over ten years. Admiral Sir Walter Cowan, or 'the little admiral' as we called him, was with us in a 'supernumerary' capacity.[3] In a somewhat irregular fashion he had attached himself to our commando (and became our mascot). Having spent his retirement in the hunting-field he now wanted to end his days on active service. In fact his greatest ambition was to be killed in action. This was not granted him. Life (and death) are not as easy as all that! However, he was later captured at Tobruk and taken prisoner. But this veteran of the Battle of the Nile (1898, where he commanded a gunboat), former Naval ADC to Lord Roberts, later decorated at the Battle of Jutland was, as can be imagined, a source of inspiration to the men as he blazed away with his Tommy-gun at the oncoming dive-bombers. But he paid us soldiers a handsome compliment when writing about the incident shortly after:

> 'It's been such a joy to me at my age to have been amongst a lot like that and to have been able to watch it all. And at sea just as good – quite a lot of them came on a jaunt in a little river gunboat most unsuitable in the open sea, bringing their own machine guns, etc. and living in the most infinite discomfort. We got properly bombed, and from very low down. All this lot buckled to and fought them off again and again – they might have been at sea all their service, and it was a perfect delight to watch the steadiness and discipline of them all and the admiration of all the sailors for them.'[4]

The soldiers took it all as a matter of course. They really believed that this was what the Navy did at sea. 'an average day in the life of a sailor'. We began to fear a rush to join the Royal Navy!

7

THE SIEGE OF TOBRUK

We returned to Alexandria to find the rest of the commando feeling dispirited and abandoned. It seemed unbelievable that such a highly trained body of men, of such superlative quality, should be thrown on the scrap heap. Was it possible that a whole brigade and their specially converted raiding ships should be disbanded and paid off? How unimaginative were the powers that be to squander their resources in this way, or so we thought.[1] For this was to be our fate. But it had not yet happened, the story was not quite over.

Jellicoe and I had conceived the idea of a two-man raid from Tobruk, on the very target which the *Aphis* had failed to reach. We had been fully briefed already, had studied the air photographs for the first operation and had all the gen we needed.[2]

There was no difficulty in collecting stores, we just helped ourselves to weaponry, ammunition, explosives, grenades and all the rest of it, notified our immediate superiors of what we were about, and took passage for Tobruk on the nightly 'destroyer run' from Alexandria. Our ship, having run the gauntlet under cover of darkness, discharged its stores in a matter of minutes and deposited us upon the shattered quayside of Tobruk harbour.

The destroyer slid out silently, still under cover of darkness. And there we were left, standing on the quayside with our bundles of equipment, in the gathering dawn.

George was a level-headed fellow, more mature than I was at the time, but with a well-developed sense of fun, but he had a deeply serious side, most helpful from time to time! The Tobruk Garrison consisted of the 9th Australian Division, with British tanks and artillery, and Indian and Polish troops, under command, all having been cut off in the original retreat. Fortress Tobruk was under the overall command of the Aussie General Morshead.

Our plan was to achieve what the commando had failed to do: to attack the German HQ at Ain el Gazala, having been landed by an 'R boat' (a light naval landing craft known as the *Eureka*) and then, having carried out our task as best we could, to make our escape. With hindsight it sounds a most perilous venture. And of course it was, but we argued that two people could achieve just as much confusion behind the enemy lines as could the ponderous presence of a gunboat with a cargo of 100 troops to disembark, with the even more hazardous task of coming close in shore to pick them up again.

We had yet to announce our presence to the Commander of the Fortress, General Morshead, and persuade him of the feasibility of our plan. Meantime we fell in with a wonderful man, Major O'Shaugnessy, Royal Engineers, a brave but modest fellow with a shock of unruly hair. He was the Port Commandant or port-operating officer responsible for unloading and shifting stores. His HQ, a bombed-out shack on the edge of the harbour, was where we made our headquarters, for we needed to be near the Royal Navy. Here we were fed and looked after. A diet of 'bully' and a load of bombs was our unfailing daily fare, as the Germans tried incessantly to sink our shipping to block the harbour. Tobruk harbour was full of wrecks, some of which we swam round in the pellucid water, during temporary lulls in the Stuka visits.

Maintaining the Tobruk garrison took a deadly toll of our shipping. HMS *Dainty*, a fine destroyer, HMS *Ladybird* (sister ship to the *Aphis*, sunk on 12 May), HMS *Fiona* and *Chakla*, former merchant ships, were all on the bottom. all one could see were their mastheads. In April the hospital ships *Vita*, *Karapara* and *Aba*, all clearly marked with the Red Cross, were dive-bombed and badly damaged. On 25 May the sloop *Grimsby* was sunk along with six other vessels which were sunk or damaged during the month. It was in June that Admiral Cunningham (commanding Mediterranean Fleet) had recourse to 'destroyers only' to supply the garrison, because of their speed. On 24 June the sloop *Auckland* was sunk and the *Pass of Balamaha* (petrol tanker) badly damaged and towed away by HMS *Waterhen*, her last voyage, for on 29 June she was sunk by bombs whilst proceeding out of Tobruk.[3]

At night our routine was to make our way to what was jokingly known as the 'best hotel in town', the Albergo Tobruk. George and I were its only visitors. It had neither doors nor windows. It was a shell.

Here, during intermittent sleep, we would get some reprieve from the constant bombing and shelling of the harbour. So the time came to see General Morshead. We found his headquarters at the end of a labyrinth of tunnels well up on the perimeter. The tunnels had been dug by former occupants, the Italians. They were pretty well bomb-proof. The name 'Jellicoe' worked wonders with the general. To our surprise and relief General Morshead accepted our plan and wished us well.

Colonel 'Gaffer' Lloyd was the Chief of Staff. This huge, gangling Aussie exuded a spirit of confidence. His HQ was in one of those underground caves into which he had managed to insert himself. It was low and crowded with men at their typewriters balanced on crates of bully-beef. Out on the perimeter six German tanks had broken through the defences. A despatch rider came hurtling down the track on which these tanks were approaching. He dashed to the dugout, lifted up the camouflage net and, breathing heavily, gasped, 'Sir, Sir! Six German tanks are coming down the road!' Gaffer Lloyd, hardly looking up, said to the agitated messenger, 'Tell the bastards not to come in here. There's too many people in here already!'[4]

Our next visit was to the 18th (K.E.O.) Indian Cavalry Regiment, holding the extreme western section of the line, their positions running down to the sea. The officers' mess was inside a stone sangar on the edge of the perimeter. It had a wonderful view of no-man's-land and the German lines beyond. Like good soldiers, the Indian Cavalry, now without their horses, knew how to make themselves comfortable. Spread across the table were copies of *The Field* and *Country Life*, of *Punch* and other journals. Providing that one did not stick one's head up too high and invite a sniper's bullet, the terrain which we might have to cross on our return journey was laid out like a sand-table before us. We noted every nook and cranny, every wadi and barbed wire entanglement. The CO promised that we could join a patrol into no-man's-land the following evening the better to see the lie of the land. The next moment I was taken on one side. I had noticed some odd looks from the officers. "Isn't that the Afrika Korps cap badge you're wearing? Where did you get it from? What do you come from? Welsh Guards? There's none of them out here." The interrogation continued for a moment or two. The Welsh Guards cap badge was a discreet affair in those days. The leek with spreading roots and leaves had been reduced to a miniature. Indeed it could have been mistaken for a palm tree, the Afrika Korps emblem. The only thing it lacked was a swastika. Now to have one's cap badge insulted in those days was a serious affair.

Particularly a leek! And I swear that if I'd had a real leek I would have enjoyed seeing my interrogator eat it raw!

The next evening we went out on patrol into no-man's-land, getting as close to the German lines as we could, for if anything happened to the *Eureka* we would have to walk back through these lines. Relations were restored. I will remember the hospitality we received from the 18th Indian Cavalry Regiment with gratitude.

We made our preparations to the accompaniment of flies, dust, bombs and the inevitable bully stew and biscuits. In the area of the harbour the time of day was 'told' by a burst of machine-gun fire at the appointed hour. It was June. The heat was numbing. Plumes of dust lazily circled up into the deep blue sky, as another shell landed out on the perimeter. In the distance a high-pitched drone signalled the arrival of another flight of Stukas bound for their target, the harbour. With a scream reaching a crescendo they would dive and release their bomb-load, accompanied by the 'phut, phut' from an ineffective Bofors gun and the rattle of small arms from our side. On one occasion, so George Jellicoe reminds me, a huge bomb landed in the room next to ours while we were trying to snatch some sleep. Fortunately it failed to go off!

In mid-afternoon, in a rare moment of peace, one tried to get some sleep. When the drone of the flies took on the nightmarish qualities of the dive-bomber, one could be forgiven for wondering how long all this was going to last? How long could we hold out? Not only here but at home? The news from home was bad. We had no help except from the Aussies, Kiwis and South Africans. The enemy were taking a deadly toll of our shipping. We were all alone.[5]

By this time other members of the commando had drifted up to Tobruk. Pat Ness, of the Queen's Bays, came on our final *Eureka* boat trip. We laid him right up on the bows with a tommy gun pointing towards the shore (at the supposed enemy). Hours later he was still in the same position as we re-entered Tobruk harbour. This caused some hilarity. Poor fellow, he was not allowed to forget it quickly.

John Pearson-Gregory of the Grenadiers was another who was lying with bad dysentery in the casualty clearing station – a sagging tent in a dust-storm – with little food or other attention. A berth was obtained for him on the nightly destroyer run to Alexandria.

The story I like best which was recalled by Morgan-Giles, was of his Senior Naval Officer who was caught in the open during a bombing raid and dived into a slit trench. His office in the building received a direct hit and his Maltese steward came staggering out of the wreck carrying his boss's tattered naval jacket. When he got into the daylight he held it up to the sky and looked up the sleeve to see whether there was anything of his master left, who of course enjoyed the spectacle enormously.

I do not intend to dwell on the three unsuccessful attempts we made on three separate nights to make our landfall. I do not think that our 'Eureka' boat was equipped with proper navigational equipment. Let me put it more crudely. It gradually dawned upon us that our skipper was a rotten navigator! In the end, in consultation with Captain Patsy Poland (Senior Naval Officer Inshore Squadron), we reluctantly agreed to call it off. But the failure of a mission is not the point of this story.[6]

Just before we left Tobruk an event took place on 22 June which later proved to be a turning-point of the war. Suddenly one morning, round the harbour, all the Brens started firing, and yet there was not an enemy aircraft in sight. The news spread like wildfire: 'The Russians have come in!' 'The Russians are in!'

The whole place went wild. *Feux de joie* pierced the air. The Germans had invaded Russia! Operation Barbarossa had begun. We were no longer alone. a dramatic ending to our little holiday in Tobruk.

8

DEATH OF A COMMANDO

The existence of the Commandos in the Middle East was now becoming more and more of a fiasco, with the consequent collapse of purpose, discipline and morale. We had not seen much of our 8 Commando fellows whilst in Tobruk, but when we got back to Alexandria we heard that a party of about ninety-six under the command of 'Bones' Sudeley had been patrolling beyond the perimeter.[1] He became badly shell-shocked whilst there and had to be evacuated back to Alexandria. In order to vindicate the situation, Dermot Daly ordered the entire party to return back to base and set about raising a new force which he himself was going to lead. Dermot did not lack courage. Then came the order for the disbandment, and the further expedition was cancelled. During this confused time the remaining officers held a council of war in the Cecil Hotel in Alexandria.

No one really knew who was in command at that stage, who was with us or who was not. But it was felt that another attempt should be made on Tobruk. We had a heated discussion, in which I declined to return (having only just got back!) which in retrospect seems rather cowardly, but on the grounds that the enterprise was misconceived and with such large numbers was a forlorn hope. George had already rejoined his own regiment. Nevertheless Dermot's advance guard left under Philip Dunne, but no sooner had they reached the Fortress, than the order for disbandment was received.[2]

Although GHQ Middle East at Cairo had largely been responsible for our present predicament, it is also true to say that the Commando was earning the reputation of being a law unto itself, and the behaviour of some of its officers was bizarre in the extreme. David Stirling had knocked out a cab-horse in the streets of Cairo, in protest at the gharry-drivers exorbitant fare. Peter Milton, whilst lying in bed at Shepheard's Hotel, had fired at a passing pigeon with his revolver, shattering the window and hitting the house on the other side of the street, causing a minor disturbance both in the hotel and at GHQ.[3] To crown it all, Harry Stavordale, then acting adjutant, had discovered a much quicker and more satisfactory means of communication with his scattered troops than through the military signal network. His traffic passed exclusively through the Egyptian State Railways (ESR) Telegraph system (the Egyptians then being neutral!).[4]

A horrified senior staff officer at GHQ wrote the following memo.

'A great deal of disorganisation and disorder is being created at the present time by Commanders . . . of LAYFORCE flagrantly disregarding orders.

'On Sunday last a copy of the following telegram was handed to me by Q (Movements), it had been received by their [the ESR] representative at Headquarters, Canal Sub-Area South and referred by him to GHQ ME. This telegram had been transmitted over the Egyptian State Railways Telegraph in "clear". It read as follows:

'"To:- O.C. Commando Base Depot, Genefa.

From:- Alex (via ESR Telegraph).

Please tell all Irish and Welsh Guards with exception of L/Cpl HALE to report to RTO Alex to rejoin B Battalion Lay Force.

(Sgd) STAVORDALE"

The staff officer added

'"It is obvious that the responsible officers of Layforce and Commandos do not realize their responsibilities in abiding to regulation or in the accepted method of addressing and despatching correspondence. . . . In any case the sending of a message in "clear" . . . is extremely dangerous and it is considered that the officer concerned should be suitably dealt with."'[5]

Harry Stavordale was a huge ambling figure, who would have very soon brushed aside the staff officer's strictures.

This was just the kind of attitude, from just such a kind of person, which David Stirling believed was losing us the war, and which inspired him to cut loose from all this military imbroglio. Although I must say the staff officer (could he have been Waugh's Major Hound?), had a point concerning security!

In his Diary Evelyn Waugh speaks grudgingly of No. 8 Commando,

50

'After the RM [Royal Marine] Brigade the indolence and ignorance of the officers seemed remarkable, but I have since realized that they were slightly above normal army standards. . . . The troops, however, had a smart appearance on inspection parades . . . the officers were clearly greatly liked and respected. But there was very high gambling, poker, roulette, chemin-de-fer every night.' But in comparison with No. 3 Commando, with whom we had shared the ship going over, No. 8 was 'boisterous, xenophobic, extravagant, imaginative, witty, with a proportion of noblemen, which the Navy found disconcerting.'[6]

But we younger ones took our more senior officers at face value; hard-drinking, hard-gambling they may have been, but they certainly had flair. We looked upon their other idiosyncrasies with an amused curiosity. Despite the utter confusion within GHQ and between GHQ and the War Office in London, there were, however, some valid reasons for this decision to disband, put, rather poignantly, in papers now in the official archives.

The first signal is from the CIGS in London to General Wavell in Cairo, dated 22 June, 1941:

'Understand LAYCOCK's Bde of SS troops has been disbanded. If so I suggest that you might return him early to the UK where his knowledge and experience of SS operations would be useful.'

There follows a rather plaintive message from Laycock to Director of Combined Operations in London,

'Repeated cancellation of Combined Operations caused continued inactivity of SS Bde from arrival here until recently. Past three weeks witnessed extensive use SS tps resulting in successful actions but such heavy casualties that disbandment now ordered.'

He went on to describe how 7 Commando and ME Commandos fought fierce rearguard actions in Crete, but seventy per cent failed to return to Egypt. How 11 Commando (Colonel Pedder) had carried out a very successful and daring raid in Syria on the Litani River against the Vichy French, but Pedder was killed and twenty-five per cent of the unit were killed, wounded or missing. 8 Commando was now executing raids in the Western Desert.[7]

Now a very curious series of signals is exchanged, as to what promises and undertakings were given to the Special Service Volunteers when joining. Apparently the engagement was for only six months (later extended) for an attack on the Mediterranean island of Pantellaria, and now everyone had a right to return to the UK or to their own regiments.

This was news to me. I heard of neither option at the time, either of a limited engagement or of the right of repatriation. Unbeknown to us the following signal had already been dispatched to London from GHQ on 19 July:

> 'Glad if you would consider early return to UK of u/m officers... together with as many of their original OR's as could be spared. Lt. Col. Daly SG, Lt. Collins CG, Capt. Dunne RHG, Capt. Usher SG, Lt. Astor L. Gds, Lt. Stirling Scots G, Lt. Berry RHG, Lt. Mather WG, Capt. Lord Milton GG, Lt. Lewis WG, Lt. Buchanan GG, Lt. Langton IG, Lt. M. Brown GG, Capt. Lance, Somerset LI, Lt. Lord Jellicoe CG, Lt. Barkworth Somerset LI, Capt. Griffiths-Jones CG, Capt. Kealey Durham LI.'[8]

How strange that no other option was given to us officers. However, this order was soon countermanded, and we find General Arthur Smith (Chief of Staff at GHQ) and the senior guards officer in the theatre urging the commander of 22nd Guards Brigade to take any surplus guardsmen on his strength (concerning which the Brigade Commander had serious misgivings!), Arthur Smith writes:

> '[they] have had a terribly raw deal since they have been out here. They have been pushed around from pillar to post, promised this, that and the other, and through nobody's fault have been continually disappointed. . . . They have now been sent to the IBD [Infantry Base Depot] where they will languish and deteriorate.'

He adds as a parting shot, 'PS. The addition of Grenadier, Irish and Welsh Guardsmen to our Order of Battle may well muddle the Axis!'[9]

However, this confused situation was just the kind of climate in which the more enterprising officers thrived. Certainly none of our friends fell prey to the dreaded Infantry Base Depot. The confusion acted like a tonic to some, in particular David Stirling, who was planning a light raiding force of his own to penetrate deep behind the enemy lines. He had completely recovered his *élan*, had been to Tobruk (and the IBD), recruiting some of our best men. He already had a nucleus therefore before he went to GHQ to get support for his idea. Bluffing his way past the security guards, he came face to face with the Commander-in-Chief, General Wavell. So astonished was this individual and so intrigued by Stirling's idea that he gave the go-ahead for a small raiding party, essentially different from the Commandos, in that they would drop near their target area and be picked up by the Long Range Desert Group.

At this stage I was wondering what to do. Not having a regiment in the Middle East there was no obvious answer. David Stirling had this hare-brained scheme, which like all the other schemes, seemed doomed to failure, so disenchanted had one become. David tried to recruit me, but like most other officers from the Commando I turned it down.[10] We really could not give it credence, and we thought we knew David too well for it to work. Another fiasco was the last thing that anyone could take. I remember having a long talk with David in, typically, the large central lobby of Shepheard's Hotel. He was all afire with his idea and speaking with great enthusiasm. But I was too jaundiced to accept, even though I was ratting on my close companion of the last twelve months. I was lying back gazing at the ceiling. The frieze running round the hall was an Egyptian version of an eagle rising; it was a pattern that was to become familiar as the badge of the SAS.

I had another tempting offer, to accompany the traveller and explorer, Major Philip Brocklehurst (who had attached himself to our commando) on a Special Service Mission to China. He had been with Shackleton in the Antarctic and had later travelled the Silk Route, on foot from end to end. He was a fascinating companion and I agonized over the prospect, walking round and round Shepheard's garden beneath the umbrageous palm trees as the night swiftly descended.

Finally, I accepted the invitation of Dermot Daly, my former Troop Leader and latterly our commanding officer, who had been given command of the 'high-powered' GHQ Liaison Squadron, later known as the Phantoms.

PART III
THE WESTERN DESERT WAR

9

PHANTOM PATROL

*'Awake! for Morning in the Bowl of Night
Has flung the Stone which puts the Stars to Flight;
And Lo! the Hunter of the East has caught
The Sultan's Turret in a Noose of Light.'*
  The Rubaiyat of Omar Khayyam, Edward Fitzgerald.

I joined GHQ Liaison Squadron in August, 1941. Dermot Daly (a Major once again) was in command. The squadron was settled just outside Cairo in a most convenient spot, a shallow wadi just at the back of the Mena House Hotel, which itself faces the pyramids. The Mena House Hotel, a rambling colonial-style building set in a garden of palm trees, possessed a swimming pool, which we made full use of.

The squadron was re-forming after losing all but nine men in Greece, and the tented camp was a hive of activity, as we collected vehicles and equipment, and prepared for desert warfare. It could not have been a greater contrast to the final commando days. Here was a sense of purpose and confidence in the rôle we had to play. In our case it was to short-circuit the normal communications system between the front line and the Commander of Eighth Army, so that he had an alternative and up-to-date view on the progress of the battle.

We were divided into about five or six patrols, each consisting of an officer, five men and three 15cwt trucks. We were equipped with the standard No 11 wireless set, augmented by a Wyndham aerial, each message being encoded into high-grade cypher.

There was a lot to learn. Driving and surviving in the desert was an art in itself. Sand mats and sand channels strapped to the vehicles were used to extract vehicles that got bogged down in soft sand. Camel tanks provided an abundant supply of fresh water. A canvas sack containing water, hung in front of the radiator, kept it cool on the hottest day. Navigational aids were the standard prismatic compass and the newly designed Bagnold sun-compass, plus the complicated Azimuth card for calculating the fall of the shadow from the needle of this mobile sundial.

The officers, on the whole, were of a more intellectual type than Dermot and I had been used to. The men were tradesmen, wireless operators, fitters and drivers. We cautiously concealed our ignorance of all these affairs.

Intensive trials of men and equipment now began, and each patrol departed into the blue for the shaking-down process. Frank Thompson and I decided upon a joint patrol, and the area we chose was the Red Sea Hills where we intended to investigate the fabled Coptic monasteries. This was pure escapism, but Frank Thompson was a delightful companion. An Oxford educated classicist and poet, he professed to be at that time a Communist with a strong attachment to the war aims of the Soviet Union. It was all quite light-hearted, and I doubt if he was a paid-up member of the Party. No one paid much attention to this; it was all a bit of a joke and his strongest characteristics were those of a patriotic Englishman with a sentimental attachment to the English countryside. As he wrote wistfully,

> 'At home the blackthorn will soon be out. Blackthorn symbolizes for me, more than any other flower, the peculiar loveliness of the English spring. It symbolizes, too, the light-hearted strength and cleanness of spirit which has been one of England's best features. ... Rather stilted,' he added, 'but I guess you know what I mean.'[1]

Frank's other feature was an extraordinary scruffiness and untidyness of dress, which rather went with his character. He held a contempt for the outward conventions, but this did not prevent him having all the characteristics of an excellent officer. Whereas he was to decry the class system, he had to admit, 'There's no getting away from the fact that regiments whose officers are most blue-blooded – the Guards, old cavalry regiments – have proved themselves among the very best fighting regiments in the British Army'.[2] However, his philosophy was all a bit different from what I had been used to in No 8 Commando!

Our trip to the Red Sea Hills was one that I shall always remember in its complete other-worldliness. Apart from our military equipment, we could have been miles away from the war. We camped out on the Gulf of Suez, with the massif of Mount Sinai on the other side. Next morning we sped down the sparkling Gulf with the desert surface as flat as a pancake. Blue mountain horizons on every side made one feel that this was the original glad morning when the world had first begun.

From a point on the map marked Zafarana, we turn inland into the red-hot hills. In their barren starkness there is nothing to rival them. We bump along a camel track, slowly climbing, until we pass over the summit of the Red Sea Hills. Now we are facing the valley of the Nile, a blue-green smudge in the distance, down, down again, but still many miles to go. In this most desolate landscape we suddenly round a bed and see in front of us the object of our search, Deir el Antonyus (the monastery of St Anthony). High mud-brick walls enclose it; all that can be seen above its walls are the densely packed tops of palm trees, stiff like a shaving brush, and like soap bubbles the white cupolas of its devotional buildings. A marvellous sight in the middle of nowhere.

We hammer on the massive wooden gateway. (Where did this vast timber come from, I wonder?) And after an interminable time, with much withdrawing of chains, creaking and groaning of the protesting woodwork, the door opens and we see a diminutive Christian Coptic monk. We feel we have opened the box marked EAT ME! For suddenly everything is very small, or we have grown very large. We can hardly move inside, but it is cool in the little palm and cypress garden, and the many chapels give out an exotic scent of frankincense and myrrh. The few monks in their shabby black are very poor and very old, but we share with them, and they with us. We spent two nights at St Anthony's, the men outside the walls with their vehicles, Frank and I in minute white-washed cells. This was our last escape from reality – and a gentle baptism into the desert navigation and lifestyle.[3]

The November push was now about to begin. The patrols moved up into the desert each to their alloted place. My task, I was told, was to make my way to the oasis of Jarabub (a Senussi holy place about 100 miles south of the coast and the southernmost tip of our line), and just north of the Grand Erg or Great Sand Sea. Here I was to simulate the signal traffic of an armoured division! As this had to come out of my head I cannot believe it was very effective. Without too much difficulty and by use of map and sun compass we found Jarabub. The spot chosen consisted of a shattered palm tree and a holy man's tomb with recent signs of military skirmish. We settled our three vehicles across the track facing westward, and for four days, timed to coincide with our advance in the north, we transmitted bogus messages on the air. It was silent and eerie down there. Except for the tap, tap, tap of the morse key there was no sound, absolutely nothing, and nothing to do. Like a drowning man I began to re-live over again my past life; memory came to my rescue in the empty void which surrounded us, only enlivened by dust devils which we took for an approaching army coming to investigate our remorseless chattering.

Having fulfilled our obligation our orders were to report to the 4th Armoured Brigade, under Brigadier Alec Gatehouse, now fully engaged in the battle. In fact we were searching for a battlefield, somewhere to the north, without a clue where it might be. Would we be too late and would it all be over? We headed north on a compass bearing, at first over pure, clean desert untouched by war. Then we began to come across the detritus of war, pieces of discarded equipment, a few burnt-out vehicles, the tracks of many vehicles, but not a soul in sight. At last we came upon three men brewing-up beside their truck in the middle of nowhere.

'Any idea where 7th Armoured Division is?'

'Not a clue, mate, but try over there.'

He waved his arm in a general direction, and added as an afterthought, 'Follow the line of petrol cans until you come to the dead camel, turn right for about 15 minutes. You'll come to some burnt-out vehicles. Near them is a track. You're bound to find some blokes there.'

We became dimly aware of distant gunfire. We followed the sound of the guns not really knowing on whose side they might be. More abandoned equipment, burnt-out tanks, some still burning; they seemed to be ours, for we could see the British battledress on the dead gunners. We aimed for a knot of vehicles silhouetted against the horizon. On coming close to, it was a ring of British tanks drawn up in close leaguer in broad daylight; it was late afternoon. We had evidently arrived at a dramatic moment. It was all that was left of the 7th Hussars.

Some were standing on their tanks. Some wounded were being dragged out. Urgent exchanges were taking place.

'How many runners?'

'Lost most of the squadron!'

'Tank strength?'

'Nil.'

'Any fuel left?'

'Hardly any.'

'Ammo?'

'Racks empty.'

The names of comrades were called out. There was no answer. I had reached the eye of the storm. It was almost indecent to be there with my clean and unsullied vehicles. Then I saw my school chum, Hussar Richard Thornton, with one tank left, an exact contemporary at Harrow. A strange and incongruous reunion.

10

SIDI REZEGH – BAPTISM OF FIRE

*'Your Excellency! Your Excellency! Your Excellency!...'
the groom kept repeating persistently while he shook Pierre
by the shoulder without looking at him, having apparently
lost hope of ever rousing him.
'Eh? Has it begun? Is it time?' Pierre asked opening his eyes.
'Hark at the firing, sir,' said the groom, an old soldier.
'All the gentlemen have gone already, and his Serene
Highness himself rode past long ago.'*

Leo Tolstoy, War and Peace

The initial advance had taken place on 16 November, 1941. The whole of Eighth Army moved forward from its positions east of the 'wire' and crossed this old frontier line into former Italian territory. Those who witnessed it said it was an amazing sight; the desert seemed to move. Most of the advance took place under cover of darkness, and the rough going in the south caused difficulties for the left flank of the phalanx. My patrol at Jarabub was about 100 miles further south and slightly forward of the old frontier line.

The operation codenamed Crusader was to avenge the abortive attempt under Battleaxe to relieve the garrison of Tobruk last June. And it was to destroy the enemies armour, thereafter to drive the Axis Forces back into Tripolitania.

The drive towards Tobruk by the British armour took place on the 18th and 19th of the month. At first Rommel did not believe that this was a serious push and was ill-prepared to meet the attack, enabling elements of 7th Armoured Division to reach the strategic high ground of Sidi Rezegh, which dominated Tobruk's fortress and harbour. (Its strategic importance only dawned upon us after we got there!) Once our forces were near enough, the garrison with its I (infantry) tanks was to break out to meet them. How I hoped they might be successful, with my memories of Tobruk only six months ago.

Just as the spearhead, 7th Armoured Brigade, was driving north towards the relief of Tobruk, a Panzer attack came from an unsuspected quarter. The German tanks had overrun the British brigade's supply column (B Echelon), and these, frantically trying to get out of the way, were at first ignored by the Panzers and then carried forward by the momentum of the armoured thrust. The British tank crews of the 7th Hussars could hardly pick out a target in this mêlée, such was the dust and confusion. The Hussars were picked off one by one by the German anti-tank gunners, who possessed weapons far superior to our own. Barrie Pitt described it thus:

> 'During the holocaust which followed, all but ten of the old cruisers (and these the ones that had broken down before battle had joined) and all the Hussars' Crusaders were destroyed; not just knocked out with some possibility of recovery and repair, but completely wrecked as the Panzers rode over their positions and pumped shell after shell into their smoking and immobile hulls until they were reduced to scrap iron. Between the wrecks, surviving crew members dodged from cover to cover, carrying wounded, dragging burnt and pain-wracked comrades out of hatches, falling under the hail of machine-gun fire; 7th Hussars was not to be seen again in the desert, although, re-formed, it fought in Burma.'[1]

It was at this moment, or shortly thereafter, on 21 November, 1941, that I had met up with the remnants of the 7th Hussars, as described in the previous chapter. I knew many of the officers from Cairo days to be distinguished by their leather bandolier slung diagonally from the right shoulder. And now it had come to this. They were a professional regiment with a very fine reputation. This type of action was to be the typical pattern of armoured warfare in the campaign that followed: an unseen enemy emerging from an unexpected quarter, usually from the direction of the setting sun, so that our crews were temporarily blinded. This was a favourite tactic of the Panzers, for the on-coming darkness put a finite end to the battle.

The rest of 7th Armoured Brigade, under Brigadier Davy, had fared little better, and they were no longer an effective fighting force. 22nd

Armoured Brigade, made up of Yeomanry regiments and led by Brigadier Scott-Cockburn, had also received a bloody nose. But such was the confusion of desert warfare that General Ludwig Cruewell, the commander of the German Afrika Korps, 'was deeply worried . . . and thought himself surrounded by immeasurably superior forces'. The 4th Armoured Brigade, the third of the trio in 30 Corps, I was now to seek out – but how to find them?

It was no good trying to find Brigadier Alec Gatehouse, its commander, that night, so my patrol dossed down in the desert, having sought out a friendly leaguer for protection.

That night it rained and sometime during the next morning we came upon 4th Armoured. I was slightly apprehensive about the reception we might receive. GHQ Liaison Squadron and their patrols were new to the desert. I thought that I would either be cold-shouldered or would have a lot of explaining to do. It was the very reverse. I was warmly welcomed by the Brigadier and immediately made to feel at home. It was Gatehouse's battle HQ, lying just behind his armoured regiments. This consisted of a troop of tanks and an armoured command vehicle (ACV – a new-fangled toy), the Brigade Major (David Silvertop), and a Staff Captain (Geoffry Hooper). My three 15cwt trucks were the only unarmoured vehicles, I noticed, and they added an unnecessary clutter to this self-contained mobile HQ. We got over the difficulty by wide dispersion. My vehicles were several hundred yards away, and each a hundred yards from the next.

When I needed to keep in touch with things I walked over to the command vehicles, and if a tank engagement was going on it was quite easy to dodge the 'overs'. They were solid shot and you could see them coming! More exciting was an unexpended round skidding across the flat desert surface like ducks and drakes. If caught without my transport and a move was suddenly ordered I was sometimes invited to jump up on the back of the Brigadier's tank, a somewhat dubious privilege although in this exposed position one could hear the cross-chat on the intercom between the armoured squadrons and have a bird's eye view of the battle.

Alec Gatehouse was a charming, debonair fellow and completely unflappable when it came to a crisis. To outward appearances he was like an amiable teddy-bear, but he was much more than that, being much respected by the men under his command, in whom he took a protective and fatherly interest. As for them, there were no men I admired more than the tank crews (RTR and Cavalry) in the Western Desert. Trapped in their steel boxes, they were prey to the more powerful armament of the German tank and anti-tank guns – sitting ducks – if it was not for their panache and skill.

Each evening at last light it was the custom of both sides to withdraw a little and form close leaguer, usually a column of about two or three vehicles abreast, with a protective screen around them. After a hard day's slogging-match neither side was in the mood for any silly games at night at that stage of the war. Indeed the leaguer had to be recognizable for replenishment purposes, and commonly displayed a 'Leaguer Light' on a long pole. We could often see the enemy's light. Tanks that one had been engaging earlier in the day were now equally in need of rest and replenishment.

The leaguer (or 'laager' as it was sometimes called) broke up before first light.[2] The armoured regiments took up battle positions, and there was just enough time to have a brew-up (with a bit of luck), before the day's battle commenced. In winter the men huddled round a makeshift cooking stove, a mixture of sand and petrol in a cut-off petrol can, with some holes punched in its side. In summer the burning sun on a tank's armour plating could be hot enough to fry an egg! The South African armoured car regiment was adept at hunting gazelle, and a common sight was a shot gazelle strapped to the turret, to provide a welcome change of diet that evening.

In theory an armoured brigade had some 25-pounder and anti-tank artillery in support, but no infantry. The consequence of this was that ground, once captured, could not be held; indeed, at that stage of desert warfare that was not the intention. It was tank against tank, the object being to destroy the enemy's armour. An example of this was the extraordinary battle in which the 8th Hussars took part on the morning of the second day (19 November). Using the tactics of the old-fashioned cavalry charge, they drove straight at the enemy in their small but mobile American Stuart tanks (Honeys) and they engaged in close-range individual duels with the heavier tanks of the enemy, rather reminiscent of the English ships against the Spanish Armada. Indeed there were many similarities with war at sea.

The terrain which was the setting for the forthcoming battle was confined by two shallow escarpments running east-west. Immediately below the northern escarpment ran the desert track known as Trigh Capuzzo, and beyond that was Tobruk itself, fenced in by lines of fortifications. In between the two escarpments (each falling toward the sea) was a desert airfield or sandy landing ground which dominated the approaches to Tobruk. However, the rise and fall of the ground was almost imperceptible – it was all flat desert to us, pocked-marked by camel scrub, no more than 18in high, the only cover one could get.

I joined 4th Armoured Brigade somewhere east of the airfield. They were lucky to have more than 100 tanks (runners); the other two armoured brigades had already been shot to pieces, although the much-battered 22 Armoured, plus the remnants of 7 Armoured Brigade, were even now battling it out with the Panzers on the edge of the airfield to our west. We could hear the dull thuds as solid shot hit armour. Columns of black smoke rose into the air and the red glow of tanks 'brewed-up' could be discerned. There was an acrid smell of cordite, burning vehicles and oil that drifted towards us, as we made our way towards the scene.

'Strafer' Gott, the Divisional Commander, held two quick conferences on the airfield that day, 22 November, with his Brigade Commanders. At the first one he cancelled immediate attempts for the relief of Tobruk. At about midday this one was interrupted by the ominous sound of approaching Panzers and the meeting had to scatter rapidly, the position being overrun. For the rest of that day utter confusion reigned at Sidi Rezegh, it was difficult to tell friend from foe and the ghastly backdrop of burning tanks, exploding shells, the thump of our 25-pounders and the whistle and crash of the German 88's heightened the drama of the scene. The whole was compounded by the cold wind and the bleakness of a desert winter's day. Regiments became split up, squadron out of touch with squadron, troop with troop and tank with tank, so action was totally unco-ordinated. It was Jock Campbell's efforts, in which he personally led tanks into the attack, standing up in his staff car and waving them on, which saved the day and prevented us from being destroyed piecemeal.[3]

It was now about 4 p.m. The battle had raged most of the day, and now we had a lull. Would the Panzers call it a day and withdraw? It seemed like it. Gatehouse's battle HQ had fortunately remained intact. He was temporarily absent at the second meeting with Strafer Gott. A leaguer light had been prepared for his return. I was standing by the ACV chatting to the occupants when suddenly there was a commotion on the horizon. We realized that we were being attacked and the German tanks were right upon us. There was no time for defence. The headquarters was scattered to the four winds, as was our armoured screen. Those of us who had time to reach our vehicles leapt in and drove like mad. The Germans had reported the HQ captured including the Brigadier, but he was to turn up later, saved by this lucky meeting. When the dust had settled I found myself in a small column consisting of:

One Honey tank
One 25-pounder gun + crew
A group of Scots Guardsmen (under Captain Ion Calvocoressi)
Our Commander Royal Artillery – Brigadier Linden Bolton
Myself with a patrol vehicle.

We did not know quite where we were, but it was clear that we had been overrun. At dusk we formed a little leaguer and consumed what rations we could find. We tuned in my wireless set to try and re-establish contact. All we heard were the seductive tones of *Lili Marlene*.

The next morning we awoke to an empty desert. We had no idea in which direction we should head but set off into the blue hoping to find friendly troops. The desert was scattered with lost detachments, some British and others Axis. We mostly took evasive action when we were not sure of the identification of the column, although we had some means of defence.

Then one of those things happened which acts as a catalyst in one's memory. The column had halted on the edge of the escarpment with the leading vehicle hesitating on the very brink. Vehicles had been down it before, but it was a bit of a drop through soft sand. Intending to give the hesitant column a lead, I took it *schuss* in my vehicle and the other vehicles followed me. Up came the Brigadier,

'You bloody fool, what did you want to take them down there for?' he cried. 'We'll never bloody well get up again, and here we are pinned to the ground in the enemy's own back yard!'

I tried to explain that I was only trying to be helpful, as the column had evidently stuck and no one came up to give a lead.

'Bloody fool,' he continued to mutter, and then he adopted a more rueful expression, thumping me on the back he said,

'Bloody good try! But you made a balls of it!'

As to whether I made a balls of it or whether Linden Bolton might have done so if he had kept the column on the Sidi Rezegh plateau we shall never know. But shortly afterwards several clouds of dust swept past the position we had last occupied above the escarpment. German tanks!

11

FORTY DAYS ON

I need not have worried about missing the battle on my way up from Jarabub – it lasted another forty days!

There followed, after the fracas at Sidi Rezegh, a period of about three days when the organization of both sides seemed completely shattered. Small columns, such as ours, were wandering about the desert looking for parent units or other friendly faces. There were minor clashes between these crippled remnants. Frequently one side could not be distinguished from another, as by this time both sides were making use of each other's captured transport. There were many cases of one side attaching itself to the column of the other, which had neither the ability to take prisoners nor any other effective action, and simply sent them away.

A good example of the type of confusion that reigned was that of a New Zealand infantry brigade, under Brigadier Barrowclough, which, after an all-night drive, at dawn decided to halt. As usual they formed a leaguer.

> 'Daylight always reveals in a great leaguer an apparent confusion with vehicles of many kinds facing in all directions, each like a domestic household – waking, washing, cooking and not minding its neighbours. And so it was this morning. . . . The war could wait until after breakfast!'[1]

As Barrie Pitt has put it,

> 'It was at this point that two important discoveries were made. The first was that the guides had veered off course during the

night and, instead of avoiding Bir el Chleta, the brigade was precisely there; and the second was that sitting in the middle of the brigade leaguer were Cruewell's Afrika Korps headquarters, complete with almost all his wireless vehicles and the whole of his cipher staff.'[2]

The capture of Gatehouse's headquarters, which had compromised the whole of the cypher codes for 7th Armoured Division, was not so disastrous when compared with this! Like Gatehouse, Cruewell had had the luck to leave his HQ only a short time before. But the 5th South African Brigade, further south, was at the same time completely destroyed and knocked out of the battle.

By about the third day, after being overrun at Sidi Rezegh, Gatehouse had managed to re-establish his HQ, having been lent two tanks (one for the forward wireless link to regiments (3rd and 5th Royal Tank Regiment and 8th Hussars), and one for the rear link to Division). He was therefore operational again. His tanks, by then about 100 strong, were our sole reserve of armour left in the desert.

Meanwhile our small column had crept along the escarpment in an easterly direction and eventually found a place where we could climb up again. We had many minor adventures during our brief period of freedom before joining up once again with Gatehouse.

Rommel now decided on a daring stroke. While we were still in a state of confusion he set out on a dash for the Wire in the neighbourhood of Sidi Omar, with the object of driving on to Egypt with the British in disarray way behind. But the British had been able to re-group, salvage some of their tanks and receive replacements. At this moment they made a successful drive for Tobruk, which was eventually relieved and brought Rommel scurrying back again.

Rommel now realized that his supply position was desperate (the loss of Tobruk being an important factor) and that he had no alternative but to withdraw to shorter lines on a properly defensible position. It had to be El Agheila, on the Gulf of Sirte. Then began a chase which never quite succeeded in cutting off the retreating Axis. At this time many of our moves were made at night as we by-passed the great hump of the Jebel Akhdar (the 'green mountain'), and cut across by the Trig el Abd aiming for Agedabia, thus isolating Benghazi.

Desert driving at night was a surrealist experience. Minute irregularities in the desert surface were magnified into enormous features – a small ridge became a distant range of mountains. Some rocks became a squadron of tanks, camel scrub a forest. All the time one's mind was hallucinating upon these imaginary landscapes, groping towards something familiar.

At night one could not use lights of any kind; we drove in close convoy. The dust was choking and the vehicle in front frequently stopped, with the driver asleep at the wheel. If, in fact, he had failed to move at the last 'start-up' this could lose us half the convoy.

All those who went through these desert experiences found it a mesmerizing place. Its very vastness accentuated the strange homeliness one found on every side. One did not have to travel far to find a friendly camp fire. Everyone was welcome. As one sat round with a mug of tea laced with a splice of rum, with the vast canopy of the heavens overhead, shot with a myriad of stars, one began to feel one never wanted to leave 'God's own country'.

Before departing from 4th Armoured Brigade, I must give a South African perspective of its commander. 1st South African Brigade reported that it was under attack and Gatehouse answered the call for help.

> 'Just in time . . . in sailed Brigadier Alex Gatehouse, that gay cavalier of the armour. His top-booted legs dangled from the turret-top, a Scots plaid travelling rug lay across his knees, for the day was cold; later one was to see Gatehouse with that rug belted round his waist like a kilt, riding into battle seated in an armchair strapped to the top of the tank. Gatehouse of the heavy head, the hawk nose and deep-set eyes was a man after Pienaar's heart, and in later days he often remarked, "Alec Gatehouse is a great tank commander, the best in the Desert, I will fight with him anywhere in tanks".'[3]

But Gatehouse on this occasion did not reciprocate, and later remarked that 'Dan Pienaar was, in my opinion, in a highly excitable state, and it was very difficult to discover what he wanted'.[3]

I left 4th Armoured Brigade just after Christmas, 1941, and was sent with my patrol to 13 Corps Headquarters then at Antelat (no more than a mark on the map) to cover their salient. Here I had the great pleasure of being reunited with Dermot Daly whom I had not seen since the battle began, although he was constantly receiving my signals and passing them on to the Army Commander, General Ritchie.

Dermot in his shaggy sheepskin coat was suffering dreadfully from desert sores and both hands were bandaged. In fact I had to send a signal back to Army HQ, 'Please send Dermot's ointment'. This *en clair* message caused some confusion at Army HQ which took it for a coded request for reinforcements! Dermot had just left in his pick-up for Corps headquarters, a few hundred yards away to see John Harding (then BGS). He never re-appeared. We searched high and low, but there was absolutely no sign of him. We could only assume that he had been 'put in the bag' in a snatch operation. In fact the enemy were now dangerously close. It was the beginning of Rommel's counter-offensive which began on 21 January, 1942, a few days after my twenty-third birthday.

A few months later Dermot resurfaced in a PoW camp in Germany. To me his was a great loss and, although he had his weaknesses, he was a most endearing character and I was very fond of him. Always the boxer, with a boxer's characteristics, he was also a guardsman of the old school. In London, even in wartime, his regulation dress was bowler hat, blue suit, carnation in his buttonhole and a rolled umbrella. Even after his release from prison he would appear in this gear. We had been together now for eighteen months, quite a long spell for wartime.

Now the fat is in the fire. Our precarious hold does not last. A new armoured division has joined us, straight from England, the 1st Armoured Division. With no time for desert training, it is put straight into the line. In three days its armoured element, 2nd Armoured brigade, has taken a terrible pasting and lost seventy tanks, which really knocked the division out of the battle.

During this confusing time while we were poised on the brink, something like the flash of a kingfisher caught my eye, a scout car with flying pennant dashed past. In it was an elegant young man, with red 10th Hussars sidecap with Prince of Wales's feathers (they were fresh out from England), and yellow knotted neckerchief, like some exotic bird in the drabness of the desert landscape. It was Simon Elwes, the portrait painter, the darling of the London scene, who, like me, had left Sandown Park, in his case to transfer from the Footguards to the glamorous Hussars. He was later to have an even more glamorous job painting a portrait of Farouk's Queen, Farida, in Cairo!

We were now on the run. Orders came that we must abandon our recently won positions and retire, in as orderly a manner as possible, to the Gazala line. This dash across the desert became known as the 'Msus Stakes', named after the pivotal position which we had been forced to abandon.

My memory is hazy about the Gazala battle where we halted the German and Italian attack. All I do remember is being sent down to join the Free French, led by General Koenig, during his redoubtable defence of Bir Hacheim, the southernmost bastion of the Gazala line. General Koenig was a charming example of the old school of French officer, who made such an heroic stand at Bir Hacheim that the enemy left it severely alone. The whole of my time at Bir Hacheim was spent in a sandstorm of such ferocity that we were hardly able to eat, let alone see to move. The sand got into everything and the darkened sky resembled a London pea-souper. This natural phenomenon, which occurred from time to time, was exacerbated by the fact that the surface of the desert had been churned up, by the passage of tanks and other vehicles, to such an extent that the lightest storm was enough to still all movement in that benighted country.

With spring came a lull in the fighting and the patrols were called in back to base, then at 8th Army headquarters, George Grant, our second in command when Dermot disappeared, had now taken over. 'Foxer' Grant was so named because his colouring resembled that of the fox, auburn hair and moustache to match. Clad in a white sheepskin coat, he was a fine sight. Sane and level-headed, he was the very antithesis of Dermot, and the fact that his yeomanry regiment had been converted to signals gave him a professional advantage.

This was the first time in five months that I had met up with the other patrol leaders, who each had his own individual adventure to tell. A leprechaun-like figure known as 'Herbie' Herbison was by far the oldest, and the most popular, a bit of an old roué, fond of his whisky, and with many stories to tell.

Living in a tiny mess tent there was plenty of badinage. Jasper Backhouse, another Yeoman, had a curious idiosyncracy. He could not bear to be woken from his bed and went berzerk if shaken out of his sleep. It became quite a game and, even if the column was about to move on, he could be seen still in his underwear pursuing his tormentor across the desert. Frank Thompson was reading Greek poetry and dreaming of the egalitarian society to come – from the safety of the officers' mess tent!

Come the spring and the rains the desert suddenly bloomed. Instead of a sandy waste it had become a meadowland of wild flowers, drifts of blues, yellows and reds. At one time the North African coast had been the granary of the Roman Empire. One might walk in shade, it was said, from Alexandria to Tripoli. Were these seeds so rudely disturbed by the churning tanks, the very ones that had lain dormant for two thousand years?

12

OUT OF THE LINE

Our Squadron had now been in the desert nearly six months and the time had come to be moved out of the line. Most of us were suffering from desert sores, the equivalent of vitamin deficiency, although the term was then unknown. To protect the brittle skin, our hands were bandaged, for even shoving ones hand into a pocket could remove the back of it and leave a raw mess.

As there was no water for normal washing purposes, although we did shave, our clothes were in a deplorable state, and a temporary lull made our withdrawal that much easier. We now considered ourselves to be thoroughly desert-worthy, able to sleep under the stars, to survive on bully and biscuits, to cook on the flicker of a flame and, with the aid of a prismatic compass and the dog-star, to find our way by day or by night; and there was a camaraderie in those wide open spaces which is now almost impossible to believe or re-create. Those regiments fresh out from England, with their pale skin, were treated with amused contempt for we knew that they, like us, would have to learn it the hard way.

It was therefore a strange metamorphosis, the journey out of Egypt into Palestine. Straight out of the desert we hit the greenery of the Nile Delta, sweet with tempting water melons, those deadly fruits which could play havoc with one's guts. Then, plunging through the oriental clamour of Cairo with its suffocating dung-laden air and a hundred strange cries, we crossed another stretch of desert before reaching the Suez Canal. Purged as we were of any impressions except those of our primitive existence, these new sights, smells and sounds made a profound impact on the subconscious and, like an undigested meal, kept on returning to the imagination.

Next we had to cross the arid Sinai Desert, where tongues of creeping sand licked the slender ribbon of asphalt which was the sole link to Palestine and regions beyond, which might become our northern front. For if the Germans broke through the Caucasus we would be hard put to stop them pouring down into the rich oilfields of Iraq, a pincer movement which would end at the Canal and Cairo. This area was notoriously insecure, with incipient terrorism in Palestine, in the Lebanon and Syria the unreliable Vichy French who had reluctantly laid down their arms, and rebellious movements in Baghdad and Teheran.

Under the auspicies of GHQ Jerusalem, then located in the King David Hotel, our Squadron, equipped with long-range wireless sets, were to report on the political situation in this troubled area. First, on whether the Vichy French had truly surrendered. Second, on a dispute which had broken out between two bedouin tribes across our lines of communication with the southern Russian front. And, thirdly, we were to report on the Turkish-Syrian frontier area which we might have to cross if things deteriorated in Turkey.

One or two huge whaleback sand-dunes had already blocked the asphalt road which necessitated tiresome detours. In our present timescale, where we are now approaching the millennium, it is salutory to recall that our tiny convoy was following in the tracks of Allenby's expedition, a magnificent host of horse and foot which drove the Turk out of his 500-year-old domain in the Holy Land. This fantastic cavalcade, the last the world will ever see, with all its problems of watering the multitude of horse, camel, mule and man, passed this way only twenty-three years before, in 1918. Indeed, perhaps not so strange if one remembers that, in 1940, the last cavalry division ever formed, armed with sword, lance and holstered carbine, was shipped out from England to help quell the Arab revolt in Palestine, the country we were about to enter. When, shortly after, the division was disbanded, many of the horses, the cream of the English shires, had to be shot.

As we emerged out of the desert and into the rolling country of southern Palestine, with all the old familiar domestic sounds of flock and farm, with water and fruit abundant, we really felt that we were entering the land of milk and honey. And in our bivouac outside Jerusalem the pungent tang of herbs, the crisp, cool air and the luminous stars completed this impression.

My first assignment was to report upon the skirmish between the Howeitat and the Rualla tribes. I stayed with both sides and was received with great courtesy, and traditional hospitality, in their black bat-winged tents with all their people and flocks gathered around. As I have remarked, the days of Lawrence of Arabia were not that far gone, Lawrence's arab revolt being the other wing of Allenby's advance. These people bore all the marks of that epoch. Only a fool would not be stirred by the romance of these Arab tribes. I was privileged to accompany the Howeitat tribe on the march, and rode in style, mounted on a magnificent she-camel, into the ancient ruins of Palmyra, my patrol vehicles joining me later. I heard the haunting banshee song of the camel riders for the first, but not the last time.

To investigate the frontier area between Syria and the Turkish border, I attached myself to the Royals Armoured Car Regiment (Royal Dragoon Guards), who in typical fashion had made themselves comfortable and at home in this unlikely area. They had re-acquired a number of horses and deployed several mounted patrols, one of which I joined for an early morning ride. It was, in point of fact, country of the most romantic beauty, unsullied at this time by any such thing as a tarmac road. Olive groves and pine-clad hills invited one to lie in the shade and doze away the heat of the afternoon sun, as if this was life as it had always been. The desert war seemed a million miles away.

In order to fulfil my mission, which was to make a series of reports on the roads and tracks leading up to the Turkish frontier, I decided to take my patrol a little bit further north. Any maps that existed were of very poor quality, usually a revised French version of an original Turkish survey, carried out in the days of the last Sultan. However, we expected a series of frontier posts with a no-man's-land in between. Our little convoy of three vehicles had been following a dirt track across this undulating country of olive grove and maquis for some time, rather longer than we should have done if we had had our wits about us.

Rounding a bend at last we came upon a frontier post. But these men were in strange uniforms and came running out with their rifles! We were two miles inside Turkey and we were quickly surrounded. In the confusion of the moment I remembered the high-grade cypher books that we carried and managed to drop them into the camel tanks holding our water supply. Another of our party, a corporal, disappeared, having asked to relieve himself behind a bush. We did not know what had happened to him. Evidently they had not counted us so far, so presumably his absence was not noted.

The commander of the post would not release us and he did not know what to do, so he sent off to higher authority. 'Ankara!' he said. I was put in a small cell and through its minute window I saw the messenger ride off on a black horse – to Ankara! Or more likely to the nearest centre of civilization where there might be a telegraph post. I saw him galloping up the white winding road in diminishing clouds of dust. What a fool I had been. But it was a minor incident and would probably cause no alarm. In the evening I saw a black horse galloping down the road from whence he had come, in increasing clouds of dust. The messenger had returned! What news? We were to be released! Rather shamefacedly and somewhat relieved we made our way back to regain the Syrian border. The hero of this episode was the corporal who by his *ruse de guerre* had evaded capture and run across country all the way back to the Syrian border to give the alarm.

Many years later Bernard Fergusson, that be-monocled Highland officer, told me that he had been the staff officer on duty at GHQ Jerusalem that night and the lines were buzzing between Ankara and Jerusalem. The Turks were deeply offended that an armed British patrol had violated Turkish territory at a moment when secret diplomatic negotiations were going on to persuade Turkey to join the Allies. 'Do you realize,' he said, 'that you almost caused Turkey to join the wrong side?' As for the men of the patrol, they loved it. This was real adventure, what war was all about!

PART IV
DESERT JOURNEYS I

BEHIND THE LINES
WITH THE SAS

The Lie of the Land

The Great or Kalansho Sand Sea is one of four, each about the size of Ireland, which cover vast areas of the Libyan Desert.

The Qattara Depression lies to the east of the Great Sand Sea, some 40 miles south of the Arabs Gulf on the Mediterranean coast. This depression is four times the size of its nearest equivalent, the Dead Sea and Jordan Valley depression, measured at sea level. The floor of the Qattara Depression (a salt bog), is the lowest point on the Continent of Africa, being 134 metres below sea level. Some vehicles were able to cross it from east to west during the war. There were two routes, one following beneath the northern lip of the Depression, and the second running across a 'bridge' of hard-going in the centre of the salt marsh itself. Enemy air attacks put the northern route out of action, whereafter the central pass began to deteriorate rapidly.

The Great Sand Sea stretches unbroken for almost 500 miles from the line of the oases, Jarabub-Siwa and the Depression, south till it meets the rock cliffs of the Gilf Kebir massif. The Great Sand Sea is 100 miles wide with crested dunes rising to 400ft above the surface of the desert. The line of dunes runs north-south in seif formation. At its southern end patches of gravel surface appear between the dunes, and it is possible to motor down these 'streets', but impossible to make any progress more than 5 miles east or west.

At the Gilf Kebir (latitude 25° north) the dunes run into the rocks of this feature. This plateau, the most remarkable feature of southern Egypt at the time largely unexplored, extends south for some 200 miles. It has a width of between 50-100 miles and the plateau is suspended 800ft above the level of the surrounding desert and is 3,500ft above sea level at its southern end, in the north merging with the sand sea. The plateau is dissected round its edges by numerous deep and gorge-like wadis. These have eaten their way back into it for considerable distances, especially in the north where narrow tongues of plateau jut out onto the desert surface, separating the deep and twisting gorges. This impassable barrier is divided by a cleft at latitude

23° 30'N, *which was penetrated by one of Stirling's parties but which did not get through. Another pass 100 miles further south, marked as 'Eight Bells' on the map (from eight conical hills) was successfully navigated. A hundred miles to the west is the mysterious oasis of Kufra. (See also p. 104)*

This, then, was the grandiose playground in which the Special Air Service (SAS) and the Long Range Desert Group (LRDG) carried out their operations. The strategic importance of the features I have described can be readily imagined, for the Alamein Line plugged the one open gap in this huge barrier. One should not be deluded, however, by the importance of place names. These usually signified a small cairn, a holy man's tomb or, in the coastal area, some ruined buildings.

13

THE ESCARPMENT RENDEZVOUS
THE AIRFIELD RAIDS

With David Stirling a new idea was born. It was to strike at the enemy's exposed line of communication from deep inside the desert. At first he suffered setbacks, in that 'air drops' had proved disastrous, resulting in the death of his closest lieutenant, Jock Lewis, and others killed or captured. The Long Range Desert Group, the brainchild of Bagnold, a pre-war desert explorer, had meantime been successfully carrying out its principal rôle, that of 'road watches' behind the lines to gather vital intelligence about enemy movement.[1] The LRDG readily came to the aid of Stirling as a kind of drop-and-carry desert taxi service. Their expertise was desert navigation and so they could be relied upon for an accurate theodolite 'fix' to within walking range of the target. This had never been the case with submarines or patrol boats, so restricted by the vagaries of the weather or vulnerability to air attack.

I had run into David several times during the winter campaign on his way to and from operations. His attacks on enemy airfields behind the lines, at first a closely guarded secret, were now becoming widely known. I had to admit that I had been wrong in doubting that he could bring it off. In effect I had to eat humble pie in asking to rejoin him. My posting came through during our time in Syria. I was to proceed immediately to Kabrit Camp in the Canal Zone. My last sight of Syria was at a cool spring in the Bekaa Valley near Baalbek in which we bathed. One or two others, including Frank Thompson, were getting itchy feet and wanted to be off, for the news from the desert was very bad with many new reverses and casualties sustained. I left the squadron with a heavy heart. Another bond forged in the heat of war broken. Particularly was I sad to say goodbye to George

Grant who had filled so ably the gap left by the capture of Dermot Daly.

The activity at Kabrit, a tented camp alongside the Canal, was frantic. Here I met many old soldiers from No 8 Commando, whom David had recruited, so in a way it was like returning home. The ubiquitous American jeep had arrived for the first time in the Middle East. David had managed to grab the first batch. We spent most of our time between the Base Ordnance Depot drawing the vehicles and Base Workshops seeing to their modification. I think I am right in saying that these were the first vehicles seen in the Middle East with four-wheel drive – an immense improvement for crossing sandy terrain, tough, versatile and with a decent mileage to the gallon. Two men and their kit was the payload; for operations we could put an extra man in the back.

The Camp was comfortable for had it not been established by those very tactics which we were now to follow, 'hit and run raids' on neighbouring camps? Our New Zealander neighbours were to discover that many of their tents had disappeared mysteriously during the night.

Within two weeks of my arrival we were off! Our next operation was to raid enemy airfields immediately behind the German lines. This was to be the first SAS (then known as L Detachment) operation with its own transport and navigators. We used jeeps newly mounted with machine guns, and three-ton trucks to carry all our supplies of fuel, food, ammunition and explosives. Our party amounted to ten officers and 100 men.

It was now June, 1942. After the fall of Tobruk, 8th Army had retired to the Alamein Line, the final stand before Alexandria and the Nile Delta, which was only 60 miles away. In case of defeat at Alamein, and defeatism was in the air, we carried maps which would enable our party to escape south-west to Lake Chad in French Equatorial Africa, via the oasis of Kufra, south to the Sudan, or east into Sinai and the Levant, as the situation demanded.

As I wrote at the time,

'Travelling west from 8th Army H.Q. from the Alexandria-Cairo Road, we passed north of Wadi Natrun reaching the base of the Alamein line after a day's journey. Having passed safely through the line we hugged the lip of the Qattara Depression following occasionally an indistinct track marked by palm leaves. The bottom of the Depression could not be seen, only a descending series of cliffs and boulders dropping sharply until their outline was lost in a shimmer of pink. A further two days' travelling brought us to a point about 30 miles north of the Qattara Spring, 50 miles from the enemy-controlled coast at Mersa Matruh and one hundred miles due west of the Alamein line. Here was a long low escarpment which offered good cover for our 30 vehicles, and this we formed as our base for operations.'

For fourteen days and nights we attacked almost every night the airfields lying between Daba and Mersa Matruh or other opportunity targets. Our tactics were to drive as close as we could to the enemy airfield and then walk round the dispersed aircraft and place a time-bomb in the cockpit or on the wing. At that stage of mobile warfare, with the constant moving of forward airfields, the enemy had not the means of establishing proper airfield defence and the planes were seldom guarded; neither were the cockpits locked.

George Jellicoe, Stephen Hastings and I, departing on one of these operations, were detected by enemy aircraft, got properly strafed, losing two of our three vehicles. The remaining jeep was holed in the radiator, its tyres slashed and the vehicle resting only on its wheel hubs, but the engine still running. We made the 30-mile journey back to base with nine men up. A bright idea led us to plug the holed radiator with plastic explosive from our unused bombs. For water we relied on mother nature. Each man would relieve himself into the radiator in turn. It worked! But it smelt like a chicken coop!

These constant night operations took their toll, for those who were called upon nightly began to suffer from a drastic loss of sleep. It was impossible to sleep, except for a fitful doze, by day because of the heat and flies. At night we were always on the move or on operations. In the last days of the fortnight we had become a party of sleepwalkers, with men dropping off at the wheel or on their feet. Not an ideal way of sending an army into battle! This does not mean that blame attached to Stirling. We were all in this together and all of an equal mind, both officers and men. But Stirling was the natural leader in daring, imagination and execution of the plan. and most important of all, we were actually winning our private war against a ruthless and efficient enemy. Stirling was proving a dynamic leader; gone were the days of lethargy and idleness. His leadership technique was a peculiarly gentle one with a diffident and charming manner which made many of his more audacious exploits difficult to resist. Some of these plans had the element of a huge practical joke played upon the Axis forces, so unexpected were the attacks and so helpless and confused their reaction.

After two weeks of such operations, supplies and vehicles began to run out and had to be replenished. Several of our jeeps had been damaged or lost in air attacks. David decided to leave a small retaining force at the Escarpment Rendezvous, Stephen Hastings, myself and the Medical Officer Malcolm Pleydell a total of thirty officers and men; the remainder returned with all speed to Cairo. A fast party under Stirling managed to force their way down the camel track at the Qattara Spring, drop into the Depression and reach Cairo in two days. The heavy party travelling on top of the escarpment filtered through the base of the Alamein line and reached Cairo intact in three days. Two hectic days were spent in Cairo refitting and collecting new vehicles, and then the new force of about twenty-five jeeps returned by way of the Qattara Depression.

It was an eerie experience once the others had departed. Silence descended upon the desert, the heat clamped down upon us as we lay as if stunned in the comparative cool and security of our caves. We banned all movement by day, and the twilight hour we spent removing telltale tracks round our hideout. At that stage we had no idea whether Stirling's group would ever reach Cairo, when they might return, or what action we should take if surprised.

Stephen Hastings and I shared a cave. He was another recent recruit. He had come from the 2nd Scots Guards and had spent a year with his battalion in the Western Desert. The rôle of an infantry officer in this kind of mobile warfare was not an enviable one.

Steve and I, in one of those brief wartime relationships, got to know each other very well, and then we parted, never to meet again for the rest of the war. His companionship was one of those unexpected wartime bonuses. He was an incurable romantic, his Scots ancestry having bitten deep into his psyche. His repertoire of ballad and song, including of course a rendering of the sentimental but haunting 'Lili Marlene', kept our spirits up. Another bonus was his knowledge of and sympathy with the French. A section of Free French soldiers accompanied us and enlivened our operations. Among the names I remember were Le Grand, Zirnhold, Martin, Harent and Klein.

We took it in turns to keep watch, on a vantage point above our cave, where the dust devils and mirages played games with the imagination. Hostile aircraft were about, but they never spotted our location.

In the early morning Steve and I would walk down from the French cave, which was at best a pile of boulders, to our 'daytime cave' near the cookhouse. Here we would spend the remainder of the day. It was a long and low grotto with a floor of soft white sand. At one end a great lip curved over, touching the ground and forming a cool enclosed space, whilst at the extreme end grew a stunted palm. At best it would only contain three men lying down, but there was just room for a mosquito net to be suspended from the eaves which covered us quite easily. Once in it was a question of exterminating the flies and settling down to some of the unsuitable books which we carried, Thackeray's *The Virginians*, Lawrence's *Seven Pillars of Wisdom*, or Hemingway's *For Whom the Bell Tolls*. Above our heads were embedded a variety of marine fossils and shells and we had the leisure to consider in what strange manner they had arrived there.

But for the most part we let our imaginations run riot upon the theme of 'the ideal day in Cairo'. This became a kind of castle-in-the-air, combining every luxury and diversion that the mind could conceive. It became known as 'Comforts Day' and whiled away the interminable hours.

Our tranquility was disturbed twice. Shortly after the main party had left for Cairo, the navigator of Robin Gurdon's LRDG patrol, Tinker, which had been operating in the coastal area, flopped down in our cave. He had been an officer in the Merchant Navy and was an expert navigator. He always wore a little white Arab skull cap and was a calm and reliable man. On this occasion he was badly shaken as he told us that Gurdon has been killed and one man badly wounded by strafing. He blamed himself because he had missed our hideout and had spent several valuable hours in searching for it, during which Gurdon had died. After that there had been an argument in the patrol as to the course they should follow, which he knew was the wrong one. We hurriedly dug a grave down in the flat, and Pleydell took the wounded man into his expert hands.

A few days after this an LRDG officer who had been out on a watching patrol at Sidi Barrani came tearing in with stories that there were German patrols in our area, which had already been chasing him. This proved untrue and we sent him off with the wounded man and the officerless LRDG patrol to Cairo.

After eight days our food and water situation was serious and we began to get anxious about our fate, so we were relieved to hear a great rattling on the escarpment above and to see thirty brand new jeeps coming bumping down, complete with fresh crews and four Vickers (K) to each vehicle. David stumbled into our grotto bearing a pint jar of eau de Cologne, Turkish delight, cigars, tobacco, new pipes and an exhaustive store of plans for the future.

There was much rejoicing as we greeted parted companions, and even more rejoicing over the goodies they had brought. Nothing had changed in their absence. Here we were, still undetected, approximately 100 miles behind the enemy's lines, and 30 miles from the coast, but all the new kit and equipment David had brought and his dashing plans for the future changed our outlook completely.

As the enemy was now getting wise to our walk-on tactics, for the next operation David planned a mass attack on an aerodrome using our full armament. This consisted of two pairs of twin Vickers (K) machine guns (as used by the RAF) per jeep. With fifteen jeeps earmarked for this operation, it made a total of sixty machine guns, a formidable firepower.

The question was, which aerodrome? Our 11 set was kept busy with reports from 8th Army HQ on the present use of enemy airfields, but such reports were so confusing that David became exasperated. He sent a strongly worded signal back to Army HQ which unfortunately fell into the hands of the new Army Commander, General Montgomery, instead of General Auchinleck for whom it had been intended. The peppery general was not amused by these threats from 'the Boy David' whom he had never heard of before.

George Jellicoe, Sandy Scratchley and Paddy Mayne, my companions on the previous operations, had returned with the reinforcements. Also Chris Bailey, a most useful man who had kept an inn in Cyprus before the war with a renowned kitchen. He had transferred from the Cyprus Mule Company to the 4th Hussars and had just spent a year at 8th Army headquarters, so that his advice was invaluable.

George Jellicoe, following our abortive raid from Tobruk, had just carried out a daring raid on an aerodrome on the north coast of Crete. He and a party of French had been landed by submarine, had destroyed nineteen German aircraft, had made their way across the island to the south coast, where according to a pre-determined plan they had been picked up by a caique.

David Russell, who had recently arrived in Egypt with a Scots Guards draft, also joined us. I described him as 'a wild and independent character with a zest for life, but better at giving orders than taking them!'[2] The new intake was completed by an RAF liaison officer named Pike who was there to help with air supply. He had followed the almost irreplaceable Derek Raumsley whom everyone loved. Pike, an Australian, proved a worthy successor. He was deeply impressed by our aircraft score and could not get over the sudden departures armed to the teeth, and a few days later the arrivals back, waterless and on foot. Such a reaction boosted our morale, ever a sensitive emotion.

It became apparent that the most likely airfield to attack was LG 21 at Fuka,[3] 50 miles away near the coast. There was one day for preparation and rehearsal. We had discovered a new cave about a mile up the escarpment. It was long and low and in it we could fit twenty jeeps side by side. When they were all safely stowed away we hung camouflage nets from the overhanging lip of the cave right down to the ground. Thus we were completely invisible.

The cave, I wrote, rather reminded me of the scene in the film *Snow White and the Seven Dwarfs*.

> 'There was much hammering and clattering and singing as new wheels and tyres were fitted. The Vickers guns were stripped and cleaned, magazines loaded, engines taken down, and explosives made up. At one end of the cave two four-gallon petrol cans containing bully stew were sizzling over a large fire. At the other David was poring over maps and figures. George (who was in charge of the commissariat) was, with a great tin of acid drops in front of him, trying to work out the impossible problems of supply. Paddy, fast asleep and unrecognizable entwined under a large mosquito net, with his head under one jeep and his feet under another. All around in the soft sand lay tins of tobacco, sweets, pipes, jars of eau de Cologne (there was no water for washing), and last year's glossy magazines. George had thoughtfully spent £20 in Cairo on these luxuries, (£150 in today's currency) for which he would never be repaid. His characteristic mixture of ebullience and level-headedness were a great addition to our party.'

That same evening, 20 July, we carried out our dress rehearsal. We drove out into the plain as the light faded, formed up into two columns of seven jeeps each, with our leader, David, at the head and centre. We were fifteen jeeps all told, each jeep, as planned, mounted with four Vickers (K) guns, with two gunners and a driver. The officer drove the vehicle in order to control his lethal machine, and taking care, in my case, not to lean forward or backwards into the line of fire. The magazines of our sixty guns contained a mixture of ball, armour-piercing, tracer and incendiary bullets. We practised forming line abreast and line astern, opening fire on David's green Very Signal and following exactly in the tracks of the leaders, for each gun was firing outwards. When we opened up the noise was deafening, but, apart from one French jeep running amok, the practice was successful. We now only had to get there.

14

THE MASS ATTACK

The following day we continued with our loading, everything we would need for that night's operation. In particular the stowage of spare ammunition drums which had to be within ready reach. Of course we were overloaded, we always were, and this took its toll of tyres, springs and sometimes sumps. A sump could split open like a ripe melon, spilling its contents on the sand, if at night one hit an unseen rock.

'We left the escarpment RV at last light and climbed up the rocky cliff in our two columns. There was a full moon and so driving was comparatively easy. David led off at a terrific speed and it was not long before we were suffering from punctures. We had fifteen before we reached our objective, and for each one a halt of five minutes had to be made. One jeep and its crew had to be abandoned on the way owing to a cracked sump, and at this halt David gave us our final instructions. "Right lads, we haven't got much time. At the edge of the aerodrome form a line abreast and all guns spray the area. When I advance follow me in your two columns and on my green Very light open fire, outwards at the aircraft – follow exactly in each other's tracks, 5 yards apart - speed not more than 4 mph. Return to the RV independently moving only by night." He spoke casually as if putting us into our butts for a grouse drive.'

Michael Sadler, a young Rhodesian from the LRDG, was navigating. After 50 miles and three compass legs we hit the target off exactly. But what with the breakdowns we were rather late and had only two hours left before dawn.

'We descended across an old battlefield, where some of our corpses were lying still unburied, in the full moonlight. The burnt-out tanks and corpses looked cold and comfortless, and I took another swig of rum. Then we heard an aircraft overhead – it was circling low. Suddenly all the aerodrome landing lights were switched on and we saw our target perfectly illuminated, and the German bomber came in to land. The noise of its engines drowned our own. A hundred yards more to the aerodrome edge and we formed line abreast, halted and suddenly fired our sixty guns. A minute's fire to spray the defences and then we followed David in our two columns. In one minute we were amongst the parked aircraft – Messerschmitts, Stukas, Junkers and Heinkels lay all around us. The green Very light went up and we wound slowly like a snake, firing at the aircraft as we went. Clouds obscured the moon, and one after another the planes burst into flames, but not a gun was fired on us. We fired into their huts and tents, and we could see one or two figures running helplessly about. Some of the aircraft would only be fifteen yards away, and as I passed them at the end of the column they would glow red and explode with a deafening "phut" and there would be great heat.'

We had passed through the dispersal area, and were swinging round for a second visit, when an Ack Ack gun some 300 yards away opened up on us wildly. Our port-side guns returned the fire, but the gunner had hit one of our jeeps in the centre of the column as we drew away, the shots passing over our heads. Then we stopped:

"Switch off!", came the cry. We were still in the middle of the aerodrome, but there was dead silence. Then,

"Anybody hurt? Are you OK? Any ammunition left?"

"Only one drum!" came from somewhere.

"Any ammunition? Any ammunition?" went echoing down the line, then,

"OK. We're going to start off now. Start up!"

And the cry went back down the line, "Start up! Start up! Start up!"

As we moved off the aerodrome Paddy Mayne spotted an untouched bomber and, jumping from his jeep with a bomb in his hand, ran up to it and, placing the bomb in its engine, ran back and caught us up.

We had burnt thirty aircraft, damaged more, and lost one jeep and one man, a Frenchman, killed. The whole thing had taken fifteen minutes. Then we melted into the desert in two's and three's, as arranged.

'I stopped to have a look at my party. Three jeeps, two of which had irreparable punctures, eight men and one wounded. There was about 1½ hours' darkness left, then the sun would rise and we must seek cover for the day. We drove very fast watching the stars for our direction, and watching for that paleness to appear which meant dawn. I wanted, if possible, to cross the telegraph track before light, but I didn't want to stop anywhere near it. The stars paled and the dawn came, and with it a blessing. A great white blanket of mist engulfed us so that we were able to continue driving unseen. As the sun rose the mist lifted, and there, only a few hundred yards away was the telegraph track. We became fearful of aircraft but took the risk and tore down the track on our tyreless rims bumping and rattling over the rocky surface until we came to three stones placed in a triangle which had been put there the night before to serve as a guide for our return. Here we swung west on a bearing 320 degrees trying to put a mile or two between us and the track. Running parallel with us to our south was a long low escarpment, which offered good cover. To our front was short and patchy scrub. The escarpment might be dangerous, so we found a patch of camel thorn rising not more than a foot – dispersed our vehicles amongst it and camouflaged up.'

We felt very bare and exposed in this spot, but decided to revive our spirits with a little breakfast.

'No sooner had the tea come up to a boil and the sausages started sizzling than the first aircraft appeared. "Aircraft," someone said in that quiet and urgent voice which we had learnt to dread, and we all froze whilst it passed harmlessly over – a Stuka weaving and searching its way down the long low escarpment. I told the men to scatter themselves 400 yards away from the vehicles and not to move, put a few finishing touches to the camouflage, sorrowfully left the breakfast and then walked slowly away myself looking over my shoulder for aeroplanes and stopping and listening every few paces. I took a rough bearing on where we had left the jeeps and then chose a meagre bush, which seemed to rise almost 18 inches, spread my handkerchief over two of its twigs and lay my head on the piece of ground on which the shadow was cast. Soon the sky became alive with aircraft circling angrily round and round, like a swarm of angry bees, out to seek vengeance on the destruction of the night before. We got no shelter from the July sun, and we could not visit the vehicles for food or water, and so we lay counting the minutes and watching the sun creep across the sky. We could see fires in the distance and watched Stukas dive again and again at unseen targets and the black smoke curl angrily up across the horizon. Our position was so exposed that although the aircraft flew directly over us, they never spotted our vehicles – searching instead into the shadows of the escarpment and into the rougher ground to our north.'

After twelve hours of terrific heat, the sun seemed to lose its intensity and quickly sank below the horizon in the direction that we must follow.

'We waited for another fifteen minutes as the darkness fell upon us. Our spirits began to rise and our bodies glow with the stimulant of a day's exposure to the sun. After a short search we found our jeeps, lit a fire for a cup of chi and stew, changed the wheel hubs upon which we had been running, for new ones, then squatted down in the sand around the fire with our mess tins in front of us. We ate in silence.'

The eight young men in the circle around the fire were already veterans. Corporal Lily, a Coldstreamer from commando days, stared in silence at his empty mess tin. He wore a head cloth tied pirate-fashion round his forehead, he had a long drooping moustache and a black beard. How splendidly those pre-war guardsmen stood up to this irregular warfare, I thought. Lily was a bit of a philosopher and had a motherly streak. He was concerned for the wounded men, and young Dalziel (one of my former commando lads), and for the rest of us, I do believe, from the fatalistic expression on his face. Corporal Lambie was with me again, always a steady and uncomplaining man. The others I did not know so well, but they were all desert-hardened, understanding how to use those unpromising elements, the sun, the moon and the stars to best advantage. So we were a silent circle, each brooding on his own thoughts, resting for an hour until the moon had changed from orange to silver, and the desert had been flooded with a light almost as bright as day.

'We threw off the camouflage nets, filled up with petrol and water and put the wounded man in an easy position in the back of one of the jeeps. Then I walked out with my compass and took a bearing of 320 degrees and found a corresponding constellation of stars, on which we could drive. It should only be a matter of 18 miles to the escarpment RV. It should also be easy to find because we couldn't miss the escarpment, and once we had found it, it was only a question of turning right or left until we came upon our people. Luckily we found our tracks of the previous evening so that now we knew we were right. They were quite easy to follow until suddenly we lost them completely and so continued on our old bearing. After thirteen miles we were a little surprised to arrive at our escarpment, at least it looked like our escarpment as there were hundreds of jeep and 3-tonner tracks running in all directions. And there also were the wadis up which the vehicles had been run and camouflaged. And yet it was deserted and not quite the same. We got out and examined the tracks closely – they couldn't have been a day old. How very mysterious! Perhaps we were too far down. So we drove up the cliffside for 3 miles and down it for 3 miles and saw not a sign of life. It was the same escarpment and yet it wasn't the same escarpment – not quite the same. It was deserted. Could they have all moved away and left no one to pick us up?

'As soon as we had stopped, all the men except Corporal Lily and myself had nodded and dropped off to sleep, and so we thought quietly for a few minutes and then decided to drive on for five miles further. That distance would tally with our milometer reading. And yet we couldn't understand why they had left our escarpment, because it was our escarpment in almost every detail, and if it wasn't why all the jeep and 3 tonner tracks? It was a mystery which was not attractive at three o'clock in the morning. All the usual uneasy feelings began to creep into the back of my mind. Supposing we are lost, and our petrol gives out – which it will do after a few more miles; and then the wounded man – he won't be able to walk. But then fatigue came to the rescue. To concentrate on driving and watching the stars was enough – there was no room for hopes or fears. And then there was always only one answer to these kind of vital problems, and now it was to drive for five miles, to stop and wait for the morning. Tomorrow could take care of itself. We pulled up after five miles in a small depression, and then suddenly, light of heart, we unstrapped our bedding, laid it out on the sand and slept.'

After an hour I awoke, roused my gunner, Lambie, and walked over to Lily's jeep and told him I was going to reconnoitre. Dawn was coming with a heavy mist and we got into the jeep, left the bedding on the ground and drove straight towards the moon which was on the exact line of our bearing. It was low in the sky and turning pink, and I was just saying to Lambie how fortunate it was, now the stars had gone in, that we had the moon to drive on, when suddenly through the mist we saw a drop and there was a cairn.

> 'I could recognize every stone of the cairn, it was the one that Steve and I had spent many weary hours watching from in the scorching sun. Yes, it must be the same one. And there, there was one of the three tonner bays – a small wadi where we left the explosives. And there, my god, was a real and solid 3-tonner draped in its camouflage net. I was right the whole time and my bearing and distances were dead correct. Why had I ever showed the men that I doubted? I told Lambie casually that I thought we were about right and didn't show my excitement, and a great smile spread over his face. We drove the half mile back to the others, shouted, "Wake up, we're home, come on, pack up and get the engines started". Then we dropped down the cliff over the familiar bumps and along the cliff edge, stirring up great clouds of talcum powder dust until we reached the long cave, and then up and into it with the three jeeps making thunder in its eaves and waking the sleepers on the ground.'

We were the first home, but then, as day came, first one and then another battered jeep came rolling in. David and George and Steve and six men arrived on one jeep grinding along on four buckled wheel hubs. They too had thought they were lost and had evidently stumbled across the same false escarpment as we had. They, for an awful moment, had thought that it was the coastal escarpment, that their compass was wrong and that the sea lay beyond. One of the French officers had been killed by the strafing of the day before. Another party had shot down a Stuka and had captured the airman who turned out to be one of Rommel's personal pilots, and a German doctor who was also in the plane.

We thought it rather odd that he should be riding about in a German dive-bomber for no reason at all. For all he could say was, 'I went up for plissure, but it ended unheppily'. These and other remarks, about his pre-war visit to 'Clicton-on-Sea', caused us intense amusement, light-headed as we were after the excitement of thirty enemy aircraft destroyed, one Stuka shot down, two prisoners, and all of us back safely except two. And there was the unforgettable exhilaration of a cool clean morning in the desert after a night of nightmare quality.

> 'In the sober heat of the day we lay flat on our backs pestered by the flies and hoping terribly that we could get some rest at last. But no, tonight we must move further south and west because the enemy would do everything he could to find us now. And this RV. We had used it for over twenty days in the most blatant fashion; it was one hundred miles behind the enemy lines and only 30 from the nearest point on the coast. Clearly it was wiser for us to be gone, and as soon as we could. And then there was something else. I was warned to leave immediately on a six-day operation to strafe enemy vehicles immediately behind their lines. And there was one other thing. A half-dismantled jeep had been left by the Frenchman's grave 15 miles away on which there were some valuable spares, which somebody had to go and get – someone who knew how to navigate, like Steve or me.'

David, Steve and myself lay in the doctor's cave. We were waiting our turn. Someone was going to be fagged to do this chore. One of us had to go. It was either Steve or me.

David said slowly, 'Carol, no, Steve, will you go and collect those spares?' I thought, 'Thank God for that, poor old Steve.' He was in an almost worse condition than myself and shortly he was to fall seriously sick. Stephen had not returned by nightfall. George and I went up to the escarpment top to give him a lead in with a burst of Vickers. Our nerves were so shattered that we could not stand any more of that rat-tat-tat, and fired off a Very light instead. No sign of him, so, being now ready to move, we left a jeep and two men behind to pick him up.

Shortly after midnight our convoy of twenty-five vehicles left on a westward bearing. This was our third successive night without sleep and it was a weary drive. I was sharing a jeep with George. I was driving first, whilst he slept. It was a beautiful night, the desert so soft and silvery, under the clear light of the moon, the stars so big and brilliant and the sky so deep blue. Adjusting to another sleepless night I was almost reluctant for George to take over at half way. Our little convoy spread across 30 miles of desert during the night (no lights of course). Half an hour before dawn we halted, we were missing ten vehicles. I followed the tracks back the way we had come for five miles and found the little group halted in their tracks, every man fast asleep. It took me all of ten minutes to wake them all, and by the time we had rejoined the others they were already moving off to some nearby broken ground where we would form our new RV.

'Having dispersed the vehicles amongst the wadis and scrub and devoured an enormous breakfast, we all tried to snatch some sleep. I crawled under my jeep, but the flies pestered one unbearably. But this was almost preferable to a fitful doze with one's thoughts a turmoil of bearings and machine guns, jeep wheels and Messerschmitts, Stukas and burning vehicles. And the unending question, "Will you operate on Fuka tonight? You must leave now".'

So it was decided that this night we would drive back to the Escarpment RV, and the following night set out for the rear of the enemy line. We would cover the lines with four parties, each one of two jeeps. The French in the central sector under their commander, Jordan, myself south of them, David Russell to the south of me, and a fourth patrol between Russell and the Qattara Depression. We would thus each cover a 15-mile sector, and our job would be to destroy enemy soft-skinned vehicles, anything except armour. We hoped to find their leaguers lying about five miles behind their lines, where they would be collected for the night.

In our five nights away we had some hair-raising adventures, probing to within 5 miles behind the German front line at Alamein. I took Corporal Lambie, my tried and tested gunner, with me. This was our sixth successive operation together and he was as exhausted as I was, but we were alert enough to realize that no target we could find in the dark justified the loss of the whole patrol. Finally we were spotted and surrounded by tanks escaping only by the skin of our teeth. Luck was with us and we found our way back to our old hideout.

15

CROSSING THE QATTARA DEPRESSION

We found Sandy Scratchley in the cave and he greeted us with bad news. The German prisoners that we held had escaped, patrols were out after us and the base of the Alamein line had been sealed by the enemy and was impassable. Now that our work was completed, we had orders to return immediately. The only possible route left was down into the Depression and across the marsh, allowing that the tracks and passes had not been cut by the enemy.

So after a breakfast of fried sausages and tea and a few hours of discussion, we prepared to depart. There was a pass leaving the high plateau between the Qattara Spring and Qara Oasis. Both these watering places lay in the Western side of the Depression itself. The first was approached by a precipitous camel track impossible for heavy vehicles; the second by a long but navigable pass. We had information that Qara was held by the Germans, but we did not know about Qattara. The pass itself debouched from the plain at a point just above Qattara, so that it was possible that the enemy might attempt to block it. Every moment the supposed force that was on our tail grew in size; the latest message that we received on our 11-set said 500 strong, adding aircraft also. But the fact remained that to get back to Cairo we must descend into the Depression by the Qara Pass, and, enemy or no enemy, that must be our first objective. Sandy had visited it by daylight a few weeks previously and he reckoned that he could recognize it again by night. It lay on the Bagush-Siwa telegraph line and quite near there was a small pile of petrol tins. If only the moon was not in its last quarter it would be child's play to find it.

Before we left we had to pick up Steve Hastings who was escorting two 3-tonners back from a disused landing ground near the coast. The previous night our main party had brought in the two Bombays to land there, to drop petrol and pick up seventy of our men, and then return to Heliopolis aerodrome outside Cairo. They had lit a flare path and the landing was a great success. Now the remainder of us, about thirty strong, were to bring back our fifteen vehicles, a battered collection of jeeps and 3-tonners, to the Delta.

When Steve came back the sun was well up and he had been troubled by a low-flying enemy bomber which had circled over him several times, but he could not be sure that he had been spotted. Although it was daylight we decided to risk it and push east along our escarpment immediately to get out of this unhealthy area. It was fortunate that we did this, for later we heard that an enemy force had visited our old RV a short time after we had departed.

Our escarpment faced south-west and so by following it along we were travelling south-east towards Qattara. It was the first of the steps dropping from the Plateau down towards Siwa Oasis, another Depression, but not as deep as that of Qattara. With our fifteen trucks spaced out at intervals of 200 yards we crept slowly along the broken cliff side, moving carefully to keep the dust down, and stopping frequently and switching off to listen for the sound of hostile aircraft engines. We had one alarm as a bomber passed over us very high, but as we had stopped in time he could not see our dust clouds. At midday we halted and camouflaged up all the vehicles. We would stop here until dusk and lie and rest but not sleep, for the flies and heat prevented that.

There was a high barren knob above our halting place and after lunch I climbed up this to take my turn as watch. The view to the south was almost limitless, but shimmering in the midday sun it was difficult to pick out any landmarks. There was the place where the ground must sink to the Depression, and further to the east was the route we had taken several weeks before to collect water from an LRDG Heavy Section.

When I had scrambled down off the knob at the end of my watch I walked along to the cleft in the rocks where Sandy was resting, and together we drank tea and made up a message to Cairo demanding a petrol dump to be made for us at Egyptian Post, a point on the eastern side of the Depression, for, even though we had had supplies of petrol landed for us by the Bombays the previous evening, it was only enough for us to get half way back. Any alternative route round to the south of the Depression was out of the question; even the hard-surface track following the great northern escarpment of the Depression was not feasible. On the million map was shown a red dotted track cutting straight across the central bog at a point marked Kunetra Crossing. It was a kind of bridge, we had heard, and vehicles had passed that way before.

An hour before sunset we took the risk of moving and filling up the vehicles from the petrol 3-tonners so that we could be ready to start just before the sun set and get at least an hour of travelling in the half light, for the country beyond looked broken. And then quite suddenly, when all the vehicles were out in the open, four Stukas appeared from nowhere flying at 300 feet. We all froze, and as they passed over us they simultaneously let off a burst of machine-gun fire, not at us but into the cliff beyond. They were blind and did not see us.[1]

The moon did not rise until 2 o'clock so that our first few hours of driving were very difficult. However, there was a certain amount of light reflected on the surface of the desert from the stars. After two hours of driving we hit a soft patch lying on the upward slope of a ridge. Leaving the vehicles to extricate themselves with sand channels and mats, we explored along the ridge in our jeeps and after an hour found a firm crossing and whipped the 3-tonners over with yells to their drivers to keep their wheels straight, drive faster and change up or change down. No sooner had we surmounted this obstacle than we fell axle-deep into a wide field of soft sand, again bordered on the east by another impassable ridge, and we were forced to push on north in the opposite direction of our bearing until we found a gap. Some of the bolder drivers had taken it at a dash, and, obeying the maxim of only stopping on hard going, had disappeared out of sight. Others, after extricating themselves, had followed separate veins of hard, in all directions of the compass, so that it was not until midnight that we were able to assemble the party complete again. It was essential that we should reach cover in the Depression before daylight, for none of us were in the mood to be caught by aircraft again. Our first guide was the Baguish-Siwa telegraph line, and very soon we hit it, but on following it in the right direction for a few miles we were disappointed to find that the poles lacked wire and very quickly petered out altogether.

We took an eastward bearing and hit the main line after two miles, following it down on a good track until we came into the area of the Qattara Spring. Here we found the camel track where it disappeared over the edge of the Depression for the spring below; then we cast about, carefully quartering the ground for a track leading south-west into the Qara Pass. After searching for an hour, with an uncanny sense

Sandy found the spot, and very soon we were plunging down into a gorge enclosed by great rectangular rocks precariously balanced in positions into which they had fallen centuries before, and our engines echoed noisily against their surfaces until we passed out into a gradually descending open plain below. We followed this good track for the rest of the night, often travelling at 30 miles an hour, frequently stopping and changing drivers as they fell asleep at the wheel, until at dawn we turned left off the track towards hills formed of huge up-heaved rock slabs resting in irregular positions, under which we could drive our jeeps and 3-tonners into safety.

That morning we were able to have some excellent tinned American bacon for breakfast and plenty of biscuits and jam which had been dropped for us by the Bombays. We had done 70 miles during the night and were quite satisfied. The main problem that lay before us now was finding the Qara Crossing the following night. Later in the day a hostile fighter patrol warned us that we were wise to lie so carefully concealed.

The track we had been running down went direct to Qara, from where there was apparently a good track running to the Crossing. Unfortunately we could not afford to pass through this enemy-occupied oasis, a pity because the Sheik of Qara was an old friend of some of ours and his mint tea was a nice change, after our 'chai', even though only two of the ingredients, mint and water, were on the house. And so we would leave the track about 15 miles north of Qara, swinging south-east to cut the track running from the oasis eastwards to the Crossing, which we hoped would lead us safely across the bog.

By the starlight we only got a vague impression of the surrounding land. Our route descended gradually amid broken country, and as I was navigating I had to concentrate wholly on the wheel marks I was following. It was very tiring and exacting work. After about 50 miles we swung south, the terrain, in the gentle light, having a rather park-like appearance. This scanty vegetation showed us that we were at the bottom of the Depression. At about 3 a.m. the crescent moon began to rise and we hit the track at exactly the correct mileage. We would have to hurry if we were going to get out of the flat bog by daylight, but we stopped to check our bearings, then drove on for four miles until we lost the track and on turning round we found, to our horror, that we were missing ten vehicles. The drivers had all gone to sleep at the last halt, and even the cries of 'start up' and the noise of engines had not awakened them. After an hour's search we found all ten of them standing motionless in the desert, with drivers slumped over their wheels. The situation was getting critical now. There was an hour until daylight, and here we were in the middle of the Depression with no cover within miles. We drove on fast for a few more miles, but after two bad collisions we gave up the attempt and raced back to the escarpment where we would shelter for the day. We turned back and saw in the dim light of dawn the great cliff towering before us, but it was more than two hours before we plunged into its deep shade.

Here, lying beneath the 400ft cliff, we spent our second day. We must have been about 20 miles from the Qattara Spring. It was intensely hot, but we felt secure from any enemy planes that might try and attack us. It was pleasing having cheated them so far, for there was no doubt that they had been after our blood for the past three weeks. From where we lay under boulders and wedged between rock clefts, we could see as far as the eye stretched – to the east a firm but broken coastline, to the south-east a flat gravel plain. We were unable to see any sign of bog or marsh. However, we thought it would be wiser to retrace our old tracks of the night before until we should come to the main Qara Crossing track. From here we could follow it slowly and carefully until we had passed over the bog.

That night we made our second attempt to cross the Depression. We followed the beaten track carefully until it became only a few wheel marks. Then we found ourselves following a single wheel track only, very difficult to see by starlight, and so cast left and right to locate the main route once again. A few miles more and it petered out altogether. Then we found ourselves travelling over a rough rocky surface which continued for about 200 yards. At the end of this distance lay a hard salt crust with a quaking bog beneath. We sent our four jeeps to the four compass points. Three returned and reported bog on all sides, the fourth with all its kit sunk beyond recovery, bonnet deep into the bog itself. Again only one hour till daylight. The unfortunate thing was that as the surrounding surface was hard rock we were unable to trace the route we had entered by, and so we seemed to be stranded. Then we found an outlet. It was undoubtedly bog beneath, but there seemed to be a fairly stout crust. It might lead us into a further bog. We had no idea what lay beyond, but it was our only chance. For 300 yards the surface held even our heavy trucks. Then we came to a dyke of soft mud, quite a narrow one only about 10 feet across. We put tarpaulins, steel sand channels, sand mats and more tarpaulins over this, and each vehicle charged it at top speed. It had to be done very quickly because the stationary vehicles on the near side soon began sinking slowly through the crust. In fact we were too late with our last 3-tonner, for when its turn came to take the jump it had sunk up to the axles and soon the tail board began to disappear. We abandoned it and hurried on to the next dyke. This we bridged in a similar manner, and a third, and just when we were beginning to think that to continue was foolhardy and to return was impossible, the ground began to steady. The upper surface became spongy but there seemed to be a firm foundation beneath, and before we knew where we were we had entered a wide flat gravel plain. We halted for a few moments to get our direction, took a bearing on a low constellation of stars, switched on all our headlights and raced at 50 mph towards the north-east. The dawn was just beginning to break, the billiard-table surface lasted, and we covered 30 miles in less than an hour. We raced on until we reached a large grove of acacias under whose friendly shade we finally came to rest.

Some of us had been without sleep for thirteen days and nights and fatigue lay heavy upon us, but it was better, we thought, that we should reach the Delta first rather than lie and sleep where we were, for although we had almost passed out of the danger area, during breakfast a hostile aircraft had passed high overhead. The smoke from acacia wood fires made us feel drowsy and to many of us who had not seen a wild growing tree for over a year, the scene before us was becoming rapidly more and more sylvan as tea followed bacon and tobacco followed tea, and a feeling came over us that of all places on earth this was the spot where we might peacefully spend the remainder of our days. So we pushed on through country marked on the map as 'numerous scattered groves'. It was still flat gravel country rising a little towards the east in gentle undulations with groves of acacia trees growing in the hollows. To the north could be seen the blue outline of the Depression escarpment.

It had been arranged that a relief party with petrol should meet us on the main track to Cairo, but after lunch we lost the track, for this part of the desert seemed to be a mass of tracks running in every direction. However, we continued on a Cairo bearing until we suddenly stumbled across them. Besides petrol, they had brought out dates, sweets and tobacco, and as we were excitedly exchanging news, we were disturbed by aircraft for the last time.

So we drove eastwards at speed out of the acacia country across the rolling desert plains, past clumps of tamarisk bushes, until the evening came. We drew our vehicles up in a circle, turned on the dance music from Cairo, helped ourselves to rum and limes and prepared for our first night's solid sleep. Since we had left the Western Escarpment of the Depression the night before, we had done an 80-mile night drive, and during the day we had travelled another hundred.

When I awoke the next morning I found my head resting against the rear wheel of my jeep, my bedding roll untouched in the back, and my mess tin full of last night's bully stew. Later in the day we crossed the Baharia track, and after many more miles, as the sun began to cast long black shadows, we topped the last ridge. Below us lay a wide luxurious belt of palms; through the palm trees and paddy fields ran the Nile. It was literally a sight for sore eyes. We picked up our glasses and recognized the familiar landmarks – the minarets of the citadel just visible against the blue cliffs, the Stella Beer factory below us in the palms. Wearily we dismounted our guns and turned towards the Pyramids. We parked the jeeps outside the Mena Camp Naafi. Then, after much heart-searching three bearded officers slunk up the back stairs of Mena House Hotel and ate, not out of dusty mess tins, but off clean white plates.[2]

PART V
DESERT JOURNEYS II

THE DEEP SOUTH

16

BENGHAZI
'MISSION IMPOSSIBLE'

The Journey Out
Stephen and I had barely time to fit in our day of luxury in Cairo before we were off again. Looking back, our tastes were very simple, but there was little choice. The programme included a visit to the *Hammam* or turkish baths, a delicious cold luncheon at the Gezira Sporting Club, an afternoon spent in an air-cooled cinema, a cold bath in which blocks of ice were floating, and a cold drink every few minutes, such was our state of dehydration. Watching the exotic belly-dancers on the roof-garden of the Continental Hotel ended our day, and somewhat cancelled out the effects of our blood-cooling experiments.

I spent a few days in Alexandria. The mornings I spent bathing on the beach at Sidi Bishr with Evie and Jenny Dimopoulos, two charming Alexandrine-Greek girls whom we had known since Layforce days, or reading in cool, colonial shade of the Union Club. At the Cecil Hotel I occupied the room belonging to Michael Alexander, who was a member of our sister unit, the Special Boat Section, trained to work off submarines. My occupation of his room was made memorable by his sudden arrival and departure. An MTB was awaiting him in Alexandria harbour, whence he was going to blow up a petrol dump behind the Alamein Line.

He was late, of course, departing only in a pair of gabardine trousers, shirt and desert boots, trailing his water bottle behind him bumping down the stairs. He could not decide whether to spend the last few vital minutes filling his water bottle or having a drink at the bar. He compromised by having his water bottle filled with White Ladies, and thus disappeared in the direction of the harbour. He must have made one of the fastest wartime journeys into Germany. Non-stop in fact, where, with a name like Alexander, he was considered to be a most valuable prize and confined to a really safe prison, indeed Colditz.

Benghazi had always been in David Stirling's sights, ever since he, accompanied by Fitzroy Maclean and Randolph Churchill, had coolly driven into the enemy occupied port in one of the most outrageous operations of his career. Although they were unable to do any damage on that occasion it gave a lot of useful intelligence for another day.

Now all these things got talked about in the spy-infested bars and bazaars of Cairo no doubt, so Benghazi was never to be a very safe bet for a return visit. GHQ had subsequently tried to interest Stirling in an attack on the harbour by land and sea. This too had been cancelled, and by implication at least its security grading devalued.

This new operation was again inspired by GHQ and the attack on Benghazi was part of a theatre-wide plan to threaten the Germans' position at Alamein by widespread attacks on their very overstretched lines of communication and port installations. By this stage Stirling was a rather reluctant player in the game, as his allotted rôle transgressed the basic rules of desert raiding. However, the units existence had to be justified and this was one way of doing so.

Eight days after returning to Cairo via the Qattara Depression I set out with Sandy Scratchley for the Oasis of Kufra, a journey of some 1500 miles. Both Stephen and George Jellicoe had been in hospital.

Stirling had divided his force into three columns. Ours was the heavy party consisting of twenty jeeps and twenty 3-tonners and most of the heavy stores, including a breakdown wagon complete with electric welder, manned by a REME officer and crew. In one of the forward parties were two Honey tanks of the Gloucester Hussars and we carried most of the petrol for these two incongruous vehicles, enough to reach Benghazi (at an incredibly high rate of consumption) where they were to help seize the port!

Our column numbered about seventy men, among whom were detachments of SBS, naval personnel, marines, Free French, German-speaking Palestinians and of course our own men who were volunteers from many regiments. SAS strength had almost doubled for this operation, to some 200 men, but many of them had little desert-driving experience which was to lead to trouble later on. Sandy Scratchley was in charge of the party, a wiry Yeomanry officer 'born and bred in a briar patch' we used to say. An amateur rider before the war, like many of his breed he had plenty of cavalry dash and used it on our lumbering column with not entirely satisfactory results. Our vehicles, even to start with, were grossly overladen, as we had to pick up all the odds and ends that the other two parties had left behind. Not a very good augury for our 2000-mile desert journey.

We had passed the base areas and had now hit the Suez-Cairo road and were bumping along, happy to be on the move once more. In retrospect it is ironic to look back upon those days. What a year! Marked at sombre intervals by those disastrous names, Greece, Crete, Singapore, Tobruk. For us there was one compensation. We were in a position to pit ourselves offensively against the enemy in a game in which we were confident of our skills. The defensive stance of those on the Alamein line we did not envy.

The plan of campaign after our long approach march was to enter Benghazi, a force 200 strong, at several different points at midnight. We were to destroy the ships in the harbour, port installations, the electricity and water supplies – in fact do as much damage as possible. Then leave the town before first light and make for our hideout in the hills, known as the Jebel Akhdar (The Green Mountain).

Simultaneously a force of SBS and Commandos, a scratch collection, remnants of Layforce, were to attack Tobruk by land under command of a British Agent active in those parts, John Haseldon. They were to seize the harbour, silence the guns, preparatory to the arrival of two destroyers and a flotilla of MTBs carrying Marines.

The same night Barce and Tocra were targeted by the LRDG, concentrating on the Landing Grounds. The following day Jalo Oasis was to receive an attack by the Sudan Defence Force, also operating from Kufra Oasis. It was hoped that Jalo could form a base for further harrying operations against the exposed enemy communications. General Alexander, CinC Middle East, hoped that if these enemy installations could be put out of action for one week Rommel would find himself in grave difficulties at the Alamein line.

D Day was to be 13 September. We left our base at Kabrit on the Bitter Lakes on about 20 August. Surprisingly, I led the column straight through Cairo (perhaps the only feasible crossing of the Nile). We crossed Gezira Island and, once on the far bank, took the left fork marked *Haute Egypte*. The right fork was marked, rather hopefully, Tripoli 1000 Km. 'Tripoli or bust!' might have been a motto for our unit. We would get there somehow even via Kufra.

Sandy 'Hop-along' Scratchley, as he was sometimes known, made a detour via David's flat. This belonged to David's brother Peter, then second secretary at the Embassy. It was convenient for the Embassy and GHQ. David did much of his planning there and it was a rendezvous for us all. Constant visitors did not add to the sense of security. The Egyptian sufragi (servant) 'Mo' saw it all. But he was a devoted 'nanny' to the whole family and would be the last person one would mistrust.

French Leave

As leader of the convoy I got the best of it, for the clouds of dust lay behind me. As I wrote:

> 'Passing through that ageless scenery I could catch glimpses of the Nile through the palms on the left of the road. On the right we followed the bank of a sweet water canal. We continued thus until the heavy river mist laid the dust; bull frogs and crickets began their chorus and we found ourselves driving along in the cool dampness of the evening. Then we stopped, bedding spread out on the road and evening fires lit. I discovered to my horror that all my bedding had rolled off my jeep whilst my driver was bumping around at Kabrit earlier in the day. I roundly cursed him, but slept no better for it. Amidst the sickly sweet dampness, stale dust, and mosquitos of our first night out I had a fitful sleep.'

We were travelling south up the Nile valley in order to branch off, just beyond Asyut, on to the Kharga Oasis track. Kharga lay about 80 miles west of the River Nile. This was our jumping-off point for the desert proper.

I was in better mood next morning;

> 'It was a beautiful morning's drive and we travelled fast. Before the sun reached its full power, whilst the country remained damp and misty, was the most pleasant moment of the day. The mud-brick buildings were bathed in a mellow glow, the palms shone out dark green, the doves and pigeons wheeled high into the clear sky as the unaccustomed sound of our engines put them to flight. The fellahin plodded to their labours and waved in friendly greeting as we passed. The desert could be seen on both sides of the river quite clearly now, the strips of cultivation on either side gradually getting narrower and narrower.'

A note of reality now enters my journal.

> 'The number of Gyppos who saw our armed convoy disappearing south at speed made us a little worried. If there were any enemy

agents with hidden transmitters lying up in this unfrequented part of Egypt it would be an easy matter for them to report everything they saw. Three columns of fifty vehicles each, heavily laden and armed, two light tanks and 3-tonners mounting 20mm guns could only point to an armed assault on a soft flank or rear. It would be an easy matter after that for recce aircraft to cover the likely approaches as soon as we were within range.'

Great and curious crowds collected at Asyut as we passed through. Later in the afternoon one of the French jeeps, driven by *Aspirant* Martin, fell into the sweet water canal. The French thought it funny; Sandy was furious and went for Martin: 'Martin, you are a bloody fool! How are we going to get there if everyone starts driving into the canal. You can't come any further if you're going to behave like that!'

To which Martin, his Gallic blood aflame, reddened, growling to his friend Lesec, 'Horr! Scratchlee!'

The French, devoted as they were to 'Daveed', could not understand 'Scratchlee', nor he them. This was not to be the last explosion between the two. *Aspirant* Martin, now aged 24, had been an art student in Paris when war broke out, had joined the Chasseurs Alpins and later fought with them in Norway. As I wrote, he was 'a most charming, brave and excellent person'. He still clung to his long-hooded Chasseur's cloak which he produced on cold nights.

Egyptian Post – Expect Trouble!

The Kharga track, where it left the Delta road, was unmistakable. We were glad to shake the acrid river dust from our clothes and move once more into the friendly desert. Soon we ran into an Egyptian frontier post. One of the Askaris jumped on to the back of my jeep for what purpose I knew not, until I discovered two water melons missing. We drew a safe distance away from the Egyptian Post, whose curiosity was unwelcome, and camped in soft sand at the mouth of a re-entrant to a plateau. After our meal Sandy was all for going off again immediately, but there were repairs to be done and it was decided to move off again at three in the morning. That night we posted a watch as a safeguard against the prying Egyptian soldiers.

It was cool when we awoke. Sandy led off and I brought up the rear. We had a lot of new and un-desertworthy drivers, and before we had reached the top of the plateau the 3-tonners were floundering and plunging into the deep soft sand at the sides of the narrow track. They had no idea of how to manage their vehicles under these conditions.

and the tail-end-charlie, or 'whipper in', at the back was continually going to their rescue. They would grind to a halt, rev the engine up and spin the back wheels axle-deep into the sand. The driver would stare hopelessly at his bellied vehicle until someone came to dig him out. This was no way to start our expedition. How were we ever going to get to Kufra?

The lunch halt found us widely separated and we had a long wait for the cookhouse truck to catch up.

> 'Sandy stayed collecting the remnants and I pushed on with the faster trucks until 4 p.m. when we stopped on the edge of an escarpment. Hundreds of feet below was a deep misty depression with the track winding down in steep hairpins. This was the Kharga Depression, and somewhere off in the haze lay the oasis.'

As we approached the bottom of the 300-foot cliff we found, to our surprise, an Egyptian checkpoint and a striped barrier pole across the road. Four vehicles had passed through before the excited Egyptians lowered the barrier. I got out and expostulated with the sentry who was demanding a count of vehicles, and every vehicle number which passed. It was of course necessary for the success of the operation that as few as possible knew about us. Threats and force would do nothing to make the worthy Egyptian raise his barrier and I wanted to avoid an incident for the sake of Sandy yet to come.

The immediate problem was solved in an unexpected fashion. The leading 3-tonner driver, whether by accident or design, let off his brakes and the vehicle began to roll slowly down the hill. There was a resounding crack! The barrier pole had splintered into a hundred bits. I gave the tearful sentry a note to a mythical colonel which he read upside down. The note read: 'Sandy! Expect trouble! We've broken this chap's pole!'

Once down in the oasis and opposite another checkpoint a savage-looking black armed with a long curved knife sprang onto my jeep and demanded that I pay a visit to the Governor.

Kharga Oasis – A Diplomatic Incident

The colonial administrative area we had now entered came as some surprise. Of course it guarded the vulnerable waters of the Nile at this point, and boasted an Egyptian Governor, a company of troops, and a narrow-gauge desert railway. Our planners had spotted the railway, but had been unaware of any further ramifications bearing upon our security.

I followed the black's directions to the Rest House where I met the Governor. He explained that it was necessary as a desert precaution to count all vehicles passing between the Nile and Kharga in case any should get lost! He then demanded payment for his frontier pole.

After a glass of lemonade I told him that his government must approach the British Military Authorities through the proper channels and that I was not in a position to pay for the broken pole. Again he demanded the number of vehicles that had passed. It was disturbing that our movements should be spied upon at this late stage. It would have been quite a simple thing for the Egyptian government to have reported our every move to the enemy.

> 'It was just before midnight before I was able to strip off my sticky clothes and walk naked across the sand to the spring. The warm water cascaded through a series of troughs from a fountainhead. In the top trough one could stand with the water up to one's shoulders. In the second one could sit with water up to the neck. In the bottom trough one could lie as in a hot bath. I started at the top and worked my way down and lay for many minutes in the last of these gazing up at the starry sky, breathing in the palm-scented night air and dreaming of what the future held. Presently an Arab boy walked up and stood above laughing, threw off his white jerd and jumped into the top basin, splashing and chanting merrily. I moved off hurriedly before the rest of his friends arrived.'

All next day we stayed at Kharga unloading the tins of petrol and water from the train, and making up further loads for our grossly overladen transport. Sandy and I found time to wander round the village, to take coffee with the agricultural officer on a visit to inspect the palm trees, to have tea at the Governor's house who had now forgotten the barrier pole, but who complained that last night some of our men had tried to dance with the village maidens. This oasis was casting a spell upon us and it was time to be on our way.

The next step in our journey was to take us across totally uninhabited desert, the 900 miles to Kufra. Kufra itself is a remote oasis lying 800 miles south of the Mediterranean and as the crow flies 700 miles west of the Nile. It was once the seat of the Senussi faith and, until the arrival of the Italians, the holiest place of that Islamic sect.

Between Kharga and Kufra lies the recently discovered range of mountains, the Gilf Kebir named thus by Prince Kemal El Din in 1926. The range covers an area the size of Switzerland, ending in the massif of Jebel Owenat (6,000 ft) in the south. On the western side of the Gilf are plentiful caves containing primitive rock paintings, we were told, of wild and domestic animals and figures in the unmistakable posture of swimmers. This seems to suggest that this land was once inhabited and cultivated and that it may have been on the shores of a large lake. In the 1920s exploring parties were searching for the lost oasis of Zerzura ('of the little birds') mentioned by Herodotus in his History and here may well have been the site.

There was an LRDG patrol lying in Kharga and we asked them about the onward route. They advised us to follow the track towards Dahkla Oasis due west. Leaving it on the right, one would then cut across tracks running south to the Eight Bells Pass. From the pass all tracks led to Kufra. Wheel tracks are a most unreliable guide; they might be a mile apart; any soft going would be churned up; a sandstorm or moving dune could easily obliterate them. We had a partially trained Corporal navigator, but he had no experience of desert travel. It was decided that I should navigate the party to Kufra. Much the best method was firmly to work out one's own route and rigidly follow one's own bearings. I decided to strike out across country. The only snag was that this country was largely unknown and unexplored. Our map sheets were complete blanks with no features marked at all. However, I planned to travel 20 miles along the Dahkla tracks, then turn south for 100 miles, then due west for 100 miles until we hit the Gilf. I aimed 100 miles north of Eight Bells so that when we came to the Gilf, even if we were 70 miles out, we knew to go south.

Dante's Inferno – The Volcanic Saucer
We pulled out of Kharga oasis at 9 a.m. on 24 August. The deadline for arrival at Kufra was 3 September at the very latest, for our attack on Benghazi was synchronized with all the other operations to take place on 13 September. We therefore had six days to reach Kufra, allowing time for reorganization and maintenance, once we had found the others. We were now more grossly overladen than when we left the Bitter Lakes, for at Kharga we had taken on board all the extra petrol designed to take the whole expedition from Kufra north to our objective. We estimated that if the worst came to the worst it would be enough to carry our party alone at least 1000 miles.

After 10 miles of our southerly bearing I stopped to let Sandy catch up. We had left a cairn of empty petrol cans where we left the Dahkla track. It was evident that the 3-tonners were going to make extremely slow progress; they were sticking all over the place and boiling over. When Sandy arrived we held a council of war and decided then and there that we would not reach Kufra on 3 September at this rate. We split the party into two, a slow and a fast party. Eighteen jeeps and two of the best 3-tonners went with the fast party, leaving eighteen 3-tonners and two jeeps with the slow party. The Corporal navigator was to be left with them. They were to follow our tracks and the REME officer was to be in charge. With the fast party would be Sandy, myself, two naval officers, half the French and Corporal Tutton with the wireless jeep.

We set off immediately and made good going in a southerly direction until sundown, when we stopped to brew up. During the afternoon we had passed through irregular sandstone country with conical hills, mushroom-shaped on top. They were dotted about in groups and singly, as trees in a great park. There was no sign of any vegetation until we reached Kufra. An hour after sundown we drove on. It was now hell for leather. We drove all night till five in the morning. There are advantages in night driving. So far south, we could use our headlights; driving on a star is easier than an indistinct landmark on a shimmering horizon in daylight. Travelling south, it was not necessary to take a fresh bearing on a new constellation four times an hour. For we were driving with the axis on which the heavens revolve, so one star would last till early morning.

> 'With the dawn we came to a high crag on our left rising out of the gravel plain. On top of the crag sat an eagle who regarded us impassively. Under the bird's glassy stare Sandy gave the drivers a pep-talk on care of vehicles. Then the sun rose and they all wrapped themselves in their blankets and slept beside their vehicles. Before turning in I plotted our course, which put us 70 miles south of the Dahkla track, had a tot of whisky and passed quickly out.'

At nine we were all up again cooking breakfast and preparing for the road. We had moved off through knolly, hilly country when suddenly at midday we came out onto a flat sand sheet stretching limitless on all sides. In the scorching heat of midday at the very edge of the sand sheet (and this was a jeep party), we all got stuck. Once out of this by mid-afternoon I estimated that we had completed our 100 miles south and turned due west. We drove on till evening at a good pace, but latterly climbing into rough country and striking a number of sand dunes. At last light we came to rest beneath a steep dune ridge flanked by two dark rocky hills, over which the vehicles would not pass. Here, as the cool of the evening enveloped us once more, we sat and cooked our evening meal. I had a blinding headache and was feeling sick; everyone was very tired, especially the sailors who appeared to be thoroughly disgruntled, and who were talking in a way that we would not have tolerated in our own men.

Sandy and I had a feeling that all was not right with our route. We had not expected to strike this range of hills and it appeared that they were not connected with the Gilf, which we should have sighted long ago. But our map sheets told us nothing. They were absolutely blank; the country was unexplored. The French wanted to stay beneath the dune all night; there was some point in not going blind into this uncharted wilderness. But Sandy insisted we push on and we left at 10.30 p.m.

We struck south, endeavouring to find an exit to the west, but were always foiled by the continuation of our dune which barred our way. Sometimes Sandy led and sometimes I did, but we were both spending so much time in digging out bogged vehicles and rounding up stragglers that it left little time for accurate navigation. At midnight we found the convoy split up into about five separate parties, which went charging off in different directions.

> 'I could see their headlights weaving about on all sides, some seeming to climb a precipitous mountain, others charging down precipices. With the aid of headlight and horn we had re-assembled them all in an hour complete.'

Then we set off again probing westwards with our headlights in the dark, but always being forced south by the sand. After another three hours of fruitless search we found ourselves in an apparent saucer which had no outlet. It resembled a shallow crater, and once in there was no way of getting back out again. The two 3-tonners would simply not take the slope, and just as they made some progress would sink back up to the wheel hubs in soft clinging sand. We were in an awkward position; on all accounts we must prevent the heavy party following us into this foul country. At 4 a.m. there was only one thing for it – to sleep until dawn.

At daylight we reviewed the situation. We were certainly in a deep saucer with no way out, except the way we had come, a long soft pull uphill. We were like flies in a trap, our legs stuck on sticky paper. We were surrounded by rocky crags, dark brown, hideous and volcanic. We climbed the highest of these on foot, leaving our companions to get breakfast below. There was no comment to be made on the vista that opened up on either side. Sandy put it in two words: 'Dante's Inferno!'

I can truthfully say that I have never looked upon more hideous or nightmarish country. Peak after peak of dark brown purplish rock reared itself in an unending desolate vista. They resembled giant purple fungi with roots probing into a girdle of sand. However, this was no time to admire the scenery. There was work to be done. To cut a long story short, inch by inch we somehow managed to get all the vehicles out of the saucer. We followed back our winding tracks of the night before ending up at Frenchman's Halt beneath the big dune. Once there, we made several attempts to cross the dune, using various angles, gears and speeds and pulled all the vehicles, including *les trois-tonners*, over. The going over the other side looked more hopeful, with no black hills and dunes petering out.

Split Again

But we were both worried about the slow party; at this rate the REME officer would never get them through. So Sandy sent me back to take charge of them. We were not to meet again until near Kufra.

Sandy therefore set off with sixteen jeeps and the two 3-tonners, but with water only for four days, and with about 500 miles to go. Meanwhile, I and Corporal Tutton, with the wireless jeep, no longer in contact with base, retraced our tracks towards the sand sheet. With two jeeps only we were able to travel at great speed and late in the afternoon met up with the rear party at the northern edge of the sand sheet, stuck fast and wallowing in the sand. When they were ready I led them off on a westerly bearing to avoid the treacherous country we had fallen into the night before. I calculated to hit the Gilf 150 miles north of Eight Bells. The 3-tonners floundered again and before we had been going long two foolish drivers collided in the wide, wide desert and badly dented David's 'Blitz Buggy'. We were approaching some impressive looking hills clearly rising out of the desert. About 10 miles from these we stopped and prepared our evening meal. We were missing eight 3-tonners. I went back and found them broken down or bogged, dotted across the desert for 15 miles. The last one, which needed a completely new engine, I left in the capable hands of the REME officer and his Quartermaster, Sergeant Skew. I told them that if they could not be back at our campfire by first light tomorrow morning, then the vehicle must be abandoned and the kit transferred to others. I collected other stragglers on the way back and then settled down to the first night's sleep since leaving Kharga. Sure enough, before we were ready to leave on the morning of 27 August, the REME party were back in camp, having performed the amazing feat of manhandling a complete new engine into the broken 3-tonner with only five men. It was now as good as new.

As I wrote these words from my hospital bed, three years after these events had taken place, I indulged in the following soliloquy:

'After three years I find no difficulty in casting my mind back over the journeys that we performed during those months of 1942. I can remember every day's journey that we made throughout those scorching August days, every outline of rock and sand; every bend; the deep furrows of particular wheel tracks in a particular place; the distant sound of engines, jeeps like aircraft, 3-tonners a high whine. I can remember casual remarks made; the first sight of Kufra. All these of the ear and eye I can recall. But the mood I cannot recapture. The spirit of brotherhood I know was there, but the impulse now gone. I cannot feel that mixture of fatigue and latent energy. I cannot laugh at misfortunes as I did then. Ancient pastures run dry, fertile emotions conceived in desolate places also pass away.'

'Sir – We cannot go on at this rate!'
And so on 27 August our little caravan of four jeeps and sixteen 3-tonners was making for the escarpment, seen the night before. We soon stuck deep in the sand, abstracting each vehicle in turn with the crews of the rest. We passed between the hills through a narrow gap and out into another plain beyond. Beyond the plain was the deep blue outline of the Gilf escarpment. Our midday halt was at the edge of the plain, whilst I went on, casting around for tracks of previous parties, one of which we had crossed earlier that morning. After lunch I altered bearing to a little north of west until we reached a high impassable dune running north and south barring our passage. We followed this south and, after 10 miles, found a narrow gap through which we passed. The remaining four hours of the day we spent climbing a long incline upon which everyone bogged continuously, so that by the time we had dropped down again on the far side and reached the foot of the escarpment I had only five vehicles left. Leaving the others to make

camp I retraced my tracks to round up the others. Four had serious breakdowns, so I left the REME party to spend a sleepless night carrying out repairs.

It was at this point that QMS Ward, one of my most level-headed men and my former troop sergeant in No 8 Commando, ('Daddy' Ward as he was known), spoke to me as he was unbogging his 3-tonner for the umpteenth time.

'Sir,' he said, 'we cannot go on at this rate!'

His view reflected that of most of the men, I was sure. But there was a very obvious answer to that: it was no good going back! In fact, at the end of the following day we knew that it was a physical impossibility!

17

NEAR DISASTER IN THE GILF KEBIR

'The moon has set, and the Pleiads; it is the middle of the night and time passes, time passes, and I am alone.'
                                                            Sappho

Owing to the numerous breakdowns in my lumbering party and the general state of the vehicles, it was necessary to have a complete day's halt the next day. I also wanted to check our petrol reserves; it seemed to me that we had been using an awful lot since leaving Kharga. There was all the difference between a good driver and a bad one under desert conditions. A good driver would use half the amount of petrol, have half the number of mechanical breakdowns and seldom get stuck. Unfortunately our party, being the last, was left with all the inexperienced drivers and a great deal of surplus kit.

I had chosen for our halting place a point about four miles from the foot of the Gilf, which towered above us to the west. It was broken rocky country and across our flat patch of sand had passed Sandy's party. I could recognize their tracks by counting wheel marks, and there was also the unmistakable 'cow with the crumpled horn' – a jeep with a buckled back wheel which left a wobbly track in the sand. This was the one which was involved in Martin's accident in the Delta.

All day the REME party worked on the broken-down 3-tonners. It looked as though one would have to be abandoned. I made the men unload all the remaining lorries and make an inventory of their loads, particularly petrol and water. Corporal Tutton tried in vain to contact HQ in Cairo on the 19 set. I sent the navigator out to climb a local peak to try and fix our position by theodolite calculation. At the end of the day the vehicles were more or less in running order and our position seemed to be less than 100 miles from Eight Bells Pass. But with the drivers exhausted and the vehicles in such a deplorable condition (none of them had been 'run-in' before we left Egypt), I decided not to continue that night.

An Alarming Discovery

But the most alarming result of the day's work was the discovery that we only had enough petrol for the whole party to continue another 60 miles, and then we would run out; we were some 300 miles from Kufra and rather further from the Nile valley.

At first sight this looked like a very bad piece of organization on our part, but we had not calculated for overloading, atrocious going, inexperienced drivers and wheel spin. All these factors combined to double our estimated petrol consumption. So there we were, 300 miles from the nearest human habitation, enough petrol for 60 miles only, water for five days, and no contact on our wireless set with the outside world. In these circumstances I made up my mind to travel to the limit of our fuel which should bring us into the pass, through which I believed supply convoys passed to Kufra from the Sudan. Out of our total fuel I would save enough for one jeep journey to Kufra to raise the alarm. In the meantime, with luck, we would get through to Cairo on the 19 Set. Surprisingly, everyone was in good spirits after the rest, if a little apprehensive about our future.

The following day we moved off along the route I had already recced through broken limestone country, dropping down to a flat plain which ended abruptly with the cliff face of the Gilf, black and menacing. We had to abandon one 3-tonner, irretrievably broken down, and transfer its load on to an already overladen convoy. At one moment, round a high rocky outcrop, we saw an opening. Thinking it might be the elusive pass I followed what must have been Sandy's jeep tracks which ended, I could see, in a black blob. The blob turned out to be an abandoned jeep, in fact it was 'the cow with the crumpled horn', the very one involved in Martin's accident in the Nile Delta. It had been almost completely dismantled, but there was no message attached to give us a clue. The wheel tracks, which were not more than a day old, moved giddily up the gorge but then swung round in a big U-turn and became mingled with the others. It was comforting that Sandy was having his problems too!

We continued on south, stopping, starting and stopping again as vehicles got continually stuck. Now we found ourselves in a series of parallel inter-connected wadis resembling a maze. It was while we were winding in and out of these that our tributary wadi suddenly emerged into the main gorge, a steep, winding valley 500 yards broad and furrowed by a thousand wheel tracks. This, then, must be the Kufra route. We ran down this for 3 miles, sometimes sinking deep in the churned and furrowed sand until we emerged. Before us the unmistakeable Eight Bells. Eight black conical hills four miles to the south. On our right an immense opening into the heart of the Gilf, towards which all tracks turned for the mass of black rock.

After waiting for an hour for all vehicles to catch up, we pushed on again having to leave two 3-tonners for the breakdown gang, this time it was burst radiators. We drove in towards the pass for a further ten miles and then stopped for good as there was no more fuel. The convoy was stranded.

'Something Funny on the Horizon'

No more God-forsaken spot can be imagined than this graveyard of all our hopes and fears. The pitiless sun still burned down, although it was almost evening. It was reflected off the black basalt rocks which redoubled its fury. Not a sound nor a sign of life to be seen. No bird of prey hunted in this barren spot.

One of my most admirable men, Corporal Drongin, had been a pre-war regular Scots guardsman. He had also been my troop sergeant in No 8 Commando. Together we had scrambled up the braes of Loch Fyne in crisp wintry weather – two years ago it must have been, but it seemed like an age. Drongin, well-built, with the looks of a Norseman, had been promoted to Commando RSM. He was a hard man and hard with others too. Feats of endurance were his speciality. He had travelled in bare feet all the way from Kharga. Although he was a loner he seemed completely selfless, in fact Stirling's 'ideal man'. In order to join Stirling's Detachment he willingly reverted to the ranks, but was persuaded to accept the rank of Corporal. Did he have a premonition that his time was up?

There were various imponderables about our present predicament. Point one, we had four days' water left, and this was only using it for the vehicles and for quenching our thirst. Admittedly, if the vehicles were grounded that would give us another day or two. Point two, we could not rely upon an SDF convoy passing our way within this timescale. It might be a matter of not days but weeks. Point three, if we were to send one jeep to Kufra to summon a rescue party, should I go, or should I send someone else who could navigate? Point four, it was so essential that this man get through, with all speed, and without a hitch that I wondered whether I could rely on anyone else. Finally, the whole execution of the raid on Benghazi depended upon us getting through with our vital stores and equipment on time.

These were the thoughts passing through my mind when I looked up and saw Drongin sitting on a rocky knob nearby. His glasses were trained in the direction of the breakdown party some 10 miles away.

'Do you see them?' I called.

'No sir, but I've seen something funny on the horizon,' he shouted back.

I scrambled up to his position.

'Look, sir, over there!'

I swept the horizon with my glasses. I saw something which I took to be a ruin of some sort. There seemed to be a group of stone columns, showing black on the horizon. My mind raced back to the legends of this place. Was this Zerzura, the lost oasis, the oasis of the twittering birds?

'I don't think it's anything that will interest us,' I said to Drongin. 'All we've got to think about is petrol. It may be much further than it looks.'

My mind reverted to our present plight. Dying of thirst in the desert? Scuppering the whole expedition?

'Come on, Drongin, we'll go and have a look,' I said.

We jumped into the battered old jeep and sped across the intervening distance in no time. It was about 4 miles away and hidden by a fold in the ground. As we approached we could not believe our eyes. ('No, wait until we get there before we utter a word.') It was a huge dump of petrol in the middle of nowhere, tin after tin and drum after drum of the stuff. We leapt out of the jeep, rushed up and shook the tins – they were full. And there were some large 40-gallon barrels. Some of it was 80- octane, but no matter. This must be an SDF dump. We rushed back to camp, emptied two 3-tonners and took them back to load up. There was enough of the right kind of petrol to get us to Kufra.

Simultaneously our first message came through on the 19 set. It read, 'Vital repeat vital you reach Kufra 1st September,'

We replied by demanding a petrol dump to be made at Wadi Sura, a hundred miles up on the western side of the Gilf. But the message was very disturbing. The only solution was once again to split up our party into a fast and slow one. This would mean a massive transshipment of stores. I would take the eight best lorries and drivers carrying the most urgent stores. This would include the French *'trois-tonners'* as they called them. The REME officer with the slow party would follow in our tracks, and with the help of the navigator, and God willing, would arrive in Kufra shortly after us.

There were always certain firm principles to obey in desert travel, and one of the first was to keep one's party intact, especially with novice drivers. But under the circumstances we could do nothing but split the party again.

I broke the good news to 'Daddy' Ward that we had found a petrol dump and it would be necessary to have a complete re-load overnight, and he would be in charge.

'Oh aye,' was all he said at this dramatic news, then walked off to take charge of a quartermaster's nightmare. By the light of headlamps we unloaded all the kit, sorted it out and re-loaded it again into the vehicles of the two new parties. Sorting out the different types of ammunition, explosive, fuel for the Honey tanks, oil, food and water was an exacting task. 'Daddy' Ward kept his equanimity and steadied the lads of the new intake.

I had a flash-back to Kabrit. Ward's QM stores were run on the lines of a Yorkshire village shop. You pushed open the door, which pulled a string, which rang a bell. Inside there was a counter over which you could be supplied with anything from an arab headdress to a pound of gelignite. Despite his forebodings about our onward journey, he was an invaluable man on whom I could absolutely depend.

We Split Once More
Before the sun rose Corporal Tutton and the wireless jeep, my eight 3-tonners and my own jeep were ready to leave. I was taking Drongin as my spare driver.

The pass led us slightly north of west and gradually narrowed. After we had been going for an hour the shadows of the southern wall fell upon the walls of the northern and we passed through a cool tunnel of shade.

> 'Driving in the desert is very like sailing in a ship. Passing between the tall cliffs our vehicles tossed and bucketed over the spongy furrowed sand like toy ships at sea. The pass was probably not more than 15 miles in length, and soon we could see clear through to the far side, a pink and mirage-like vista of desert in the shimmering mid-day sun.'

Four vehicles got very badly bogged as we emerged from the pass and one developed a leaky radiator which we patched up with red lead. The pitiless sun began to fray our tempers and exhaust our energy. We had now turned north and were making for a headland on the western 'shores' of the Gilf. It appeared mauve and hardly distinguishable in the far distance. At the foot of the headland should lie Wadi Sura where we planned to spend the first night, and make Kufra the next day. If all went according to plan therefore, we would be in Kufra on 31 August, remarkably enough, one day ahead of schedule.

I must pass swiftly over the events of that day. It was an absolute shocker.

> 'We bogged down continuously; we dug in the sand with our hands and with spades; we laid sand mats [a long roll of canvas with wooden battens], and ran before the moving vehicles carrying heavy steel sand-channels to lay in the path of the wheels, like slaves laying gifts at the feet of an insatiable monster. Then quickly running behind, picking up the channels and rebuilding the path of steel so the monster should not sink again.
>
> '"*Horr! les trois tonnairs!*" the French cried, "*Espèce d'espèce!*"
>
> 'Then, "She's away!" someone would cry, and away would sail the wagon over beautiful hard sand like a dignified swan, and after it would run the cursing men, each bearing a sand-channel on his shoulder; lifting it into the back, still at a run, and jumping in themselves. As soon as they were settled there would be a shudder, followed by an abrupt stop. The process would then begin all over again.'

Finally, after further breakdowns within 10 miles of Wadi Sura, I decided to go ahead with Corporal Tutton, travelling in two jeeps to see if our requested petrol dump had been made. With luck we might get a lead-in to Kufra if someone had stayed behind.

The sun had already set and, leaving one of the French officers, Bernard Haron, in charge of the column, Tutton and I drove off into the cool of the evening. We could see our landmark quite clearly – a tall pinnacle of rock rising sheer out of the desert, flanked by two smaller ones.

> 'It was glorious to be away from the responsibilities of the column for a while, even though they were still on one's shoulders. The desert can be so enticing in the evening, the long shadows so inviting, the sand so soft and cool and the balmy air caressing

one's blistered cheek. And oddly enough the ground one traverses at this hour is strangely transfigured into an enchanted land. Rocks assume immense shapes, casting grotesque shadows; distances appear twice as long or twice as short. One drives to a mountain 20 miles away and reaches it in 20 yards. One gets out to climb a rock and finds it will take several hours to reach. And all bathed in a soft companionable light. It would be hard to feel lonely in the desert at night – one's lightheadedness overcomes all dangers and all fears – even the most serious event becomes slightly ridiculous, dwarfed by the magnitude of one's surroundings'.

From these words penned 50 years ago I can still feel the spell of the desert, for on this trip we were travelling across pure, clean and unadulterated steppe. There were no flies and no stench of death; in many places our wheel tracks were the first ever made. We were making history. It was like being 'the first man on the moon', then an undreamt-of event.

The magical surroundings of Wadi Sura gave rise to a further philosophical comment.

'We camped in the lee of the tallest rock tower, lit a fire, sending uncertain fingers of light groping up its barren face. The morse was tapped out, bully sizzled in the pan, rum and lime was mixed in a petrol can and pipes came out. There are just a few moments in a year of life that one can see things in their true perspective – the efforts of the past justified, the design of the future revealed. Quite suddenly this moment of detachment is lost, never to be regained.'

When I awoke I left Corporal Tutton beneath the rock and went off in search of the others. Retracing my tracks, I found them where I had left them the night before, and ready to move with all breakdowns patched up. A few moments later, when to my dismay they had all plunged axle-deep into soft sand, a strange vehicle appeared over the horizon. I drew my jeep up alongside.
'Hello Sandy', I cried, 'What on earth are you doing here?'

Other People's Troubles
Sandy was in an LRDG truck and briefly enumerated his disasters. His party had run out of petrol when about 100 miles from Kufra some-

where north of here. He had raced on to the oasis in one jeep and returned in an aeroplane to pinpoint their position in the middle of the desert away from any landmarks, so the relief party could locate them. He dropped a note saying, 'If you are OK form a circle'. Whereupon all the vehicles milled around in nothing remotely resembling a circle; the aircraft, running low in petrol, had to return. Once back at Kufra he set out by land with supplies of water and petrol to try and find Sergeant Almonds who was in charge of this stranded party. He had been searching continuously for the past 24 hours and had not seen a trace of them.

Now he had found us. I told him of our lucky escape and the three 'vital repeat vital' signals that had come over my wireless set; that I had had to split my party in two once again, and that I thought the others would very likely get lost. Whereupon he made up a signal for David, saying that by these repeated demands for speed our party was spread over 500 miles of desert, that half of them were lost, some of them probably dying of thirst, and that he was going to call a halt for three days at Wadi Sura. If ordered otherwise he would resign his position in the SAS! Sandy was very concerned about Sergeant Almonds' party which had been left with very scanty water reserves.

Leaving Corporal Drongin, who knew the way, to lead the others to the rock stack at Wadi Sura, I departed at speed back to the wireless jeep. A few hours after my message demanding a petrol supply, a reply was received. It explained at length the incorrect procedure of our signal and the faulty drafting. Consumed with rage, I sent the most insulting reply that in my weak state I could compose. Later I learnt that David had left Cairo some time since and that this was the work of some sheltered GHQ staff officer. 'May God rain curses on his head for every more,' I ended my journal.

The next event was the arrival of Drongin's party complete – the fast section of the slow party. An hour later I spied a speck moving in a suspicious direction on the horizon and, racing towards it in my jeep, I found that it was a vehicle belonging to the slow section of the slow party! As I approached, it raced off in the opposite direction at a mad gallop, taking me, I supposed, for an enemy. When I eventually caught it, the driver, I found to my horror, knew not where he was going, from whence he had come or the whereabouts of his companions. The rest of the afternoon I spent patrolling east and west fifteen miles, catching each vehicle as it came into sight and sending it off to Wadi Sura which was clearly visible to the east. At the end of the day, to my great relief, I had accounted for them all and so returned myself to Wadi Sura.

'Men Have Been Here Before'

'Sura' means picture and the Wadi contained a number of prehistoric rock paintings such as had been found at Uweinat at the southern end of the range. Discovered only in the 1930s, they represented domestic animals and human figures swimming, which suggested the shores of a huge lake.[1] The rock pinnacles, 200ft high, stand as sentinels several hundred yards from the escarpment itself. A little to the north of these is the entrance to the Wadi, narrow and overtowered by black rock walls. There is only enough room for two vehicles to pass abreast, then one drives into a small bay with sheer cliffs on either side. Another passage connects this to a further bay, the whole complex not being more than 200 yards across. I scrambled around on the rocks marvelling what a secure fortification this would make, even for ourselves. There was no time to spend searching for the paintings, but, emerging into the hot sunshine on the far side, I determined to re-visit this enchanted spot to discover its secrets. It was clear that men had been here before.

To reach Kufra from here we must cut into the mauve headland seen the day before. A gap would then lead us into the open again whence we could take a direct bearing for Kufra, some 250 miles away. Sandy not having shown up again, we pushed off early the next morning, stopping for lunch at the entrance to the headland pass. Another urgent message came over the set. This time it was a demand for the arrival of Corporal Tutton and the wireless set the same day, and it came from Kufra. The urgency of the message was quite apparent. If Sandy's message had been received by David there must have been good reason for this new demand. There was no alternative but for me to navigate the wireless jeep to Kufra that night. I left the main party in the capable hands of the REME officer, his Quartermaster Sergeant, the redoubtable Skew, 'Daddy' Ward and the navigator. I gave the REME officer explicit instructions how to control the party, and whatever he did to keep everyone together.

Sing-Song Round a Camp Fire

With Corporal Drongin accompanying me, and Corporal Tutton following behind, we left in a cloud of dust and raced at great speed through the pass and emerged onto a gravel plain on the far side. Quite suddenly, rounding a corner, we came across Sandy, with two LRDG trucks, eating lunch. Sandy was very down-hearted, for, after his third day of search, he had not located Sergeant Almonds and the lost jeeps. I told him my news and we decided to push on together as fast as we could for Kufra. To my great relief the LRDG navigated and my memory of the final 200 miles is only a blur. We crossed flat plains of gravel sprinkled with dark patches of *serir*. We stopped some time after dark and camped on the outskirts of the oasis, weary and exhausted after 1200 desert miles. We would enter Kufra early the next morning. That night we consumed our remaining rum ration and sang songs lying round a blazing fire.

18

KUFRA OASIS AND THE APPROACH MARCH

Bimbashis and Jeep-men
Fifteen days after leaving the Bitter Lakes on the Suez Canal we reached Kufra. I remarked on this fact to Corporal Drongin as we first sighted the blue line of the Kufra palms the following morning. In which case, three days are missing from the foregoing narrative which I am unable to account for – lost somewhere in the desert sands.

The dark blue line stretched from one corner of the horizon to the other like a distant sea. As we approached, the blue palms merged into greens and browns. This was the end of the first stage of our journey – 1,100 miles from Kharga Oasis on the clock.

We drove across the airstrip and turned left up the track leading to the former Italian fort and wireless station. Here we met David who roared with laughter at Sandy's and my appearance, caked and matted with sand, like men from Mars. Turning to us both he exploded:

'Son of a gun! I thought I'd really lost you. We are going to start tomorrow.' He added, 'Can you make it?'

Here we heard the good news that Sergeant Almonds had come in two days previously. Two days after Sandy had left them, an SDF convoy had passed nearby; they waved and shouted like shipwrecked mariners until they were seen. Then they were rescued, given petrol and water and were led into the oasis apparently none the worse for their ordeal.

The whole of our expedition was now concentrated at Kufra, as well as men from the Sudan Defence Force (SDF), the Long Range Desert Group (LRDG), Commandos and Special Boat Section (SBS) who were all undertaking similar land raids. We were well behind the enemy lines and 800 miles south of their positions, and so far no one had been seen by hostile recce aircraft. It was the first day of September and our combined attacks were due to come off on 13 September.

The Benghazi expedition was still to remain split into three columns, and although there had been a good deal of shuffling about at Kufra, the columns were virtually the same as those with which we had set out. Paddy's column was leaving for the north that morning, the second column that evening, and our own, now led by David, was to depart on the morning of the following day, 2 September.

It was considered rather a poor show our being so late; the other columns had made quicker time. But there was no time for explanations about drivers and loads. We had arrived and that was the main point. I was pretty well exhausted and David had ideas of leaving me behind as rear party to recover. But I objected strongly to this and soon forgot my fatigue. Operational strain was a common complaint and the sufferers were pretty useless on active operations. Sometimes men were sent away to 8th Army for a so-called 'change'. David tried to work on the RAF principle of a 'Tour of Operations', but we were so short of officers and men that one's tour of duty was apt to be for an indefinite period.

As can be imagined, we had a hectic day of loading and unloading, studying maps, collecting personal kit, examining the model of the town of Benghazi in a huge wooden box, which had been brought all the way from Alexandria by Gordon Alston acting as Intelligence Officer. Natural instinct kept one well away from David in case he had the jolly idea of one slipping back to the Gilf Kebir to pick up a broken-down 3-tonner, and catch the expedition up at Benghazi!

'Some Friends and Many Strangers'

Here, within this circle of palm trees, were to be met all those who were to take part in these expeditions, some friends and many strangers. Tommy (or 'Tubby') Langton (an old 8 Commando hand) was one. He had taken part in the raid on Rommel's HQ under the leadership of Geoffrey Keyes who had been killed, and awarded a posthumous VC for this operation. Escaping from the scene, Tommy had made an epic journey of sixty days on foot, to reach our lines. His journey ended on rather a remarkable note.

Julian Berry, who had been a former Commando too, had by now rejoined his unit, The Household Cavalry Regiment.[1] They were on armoured car duty at the southern end of the Alamein line. His troop had been sent on patrol down into the Qattara Depression to watch for enemy movement. Julian spots through his field glasses an Arab in the far distance. Turning to his Troop Sergeant, he says,

'Go and find out what that old wog is doing, and if he can tell us anything.'

The troop sergeant jumps into a scout car and is off in a cloud of dust. Five minutes later he returns,

'Sir,' he reports, 'he thinks he knows you!'

'Knows me?' says Berry with some astonishment.

'Well go and bring him in.'

A bundle of rags hobbles up. A holy man on pilgrimage? This pathetic figure speaks:

'Hello Julian, I didn't expect to find *you* here!'

The 'holy man' is none other than Captain 'Tubby' Langton, Irish Guards Officer, former Commando, and one time Oxford Rowing Blue!

There was David Russell, recently with us behind the Alamein line; John Haseldon the spy from the Jebel (who we last met in a disused cistern outside Tobruk) who in Arab disguise was to guide in the submarine task-force who were escorting the ill-fated landing force for this raid on Tobruk.

Nick Wilder, who commanded the LRDG New Zealand patrol, a strong ally during our June raids, was bound for Barce.

Cyril Strauss, who had reached the Sudan Defence Force via a variety of postings, the 5th Bn Scots Guards, his own regiment, the 60th Rifles, and the Polish Brigade in Tobruk, was also here. He was to try and capture the oasis of Jalo. The Sudan Defence Force was from another age, each officer, Ombashi or Bimbashi, with his own driver, cook and servant, polished and waited upon hand and foot. The warlike strangers who had invaded their peace they knew as the Jeep-men. They were known to us as the Bimbashis, and their commander was Bimbashi Stubbs.

Of our own party there was Stephen Hastings, restored to health once again. Having been flown to Kufra he had gained a week of relaxation in the fleshpots of Beirut – lucky fellow!

Geoffrey Gordon-Creed was a new addition and was the Yeomanry officer in charge of the two Honey tanks which had the outsize task of neutralizing any enemy destroyer in Benghazi harbour. These tanks had to be abandoned, through mechanical breakdown, very shortly after we left Kufra.[2]

Bill Cumper, the 40-year-old Sapper officer, who was to play such an important part at the gates of Benghazi, was a former sergeant,

Royal Engineers, and an early member of 7th Armoured Division, both of which attributes he was immensely proud. His Stanley Holloway type humour was to have an ironic twist as we neared our objective.

Chris Bailey, the former Cyprus hotelier, had chosen to join us once more, as had Michael Kealy of the DLI, another former 8 Commando officer, with whom I was to share a memorable adventure a little later on.

There were many hails and farewells crowded into that September day. Whilst we were engaged thus, busy beneath the palms or swimming in the concrete cistern beneath the fort, the life of Kufra went on little disturbed. Accustomed now to the invasion by Christians, the local inhabitants were doubtless turning their minds to personal gain.

The Lie of the Land

Kufra Oasis consists of six separate groups of palms, each with its own wells. Jof is the central and largest group. To the south are Tollab, Talakh and Zuruk. To the north Hawari and Hawawiri. All these are within a radius of 5 miles. The neighbouring oases to the north-west are Ribiana, Buseima, Taiserbo and Zeighen, some 120 miles distant. From there, for a camel caravan, there was a ten-days waterless stretch, north-east to Jarabub, or north-west to Jalo. Kufra therefore held a strategic position controlling the trade routes from the Sudan to the Mediterranean. The Senussi exacted a toll from the caravans passing through. Slaves, ivory and leather would come from the Sudan, whilst arms would come back in exchange. The original inhabitants were the Tebus, a small dark people. They were evicted by the Zouias about 200 years ago, who themselves were half converted, half evicted by the Senussi, during the 19th century. Kufra was a fascinating 'lost' oasis with crystal clear salt lakes fringed with palm trees. It was on the edge of North Africa's 'empty quarter', part of which we had already crossed.

For the next stage of the journey, which was to take us some 800 miles north to a hidden rendezvous called Wadi Gamra, (this was 40 miles south-east of Benghazi in the Jebel country of Cyrenacia), we would almost be following the old camel route to Jalo. To Zeighen first of all, and then following the western wall of the sand sea until level with Jalo to our east. Jalo was occupied by the enemy and they possessed aircraft. We could not pass the western side of Jalo for fear of crossing their supply route to Agedabia thus leaving telltale tracks, so we had to pass through the 80-mile gap. Once through this bottleneck we would have a clear run until we reached the Trig el Abd, an old slaver's route, which unfortunately the RAF had sown with 'thermos bombs', an anti-personnel mine which exploded on touch. Then skirting Msus (by now a ruin) to the west, we would climb up into the broken Jebel country where at last we had good cover and would feel safe. Once spotted by hostile aircraft of course, the cat would be out of the bag. At least, they would be ready for us, and at worst, we would get a thorough strafing.

Approach March

Stephen and I, as seasoned campaigners, were appointed by David as the rearguard to keep the convoy together. We travelled in the same jeep. This was a more relaxed journey, as far as we were concerned, because no navigating was involved; we were simply following tracks. On the afternoon of 2 September we were lazing by a salt pool intending to catch the others up. The one big bonus was the arrival by air of my bedding kit and minor comforts – tobacco, dates, sweets, whisky, all stowed away. Our escape kits, ready for an emergency, were at hand, including the essential rubber tube for condensing salt water drop by drop to make it fit to drink.

Doing this tail-end-Charlie job, one sometimes got left miles behind. We had a brief halt at sundown, enough for the stragglers to catch up, brewed up and then drove all night long. It was a race against time; we had to do 800 miles in eight days, which, over unknown ground with strained and laden vehicles, was a strenuous performance. We had forty vehicles all told to look after; sometimes we were at the head of the column warning of a breakdown behind, sometimes miles back. On one occasion we found two scared men in the middle of nowhere, broken down. They were from Paddy's column. We were to return them where they belonged and, throwing extra petrol and food into the back, raced ahead to catch up Paddy's party.

On another occasion we found Martin missing. We retraced our tracks for miles and then found the tracks forked. Had he taken the wrong fork and gone on, or was he still way behind? What now? To go 20 miles south to see if he was there or to wait? Even if we went south we would still not know which fork he had taken. We decided to wait and conserve our dwindling supply of petrol. David was ahead by four hours now. If we waited another four, over good going he would be 120 miles away – outside our range. Fatefully we began to work out reserves of food, petrol and water. It was whilst we were thus employed that there was a whine and a rumble and over the horizon appeared Martin with a 3-tonner behind.

'Allo Stef! Carole!' cried Martin. 'Où est Daveed?'

At the end of the fourth night we worked out our position to be in the mouth of the Jalo gap. It was eerie and quiet and we dispersed 500 yards between vehicles. We moved on uneasily in the dawn light with the Sand Sea a few miles to our right, Jalo and its enemy landing ground a few miles to our left. With the daylight we had become aware that the country had changed; slender stalks of grass, withered and burnt yellow, gave the land a golden sheen. The ground began to undulate. The coarse black rocks of the southern desert had vanished; the gentle breeze that wafted past our nostrils told its own story. A whiff of civilization. Where had I last smelt it? Palestine!

When not employed rounding up the convoy we travelled with the rest, one driving, one reading aloud. We had read every word of an old *Illustrated London News*, we had almost finished Steve's contribution, a volume entitled *Rough Shooting*, (as if we needed such a reminder!) and we were now on to a Somerset Maugham novel.

> 'And so we continued for seven days and seven nights. Halting three times in the 24 hours – for breakfast, lunch and supper. Sometimes at the breakfast halt we would stop and sleep for a few hours. The daytime was worst with its hard metallic heat which pressed down on the top of one's head; either in shade or sunlight, it was unescapable. At night it was cool and fine and good to be alive. In open formation we swept northwards, forty pairs of headlights illuminating the land, each pinpoint conforming to the rise and fall of the terrain. It looked queer – like an irresistible force moving forward destroying the shadows in its path. How many separate forces of will power were necessary, one thought, to make the mass move?'

Pulling away from Jalo we moved carefully all day, and then all night, faster across good going. QMS Skew, our invaluable REME fitter, had the misfortune to fall from the back of a 3-tonner, whilst asleep, and broke his thigh. A most unfortunate accident, for he would have to travel 1000 miles before he could reach adequate medical attention, as well as endure the vicissitudes of our operation.

Taking it in turns to drive, the morning eventually came, misty and cool. We all drew up in hidden ground and counted our losses. It had been a good night; all vehicles were present.

Disaster at the Trig el Abd

> 'Everyone was in very good heart, we were only a very few miles from the Trig el Abd, and here we settled down to breakfast. Suddenly we heard two loud explosions ahead. Everyone pricked up their ears. Stephen and I took up a strategic position near a disused water cistern, in case of enemy bombing. David sent a jeep on ahead to see what it was.'

Half an hour later it returned to report that two of Paddy's jeeps had been blown up crossing the Trig, and that he advised us to cross as soon as possible before recce planes were sent out. We all pushed on and came to the scene of the accident. Two naval officers had been badly wounded. One had lost his leg, but Malcolm Pleydell, our MO, quickly fixed him up. It was a great loss. He had been the former Harbour Master when we held Benghazi last winter and was going to play a crucial part in blocking the harbour. He was made as comfortable as possible in the back of a 3-tonner, but died of shock before we reached the Wadi.

Once the rest of our party was safely across the track we came into the battle area of the previous winter, which I remembered well.

> 'At intervals we would come across burnt-out tanks, abandoned guns, a dump of jerry cans, and odds and ends of personal kit. It had been a battlefield – but it was of a season past. During the spring there had been very heavy rains. The tanks and trucks churned up the desert and carried on their tracks and wheels countless thousands of the seeds of wild flowers picked up from oases of vegetation. These had sown themselves indiscriminately all over the desert, so that by March it was a glorious carpet of frail and delicate flowers, which withered and died as soon as they were trodden under foot. The dried remains of these now surrounded the blackened hulks, leaving two clear bands where the vehicle had passed. Where the bands stopped, there was the scene of some disaster.'

The Jebel Akhdar

Skirting Msus on the eastern side we soon came in sight of the Jebel hills. Jebel Akhdar was a range with a higher rainfall than the rest of the coastal plain and in parts fertile enough for European farming. There were numerous square box-like Italian settlements all along the inland road. In the hills were many Senussi tents, more now than in peacetime, as the Arabs had departed from the battlefield areas of the Western Desert for the comparative safety of the hills. It was also a refuge for our airmen or soldiers shot down or left behind. It was possible to live here, albeit meagrely, with the hospitable Senussi, waiting for a suitable time to make a trek due east. During the whole of this period there must have been a permanent garrison of lost Englishmen, hiding among these barren hills.

At the end of the seventh day we reached Wadi Gamra, our chosen rendezvous and base. It was a long winding dried-up watercourse, and along it we managed to conceal all the vehicles. Not a sign could be seen from above except a few figures squatting or talking in groups. Every arm of the Service was represented, soldiers, sailors, RAF, LRDG, British spies, Arab spies and a certain number of local Arab sightseers whom we could not get rid of. We were now in position 40 miles from Benghazi, and 500 miles behind the Alamein line. So far we had not been spotted by a single hostile aircraft.

After our evening meal Stephen, Gordon Alston and I squatted round a brush fire with some local Senussi; tomorrow was Ramadan, their 'fast' period, so they made merry with our rations. We bid them gone as soon as we could reasonably do so.

The Plan
In two days' time, on 13 September, we were due to launch our attack. We would be guided down the escarpment by a pre-arranged Arab guide, and should reach the outskirts of Benghazi at Berka just after midnight. For two hours from 10 to 12 midnight the RAF would bomb the town, and under cover of this we would enter the southern suburbs, a party of forty jeeps armed with Vickers Ks and the two 3-tonners' 20mm guns according to the revised plan. There was one narrow bottleneck in the suburbs, after which we would drive straight up the main street until we came to a roundabout; then a left turn should lead us in about 200 yards to the dock gates. We would enter the docks by force, line up on the quayside, and employ our 160 machine guns to silence any opposition. Chief target would be the ships in the harbour, the lorry-borne 20mm guns having replaced the absent tanks in taking on the destroyers, if any! After this initial display of fire power everyone would disappear to their appointed tasks – one party along the Juliana Mole with explosives to blow up dock installations; another along the north mole to board any ships; others to the police station, power house, water tower, barracks. The deep sea cable to

Italy was to be cut, dumps to be blown, aircraft on outlying LGs to be destroyed, German barracks in the northern suburbs to be visited. We would destroy as much as we could and return to our hideout in the hills hopefully before first light.

All day on 12 September we spent in preparations, formed into the small groups of two or three with which we would carry out our tasks. My party was to consist of Quartermaster Sergeant 'Daddy' Ward (this was his first operation, his real job being 'Q' at Base), together with three men. Our job was to travel with the main party as far as the dockside. Not waiting for the 'fusillade', we would cut off on foot making for the submarine cable to Italy (of which we presumably had some knowledge). Having destroyed this, our team of five was to attack an Italian barracks in the eastern suburb, and finally to capture the adjacent stadium and car park, which was to be used as an assembly point for our return. I was very happy to have 'Daddy' Ward alongside me during these precarious exploits!

It says something for David Stirling's leadership that we actually swallowed these ideas and were prepared to have a go. But it is also true to say that with these kind of infiltrations the chances of success with a small self-contained group, properly armed and trained, were greater than with a much larger one. David believed, not in the big battalions, but in the single spies. As indeed we all did, as George and I had been trying to prove on the Tobruk operation one year earlier (see Chapter 7).

The first objective was the capture of an Italian fort and Radio Station on top of the escarpment. This task was alloted to Chris Bailey, the dashing cavalryman or mule-trainer who must have found it a novel rôle. He was then to visit a landing ground on the town's southern outskirts to destroy any aircraft that might be using it. Thereafter, if time hung heavy on his hands, he was to enter the town and, having reached the harbour, swim out to a small merchant ship, with his three men (like a flotilla of ducks) behind. What next? To board it and take it over!

Spies and Surprise
Surprise was the key. If we had it some of these astonishing operations might succeed. But did we have it?

On the first night an enemy aircraft passed quite close. We all froze. It appeared not to see us.

Another thing. Bob Melot, a brave Belgian officer, had been sitting in Wadi Gamra for the past week. His Arab spies who had been in and out of the town reported a newly arrived battalion of Germans and a general atmosphere of uneasiness. He and Fitzroy Maclean, veteran of the earlier Benghazi exploit, went into a huddle with our Arab informants who reported that an expected attack was the talk of the cafés. An anti-tank ditch and minefields had been laid on the western perimeter. They also confirmed that a new German battalion had been moved in. This information was relayed to Cairo with a request for new orders. But GHQ discounted such rumours as 'bazaar gossip'.[3] As a result of this disquieting news David decided to abandon the plan to enter the town at several different points and concentrate on a surprise attack at an unexpected point to the south of the town.

Stephen and I were reluctantly forced to hand over our jeep, of which we had grown inordinately fond. We were now on our feet. I selected a tommy-gun, a sheepskin coat, blanket, escape kit and two books in one haversack. This would have to last me for the next month. In the other haversack were twelve time-delay Lewis bombs, ten hand grenades and four incendiary bombs. The men would carry two EY rifles, dual purpose weapons which could also launch a grenade from a discharger-cup fitted to the muzzle of the rifle.

In old Russia (with which my family had been connected) there was a custom, before setting out on a long journey, for the family to sit around quietly each with his or her own thoughts, before taking to the road. As we lay in the wadi, all jobs done, ready to start, our minds were cleared of all the myriad practical details with which we had been concerned. We were now on our own in the lap of the Gods.

19

AMBUSH!
DEATH WADI AND ESCAPE

On 13 September at 3 p.m. a long column of vehicles left the wadi. All kit that was not stowed on the vehicles had to be left behind. Each jeep, mounting two twin Vickers, was cleared for action, guns loaded and working parts freed. Grenades, bombs and pistols were lying to hand. Everyone was at the top of their form, singing, laughing and ready for anything after 2000 miles from the Delta. We were on the job at last, and success or failure would be taken as it came. It is true that some of the men's high spirits were a little forced, but 'Daddy' Ward, perched on a pile of kit smoking his pipe like an old grandfather, was in great spirits.

Silencing the Fort
We climbed out of our wadi fifty vehicles and 200 men strong. We ran along a bumpy track sending telltale dust clouds into the still air. Soon we dropped down steeply into another deep wadi, followed it up for a mile and climbed up onto the scarp again. It was a rough afternoon's drive. But the atmosphere was one of a race meeting, as we filed along picking up outlying parties on the way. Then someone spotted an aircraft. We all leapt out and froze. The plane did not alter its course but passed low over our column. We did not know whether we had been seen or not. But we should know more within an hour.

Chris Bailey had left two hours in advance to silence the Italian fort, timed for 4 p.m., and we were to pick him up on top of the escarpment. British equipment, dotted around and stuck hard in the sun-baked mud, told us that this was the remains of Wavell's retreat in 1941. As night fell a horrible journey began over jagged boulders following the course of a rough track. We were now in the hands of our Arab guide who was to find us an easy way down the escarpment.

It was during one of these interminable halts that one of Bailey's party appeared out of the darkness, running down the side of the wadi. He wanted a doctor quick. He was the only one unwounded. The Italians in the fort had surrendered after EY rifle grenade fire. As Bailey's party entered the building the Italians opened fire. Bailey had been shot through the chest and Bob Melot, who was with him, badly hit in the shoulder. The other man had also been wounded, but mercifully they were all still alive. The fort was captured and the radio link smashed, but had it remained long enough on the air to report our coming?

A Treacherous Guide

After sending off a party to deal with the situation we continued, our spirits somewhat dampened. It was now a question of manhandling most of the vehicles down. In the pitch dark without any headlights this was not an easy job. It soon became apparent that the head of the column was badly stuck, and, upon my going forward and talking to David, the situation was plain enough. Our guide had treacherously misled us and we were bumping down into a steep-sided rocky ravine, Wadi el Gattara. Once at the bottom it would be impossible to get out; we should have been well to the south. This was serious for it was approaching midnight and we still had a good 15 miles to go.

We abandoned the guide and with difficulty extricated the leading vehicle. After that we had to clear boulders all the way, build a rough track and guide each vehicle individually over a mile stretch. Once on the good going again we were all exhausted. In the distance we could see searchlights and explosions of the RAF bomber raid. We would have to be very quick to take advantage of that. There was still a perimeter wire and minefield to get through before we reached the suburbs. It was Bill Cumper's task to clear this and he and the navigator and David were up in front.

Misgivings Fulfilled

The ground was too rough to send a jeep up and down the column whipping in. A runner was too slow. Messages had to be shouted down the line of vehicles, from one to the other until it reached the rear. As the French contingent was in the middle, a message coming up the line would inevitably cross with one coming down the line, from front and rear simultaneously, with resulting shouts and arguments. Despite the tenseness of our situation the results of the garbled messages were hilarious. Even we could appreciate that.

At 2.30 a.m. we were still running across the plain, disappointed with our progress and now freezing cold. It was being whispered that once in Benghazi we were there for keeps – no good trying to get out of the town in daylight. Four hours later our misgivings were fulfilled; single jeeps were racing back over the same ground for the deep shadows of the escarpment. The raid had failed.

What had Happened?

This is what had happened. The minefield and wire did not materialize. At 3.30 a.m. the shapes of trees and houses had loomed up. We had passed a farm. Now we were on a good track with poplars either side bordering deep ditches. We had turned on the headlights of the leading vehicle to lull the enemy's suspicions. Of course the RAF bombers had departed hours ago.

> 'I could see a white tollgate across the road now shining and illuminated by Bill Cumper's headlights. Bill had stepped out of his jeep, walked ostentatiously up to the gate, flung it up with a flourish, and with typical bravado proclaimed in a loud voice "Let Battle Commence!"'

Whereupon the hail of fire was directed at our column. There was no time to appreciate the humour of the situation. We were caught in an ambush. Sporadic fire was also coming through the trees from either side, presumably from riflemen. In front Sergeant Almonds drove his jeep through the gate. But he was soon silenced and the jeep set on fire, followed by a second jeep bursting into flames. The rest of us were nose to tail. Those who could fire fired to the flanks. The jeeps in front directed a withering fire on the enemy guns, but they were protected by concrete emplacements.

> 'After 15 minutes David, quickly grasping the position, ordered, "Every man for himself" – back to the RV. It was a scene of the utmost confusion, for we were all jammed tight on a narrow causeway, hemmed in by poplars and ditches. With guns still firing the vehicles began to mill around – reversing and turning. It was an ideal situation for the enemy to exploit, but they were still afraid of our sting. In a few minutes we were all round,

leaving the two jeeps behind still blazing, and acrid smoke drifting through the splintered trees. The enemy were still firing. As we whizzed down the poplar avenue I could see the break of day, a pale streak in the eastern sky.'

In the confusion I had lost my 3-tonner, and as the column turned I jumped onto Bill Cumper's jeep. He had been run over by another jeep reversing and was badly bruised. Corporal Drongin was slumped in the back, shot through the groin. We travelled too fast for the wounded man's comfort I'm afraid, but we had to reach cover before dawn. But dawn overtook us as we reached the farm amidst the poplars. There was not a sign of life, nor could we see any other of our vehicles. We drove up a track between two ploughed fields, caught up another jeep and quickly compared bearings. It was now broad daylight. The escarpment could be made out, blue and misty, 12 miles to our east. There was an argument as to which point we should make for – the headland or the dip. We had not gone much further when we hit Wadi Gattara. Alas, we were on the north side, so, plunging down into the wadi, we followed its course for a mile before branching east along a track. We passed a blazing 3-tonner on our way with no one about. Then we saw another jeep in the distance and found it was David, on his way back to Benghazi to look for stragglers. We told him that we were the last past the farm. But he was worried about the French and made off for Wadi Gattara. Then we saw the first hostile aircraft, an old Italian CR42, wheeling and circling towards us. They had not lost much time. We drove towards a flock of sheep hoping that we could make ourselves inconspicuous amongst them. The Italian circled over the blazing 3-tonner and then, flying over us, made for the Jebel.

'We looked back. Benghazi, a white city of towers, was suspended on the morning mist. Around us sheep grazed the dew-spangled plain, whilst above our head skylarks were poised, challenging the shepherd's pipe, sweet notes drifting and fading in the light breeze. A moment worth 2000 desert miles! Sensible also of the danger that lurked behind this fair scene, we scattered the chanter's flock. The notes faded and the vision passed, the sky was loud with the noise of our engines as we accelerated away. The giant shadow was but a few miles away, and racing, exhilarated, through the morning air, we reached its safety apparently unseen.'

Rendezvous at the 'Seat of Learning'

At this point the escarpment was steep and rocky, but our direction was right; Wadi Gattara, with bleached white stones and shrubless course, lay a few miles north. We attempted the cliff, walking in front of the jeep preparing the way and shoving from behind. It climbed as sure as a snail, over rocks and scree up the 300-foot slope. Further along the cliff we could see another vehicle with minute figures repeating the same performance. Following up a narrow watercourse towards the plateau, on rounding a bend we came across Sandy sitting on a mossy shelf, examining a battered jeep with holed radiator, three punctured tyres and buckled wheel rims. We all sat down together, ate emergency rations and felt suddenly very tired. A fine chestnut mare came grazing up the wadi, and then the aircraft came again. So far they had been concentrating on the plain, now they moved over our stretch of jebel. Luckily we were well hidden in the shadows, but we watched them dive and fire at others less fortunate.

Peace returned and we made a plan. An old *zawia* or arabic school was marked on the map as 'The Seat of Learning'. Here we had planned to have our first RV. Thoughts of cool cloisters and 'palely loitering' nuns with well laden refectory boards seized my fevered imagination. Whilst the others fixed up the jeeps and the wounded man, I set off on foot to search for this mirage. On reaching the top of the hill I found a little group of men standing around a van. It was the local grocer's van; the driver dolefully explained that he had already made his deliveries, otherwise he would be ready to serve us.

I walked on and was hailed by a Bedouin at the mouth of his tent.

'*Etneen Inglesi hena*,' he shouted excitedly. '*Hena! Hena!*' ('The Englishmen here. Here! Here!')

He made motions that they were lying down and were sick, and I followed him quickly, thinking they might be wounded. But lying dozing beneath a bush were Gordon Alston and Stephen Hastings. I prodded Gordon, who opened one eye.

'Hello, oh it's you,' he said, 'what do you want?'

'Nothing in particular,' I replied, 'I was only wondering who was underneath this bush. Do you know where the Seat of Learning is, by the way?'

'No,' murmured Gordon, still only half awake. 'Why? Are you going there? Come back and tell us if its worth it,' he added drowsily.

The high plateau upon which I stood seemed to be dotted with jeepmen, walking or riding in different directions, whilst enemy aircraft circled round. I could see about five in the air at once, Macchis, Messerschmitts and CR42s.

Black smoke was curling up from behind a rise; someone's vehicle had been brewed up. I carefully retraced my steps to the spot where I had left Sandy, Cumper and the wounded Drongin – but they had gone! On the other side of the wadi on a high hill overlooking the coastal plateau was to be seen the wireless station where Chris Bailey and Bob Melot had been wounded, whilst Benghazi was now invisible in a heat haze 12 miles to the north-east. So I walked back the mile to where Gordon and Steve lay.

'*Molto stancho ufficialli*,' ('very tired officers') muttered the owner of the tent, breaking into Italian. Then we all decided to search for our elusive rendezvous – The Seat of Learning. Taking their jeep, we followed a track, stopping and hiding away every so often whilst enemy aircraft searched overhead. We soon came to a party of jeeps and men well hidden beneath some acacia trees. A few crumbling stone walls on a slight rise was all that remained of the elusive *zawia*. This was our first place of rendezvous, but so far there were only four jeeps, Mike Kealy, and a few men. We lay all day exhausted beneath the thick bushes and trees, and all day aircraft buzzed overhead; the CR42s slow, low and dangerous, searching out every bush and tree; the 109s and the Macchis faster and not so sharp-eyed. One by one people drifted in, on foot or in jeeps. David came in the late afternoon with Lorry Pike, the RAF officer. He and David had been badly strafed all afternoon near a French 3-tonner which was finally blown up. We were tickled to death that the RAF at last knew what it was like at the receiving end. Pike was not so happy about it, however. He was badly shaken.[1]

At last light we were mercifully all complete except for some twenty men which included Arthur Duveen, Martin and Lesec. The wounded had been taken back to Wadi Gamra. Sergeant Almonds and two others were known to have been lost at the ambush in Berka, but killed or wounded we knew not.[2]

David instructed everyone to leave that night for Wadi Gamra, a distance of some 25 miles, and collect there. Kealy and myself with five men and three jeeps were to remain for another twenty-four hours to collect stragglers. As I recalled,

'That night we bade farewell to our friends, ate a meagre supper, extinguished the fire before dark and wrapping ourselves up in camouflage nets, fell fast asleep.'

Meeting the Professor

We were all terribly disappointed, particularly David, whose cherished scheme this was. If only it had not been cancelled the first time, and we had done it earlier, we might have had great success. However, we could have been worse off, for we had sustained comparatively few casualties at the ambush, and hopefully we had enough fuel intact to reach Kufra again. Our immediate problem was ground patrols. Unarmoured patrols we were confident of dealing with, but if combined with air co-operation we would be in a difficulty.

We lay as low as possible during 15 September, so low one Arab thought, who came to trade us eggs, that it was positively shaming for the British Army to be seen thus.

'*Sempre dormire*' he thought aloud, '*Machina dormire! Il majori dormire! Sempre inglesi dormire!*'

(Everyone sleeps; machines sleep; the major sleeps; all the English sleep!)

We packed him off to fetch us a hen.

All day long the aircraft circled and twisted in the brilliant blue sky. They would appear far over the red ruins, glinting and shimmering in the high sun. In our present hideout we were only afraid of the old CR42s, which could twist round every bush and tree until one could see the pilot's head, leather helmeted, goggled and it seemed, grinning, as he leant out over the cockpit. We had had so many narrow escapes from strafing that we wondered how long our luck would last. When they came close over our hideout we lay in the thickest shadow, moving not a muscle, until they had passed away. In the meantime we sat and smoked and talked. Soon our Arab returned with a fine hen, which we paid for with Italian Lira provided for this purpose. The hen would be kept as emergency rations in case we failed to join the others.

Behind our Arab came a bronzed balding figure in shorts and sandals. He was middle-aged and was clearly not Italian. He began apologetically,

'Excuse me,' he said in English, 'but are you by any chance going back to Cairo?'

Astonished, we replied that that was our intended destination.

'Well, could you possibly give me a lift? I am a professor at Cairo University, and my term begins in ten days you know. I only get the holidays up here,' he said.

1. 'Another aspiring Everest man was Sergeant David Stirling, later to raise and command the SAS' (p.6).

2. 'The veteran skier Bill Bracken represented an older generation' (p.6).

3. *Poilus* at Chamonix, still in their First World War uniforms. (see p.11).

4. Sergeant John Cripps: 'Goodbye the mountains, the bars,... the little French girls' (p.15).

5. 'Captain Frank Usher was a shrewd and canny Scot' (p.28).

6. 'Major Dermot Daly (below left) was our commander, a Scots Guards Officer of considerable experience and of pugilistic mien' (p.28). On the right is David Stirling.

7. 'Our Colonel, Bob Laycock, had a pug-like face and was a tough nut' (p.30).

8. 'My Platoon Sergeant was known as "Daddy" Ward, an uncompromising Englishman with a northern bluntness and common sense' (p.36).

9. RIP for Randolph Churchill on his departure from Lochailort, 1940 (see p.31).
Left to right: ?, Michael Alexander, Julian Berry, Kelpie Buchanan.

10. The *Aphis* (see chapter 6).

11. 'With David Stirling a new idea was born' (p.82).

12. 'Mike Kealy was another fine example of a pre-war regular officer; (p.156).

13. Admiral Sir Walter Cowan: 'A 71-year-old admiral who had been on the retired list for over ten years was with us in a "supernumerary" capacity' (p.43).

14. 'Sandy Scratchley, a wiry Yeomanry officer' (p.108).

15. 'Frank Thompson was a delightful companion' (p.58).

16. 'One of my most admirable men, Corporal Drongin' (p.122).

EIGHTH ARMY

Personal Message from the ARMY COMMANDER

1—When I assumed command of the Eighth Army I said that the mandate was to destroy ROMMEL and his Army, and that it would be done as soon as we were ready.

2—We are ready NOW.

The battle which is now about to begin will be one of the decisive battles of history. It will be the turning point of the war. The eyes of the whole world will be on us, watching anxiously which way the battle will swing.

We can give them their answer at once, "It will swing our way."

3—We have first-class equipment; good tanks; good anti-tank guns; plenty of artillery and plenty of ammunition; and we are backed up by the finest air striking force in the world.

All that is necessary is that each one of us, every officer and man, should enter this battle with the determination to see it through — to fight and to kill — and finally, to win.

If we all do this there can be only one result — together we will hit the enemy for "six," right out of North Africa.

4—The sooner we win this battle, which will be the turning point of this war, the sooner we shall all get back home to our families.

5—Therefore, let every officer and man enter the battle with a stout heart, and with the determination to do his duty so long as he has breath in his body.

AND LET NO MAN SURRENDER SO LONG AS HE IS UNWOUNDED AND CAN FIGHT.

Let us all pray that "the Lord mighty in battle" will give us the victory.

B. L. MONTGOMERY,
Lieutenant-General, G.O.C.-in-C., Eighth Army.

MIDDLE EAST FORCES,
23-10-42.

To my personal liaison officers Carol Rather

B. L. Montgomery
Lieut-General

18. *Left to right*: the author, Monty, 'Maori' Coningham, Tommy Elmhirst (see p.195).

19. The author (left) with Gordon Alston setting off for Tripoli.

20. Others of the raiding party.

21. The author, after his escape, arriving at Monty's HQ, October, 1943 (see p.239).

22. Back in England. 'I felt it was high time I got back to my regiment' (p,243).

23. In the Ardennes, December 1944, Montgomery's Liaison Officers. Left to right: the author, Eddie Prisk (US Army), Charles Sweeney, Maurice Frary (US Army), Dudley Bourhill, Dick Harden and John Poston (seated).

24. Investiture in the field. King George VI at Tac HQ, Holland, 1944.

25. 'The last of my desert journeys' (p.299). Crossing the Trans-Jordanian desert with Arab Legion guides, 1948.

And so Professor Smythe, British intelligence agent, joined our party.

Later in the afternoon a few stragglers walked in. At last light we had been told to leave The Seat of Learning rendezvous for the 25-mile journey to Gamra. It was expected that the main party would need to remain there for a week. However, we decided to wait a few more hours on the off-chance that a few more missing men might turn up. Mike was still worried about Arthur Duveen and we sent the Professor out to look for him. Some time after midnight it was time to depart.

We threw off the camouflage nets, started up the jeeps and, amid loud protestations from the fowl, followed the pale track into the night.

Although we could not use our headlights the track in front of us was perfectly clear, a dust track through scrub made by our wheel marks on the journey out. We decided to travel a short distance only to a neighbouring wadi, where we thought a few stragglers might have collected. We found a convenient bush in the broad depression, switched off and settled down to a few hours' sleep before dawn. Dawn came and we found ourselves in an exposed spot and so pushed on. We found some good bushes about 300 yards from the track and, as the sun was up, lost no time in camouflaging up. Two jeeps we drove into the bush and the third we put in some thick scrub 100 yards off. Just beyond the bush there was a hole as though someone had pushed in a pie crust. It was only ten yards across and four feet deep, but on one side a lip overhung which on closer inspection revealed a narrow cave with room for us all to lie down flat. After fixing up the vehicles, Michael and I and five men squeezed into its musty shade, which gave us some protection against aircraft. We soon made ourselves comfortable. Sergeant Kershaw had secured the hen which was protesting strongly about the emergency ration it had been offered for breakfast. Dalziel, from my old commando troop, was squatting at the mouth of the cave stoking a smokeless scrub fire, whilst the rest of us opened our escape kits to see what was on for breakfast. We found a tin of bacon and a tin of bully and with five eggs we prepared a hearty breakfast. As the embers died and the sun crept up we lay back in the depths of the cave, lit pipes and cigarettes and listened for the sound of aircraft. A recce plane came overhead high and upon a straight course, droning away in a monotone, and then silence. Arabs gathered around; the distinctive white of their dress served well as our camouflage.

A Proper Strafing
As the morning wore on and the air remained inactive we thought it safe to push on for Wadi Gamra. As we moved off our three jeeps sent up little clouds of dust into the clear air.

'Aircraft!'

I saw them first, as silver specks against the azure blue. Just enough time to wheel twenty yards off the track and run for cover. Both Mike and I dived for the same bush, which rose only a few feet above the surface of the desert. Jeeps were only 15 yards away and broadside on, the angle at which a fighter attacks.

It had all happened in a flash, and in a flash they were upon us. A slow circle – then a long steep dive shrieking louder and shriller. Then the earth hot and jumping all about one as the bullets struck the ground. As the plane zoomed up again I recognized its markings – an Italian Macchi. We could expect no mercy from them. Behind I caught sight of a man running and cursed him for a fool, for he would get singled out. But my curses ended in a prayer as the plane dived again.

'Oh God our help in ages past
Our hope for years . . .'

But the bullets cut short my appeal as they started pounding the ground all around me. One plane circling around watching now as the other dived; they had got it to a fine art. The bullets passed over our heads and they struck the jeep beyond. It would be a miracle now if the jeeps survived. Soon the jeeps on our right and left were exploding and crackling in flames. Ours was still intact. Both pilots now concentrated on us.

'Nine times we prepared ourselves for the blow, and nine times their bullets exploded around us. But as our jeep went up with an immense "Poof!" we at last breathed a sigh of relief. Perhaps they would go away now? But they came in for another dive as the débris from the explosion was still falling around us, and amongst the débris the remains of our fine hen floated gracefully to earth. This time they followed each other down, whining and screaming as we tensed ourselves for the sickening crash of the bullets. Our bush was riddled and cut down. Then Michael suddenly said, "Good God, our bush is on fire! We'll have to evacuate!" We kept one eye on the aircraft and one on the burning bush the flames creeping nearer and nearer.'

A Long Walk Home

'Then there was silence. The sky was empty! We stood up and shouted, "Anyone hurt! Anyone hurt! Everyone OK?" But there was no reply. Then gradually five figures arose from the neighbouring scrub. We had all survived.'

There was nothing to salvage from the three burning wrecks. We counted our assets. Seven men, two water bottles, seven tins of emergency rations and a tin of bully. We looked around. Black smoke drifted across the landscape and little scrub fires were burning in patches. We were in a broad, even valley with a dusty track winding away towards the east. Quite close and above us were some Bedouin tents which we had not noticed before. From the nearest of these came running an angry figure. He stopped in front of us shouting wildly, pointing to the sky, our jeeps, his tents and then us, stamping on the ground and generally registering disapproval. It seemed that his old mother had not enjoyed the performance.

Having crossed the track we sat down to make a plan. The first step was to make for Wadi Gamra where we hoped we would find our companions. If this failed we would head for the high jebel between Barce and Derna, among the stunted pines, and fall upon the hospitality of the Senussi until we found a means of getting back. This 'getting back' was over a distance of some 500 miles!

'I plodded along besides Michael. In a way, now that we were rid of all encumbrances, life had become infinitely more simple. We possessed one map, one compass, a pistol and several reliable Shanks' ponies. It was the end of one chapter and the beginning of a new one.

Soon it became very hot. The September sun beat down upon our unprotected heads. It bounced off the dry desert and hit us in the face. We did not speak. We had the men spread out in wide formation behind us so they would be scattered in case of air attack. After we had been going for about three hours we came across two LRDG trucks smouldering in a wadi. We had ordered no drinking until dark, and so we hurriedly searched in the wreckage for water tanks. We rummaged amongst the charred remains and found a tin of peas which produced a trickle of green liquid which we shared out. It looked as though they had been caught the day before. One was a wireless truck, but there were no survivors about.

During that afternoon we had to lie low on several occasions as aircraft passed overhead, but they never spotted us. Now everyone was getting very tired. The men, unaccustomed to marching or even walking, lagged far behind, and we had to halt frequently for them to catch up. We found our willpower was gradually being sapped and we walked aimlessly, the uncertainty of rescue weakening our limbs. At 5 o'clock we had to call an hour's halt. We continued somewhat refreshed but the sun's heat was still intense.

Olivey's Patrol and Grim News

Mike and I, walking side by side to control the party, became exasperated bumping into each other, so halting were our steps. Speech was superfluous so we walked along in silence. We had both seen the man, squatting on the flat of a rock at the foot of a wadi. We quickened our pace a little but gave no indication to each other of what we had seen. Michael admitted later that at that point he had inwardly forgiven me for the last time I had bumped into him. The figure was now before our eyes, as large as life. The first words we spoke were to the man himself.

'Hello! Who are you?'

'LRDG. Olivey's Patrol,' came the reply.

But at that moment an aircraft approached and we dived into a dark hole. It was a water cistern carved out of solid rock. In its cool depths we crouched until the danger passed. Our Rhodesian (for it was the Rhodesian patrol) led us over to the patrol leader, Captain Olivey, whose vehicle was so well camouflaged that we did not see it until our backs were against its rear wheel. With usual LRDG hospitality everything they had was ours. Tea was soon produced and, having slaked our thirst, we asked for the latest news.

The raid on Tobruk had apparently failed and the raids on the Jebel coastal towns seemed to have met with little more success. But most alarming for us was that Wadi Gamra, where all our party was concentrated, had undergone an all-day pasting from the air and many fires had been seen; so perhaps we had been lucky after all to have been left as rear party. Olivey was going to Wadi Gamra tonight to contact David Stirling, and then planned to return to Kufra. We would also talk to David to see what he wanted us to do.

Death Wadi

That evening we ate a large meal and prepared to depart. We travelled two to a truck perched on top of its load. And, happily tingling from the rum ration, we felt that we no longer had a care in the world! Very soon we came upon some more of our own men trying to get an old Italian truck to work. They were under a Sergeant who was quite badly hurt, having been run over at the ambush. The task was hopeless, so we sent them ahead in their jeep to try and find the doctor in the wadi. We had some rough going and some steep hills but soon came to a sentry by the side of the track. He was from David's party a few hundred yards off. David had Corporal Tutton's wireless jeep with him. He was as cheerful and confident as usual. There had been a lot of trucks destroyed by aircraft that day he told us, and Paddy and Sandy had already set off for Kufra via Jalo. He had heard no news of the Sudan Defence Force but hoped that they had taken the oasis. Paddy's party would visit Jalo on their way south as they were short of petrol and food.

The badly wounded, who consisted of Chris Bailey, hit again in the strafing, QMS Skew, Corporal Drongin and Corporal Tutton's second operator, were all too bad to move. One of our medical orderlies, who had volunteered for the job, was to accompany a captured Italian the next day and drive into Benghazi and lead out an ambulance. He had therefore bravely volunteered to be taken prisoner. Bob Melot, although badly hit, preferred to make the journey back with all its excruciating discomforts, as had also an American officer who wore the uniform of the French Foreign Legion. We knew him as 'the Pineapple', a diminutive drawn from an idiosyncracy of his. A great favourite of us all, he was badly wounded and died en route.

David himself was remaining in the neighbourhood of Wadi Gamra for a few days in a last-minute attempt to contact stragglers of which there were now not more than three unaccounted for. He suggested we continue with Olivey's Rhodesians. We left David silhouetted against the night sky and wondered when we should see him again.

Very soon we reached the head of Wadi Gamra. The night was very dark, but it was a gruesome sight. This place that had once been buzzing with life was now deserted and dotted with still burning vehicles. Burning rubber, metal and oil reeked in our nostrils. All about lay scattered kit; from what we could see it must have been a thorough strafe. About twenty vehicles were lying there wrecked. We saw no sign of life although we had expected to find the wounded. We stopped at the fork by the blazing French trois-tonners. I walked over to the place where I had dumped my kit but found nothing. The Rhodesians loaded on a few undamaged Vickers guns and we pulled out, glad to be out of Death Wadi, but carrying the stench of disaster about our clothes until well out into the clear desert air. Corporal Drongin I was never to see again; years later we heard that he had died after a few days. It could have been any one of us.

20

SOUTH ACROSS THE GREAT SAND SEA

We made good going that night in a south-easterly direction. Olivey wanted to get well away from the area so that we could travel safely by daylight. On the morning of 17 September we had halted for breakfast, when over the hill came walking a collection of queer-looking figures. They were from Jake Easonsmith's party whose LRDG patrol had been attacking Barce and had lost all their vehicles. They had walked a long way and were heading south to Bir el Garrari, 80 miles from Barce. Here they hoped to pick up a dumped truck. Six badly wounded had been sent south to Kufra in the only undamaged vehicle. They were as delighted to see Olivey's party as we had been the day before. There were twelve of them all told, including Jake Easonsmith, and with them were remnants of Timpson's Guard's and Wilder's NZ patrols.

> 'They had had the most tremendous party in Barce, destroying thirty aircraft and charging into tanks. Alastair Timpson himself (another former ski-battalion man) had been badly hurt on a razor-back dune on the approach across the Sand Sea; Nick Wilder, an old friend from Fuka days, had been shot in both legs. He was now in the "wounded" car somewhere between us and Kufra.'

So Olivey's patrol of four trucks now had twenty passengers. We arrived at Bir el Garrari in the evening and found the dumped car, plus supplies of petrol and food. We camped here the night and made a huge brushwood fire. We now considered ourselves safe from any prying eyes.

Fateful Meeting at LG 125
On the 18th the passengers set off with three trucks in charge of Henry, a new Rhodesian officer, while Easonsmith and Olivey went north again to search for a second walking party. We crossed the Trig el Abd safely (that of the thermos bombs) and that evening reached LG 125, 150 miles to the south. We drove cautiously onto the barren landing ground scattered with wrecked aeroplane fuselages. At this spot we were supposed to meet Lloyd-Owen's Yeomanry patrol, back from Tobruk. We fired a Very Light and very soon Lloyd-Owen's cars sailed into sight. It was a fascinating meeting. Here in the heart of the desert we had a member from each expedition, except of course the SDF at Jalo. David Lloyd-Owen, although he had skirmished on the outskirts of Tobruk on the Axis road, had not been able to penetrate the perimeter defences, and believed that the Naval and Land forces which he had guided in were pretty well written off. This was very sad because John Haseldon, Tommy Langton and David Russell were of this party. At this rendezvous we, the original passengers, left Henry's patrol and joined Lloyd-Owen, who was bound for Kufra. Bidding goodbye to Henry we pulled off the aerodrome for several miles and camped for the night. What were our feelings as the enormity of our disaster began to dawn upon us? A myriad of individual efforts set at naught; countless thousands of miles travelled in vain; the cost in men and material had been high. Strange to say we were relatively unperturbed. We knew, in Kipling's words, that both "triumph and disaster" were the imposters of our trade.

We made an early start on the 19th. We had four cars and travelled fast across good gravel *serir*. In the early morning it was cool and misty. After the hardship of a jeep, a Chevrolet truck was luxury. We were aiming south-east in the direction of Jarabub, my erstwhile stamping ground. That had been ten months ago, and what a lot had happened since!

First Sight of the Great Sand Sea
To our south we had our first sight of the Sand Sea, range upon range of dunes with pink dancing crests and ridges.

> 'From a distance it seemed an impassable barrier. As we approached, the foreground gradually absorbed the whole picture and we could only see the first obstacle – a large humpbacked ridge of shifting sand. The fingers of the Sand Sea lay like a huge outstretched hand upon the dark surface of the hard

desert. We drove between these fingers and, before we left "the hard", stopped to have our midday meal.'

Whilst we sat and munched our bully and biscuits we could watch the sand move. When there was the slightest breeze this would happen. The area covered by the Kalansho and Great Sand Seas is almost 1,000 square miles. They lie in the shape of a gigantic horse-shoe. The left-hand arm, starting north of Kufra, stretches 250 miles to latitude 30°. Here the top of the horseshoe swings round east, passing south of the Jarabub and Siwa Oases, then turning south for 300 miles until it meets the northern end of the Gilf Kebir.

The centre of the horseshoe is occupied by an open stretch of gravel *serir* over which one can drive in safety to Kufra. At the northern end of this, in the *cul de sac*, was Howard's Cairn, a landmark for LRDG patrols. To cross the Sand Sea was our safest option. The alternative route through the Jalo Gap was too risky, as no news had come through as to the success of the Sudan Defence Force attack.

Fortunately, the conformation of the dunes was north to south, rising to 300 feet; a single dune may run south for some 30 miles. The trough between two dunes will carry one on until one of them peters out and one can then cross laterally to the next trough. A trough may vary in width from 500 yards to 5 miles. The prevailing wind is from the west so that the usual shape of a dune is a smooth western slope rising to a flat crest over which the sand precipitates down an almost vertical eastern *glacis*. East-west dunes are formed by wind eddies which have their razor-back slope on the southern side. Even whilst eating our lunch, between ridges of sand, we could watch small sand avalanches drifting down the eastern slopes and spreading across the virgin desert like the tentacles of an octopus.

We had a tough job in getting into the 'sea' itself, but after the third attempt dropped down onto an open undulating plain, over which we were able to travel at 30–40 mph. Then into the sand again this time like a scenic railway, banking round corners and charging over the top, to subside in a heap at the bottom.

'At sunset the scene can hardly be described without superlatives. For me it was as though I had found myself on another planet. As the sun sinks, the landscape loses its harshness and is suffused in a thousand soft colours – both beautiful and misleading. When the night comes – a plain moonless night as this was – it is a night of unfathomable depth enhanced by the deep blue sky, the brilliancy of its stars, and the balm which it spreads over all cares and anxieties. All desire for sleep left one as one gazed at this intoxicating scene.'

All day on the 20th we ploughed through the Sand Sea. It was a day of pretty hard work. Shortly after midday we came to a really big east-west dune lying directly across our path. We all stood at the bottom cheering and shouting as the cars came over one by one. Over one small but sharp razor-back our car was the second to cross. As the top was unexpectedly firm we sailed over and rose into the air landing in the soft sand at the bottom. As the last car came over it leapt right into the air, as off a ski-jump, and sailed airborne over the other side. The front wheels hit the ground first, bouncing the car back on to its rear until it was almost vertical. Everyone fell out and I thought I saw at least one man run over. We all rushed up and found no one was badly hurt, but on closer inspection it seemed that the steering rods were badly buckled. So we called a halt for the night.

As the fitters busied themselves with the repairs and the operators set up their aerials and contacted HQ, the navigator was setting up his theodolite and 'fixing' our position. A sun shot, a star shot and direct reckoning by milometer and compass, would form a small triangle, the centre of which would be our position. We found ourselves to be not more than 50 miles north of Howard's Cairn. Meanwhile the evening rum and lime ration was mixed and the cooks prepared the bully stew. SAS and LRDG drew a double rum ration so there were compensations to this way of life.

The Human Element
David Lloyd-Owen, bearded and clad only in a pair of shorts, sat cross-legged in the shadow of his car composing the evening message to HQ. His extremely youthful looks belied his professionalism. He had hardly left the desert during the past two years. He had travelled the farthest west to the Tibesti mountains, the site of the legendary ruby mines. His gentle manners belied his reputation as one of the foremost patrol leaders of the LRDG.[1]

My own companion, Mike Kealy, was another fine example of a pre-war regular officer. He commanded our sister unit, the Special Boat Section, whose main task was the destruction of enemy shipping with the aid of the Royal Navy. Sections of Michael's men were spread between Benghazi, Tobruk and the Greek islands. Tall and very good looking, he cultivated a laid-back manner. Easy-going he may have been, but this only concealed the man of action. Much senior to myself, the amalgam of these qualities made him a delightful companion on such a journey.

> 'Before the sun had set Michael and I climbed bare-footed a neighbouring dune, our feet sinking luxuriously through the warm surface layer into the ice-cool sand beneath. From the top we could see crest after crest of mountainous dunes on every side. Was it like a sea or a vast snowfield? Did we know England or was this our home – with visions imagined? Had we seen shepherds and warped pines and a sea to the north? Was there an oasis of lakes and palms to the south? All we could see was eternity.
>
> 'Mike broke the spell, "Ugh!" he exclaimed, "to think we've got to dig our way through all these bloody dunes tomorrow."'

Below lay the three cars and the disabled one; faint tinkerings could be heard, above the wireless music from Cairo, as the men worked. In the few moments whilst we talked it had become night. There is no twilight in these latitudes. We glissaded down the dune to see if supper was ready. We were happy and relaxed. We dug and burrowed with everyone else during the day, but apart from that we had no other responsibilities.

> 'After dinner Michael, David Lloyd-Owen and I lazily talked away the night, idly sifting sand through our fingers, discussing much of the past and a little of the future. When the constellation of the group of stars known as The Plough turned itself on end, we knew it was time to sleep.'

RV at Howard's Cairn

At midday we emerged from the white sand on to the brown gravel. We struck due west across firm going, stopping now and then to scan the horizon with our glasses. Turning a little to the south we struck Howard's Cairn but found no petrol dump. It was intensely hot so we spread a large tarpaulin between two cars, cooked, ate and rested in the welcome shade thus provided. Presently the petrol party, which had been lying off, came and delivered their precious cargo.

Howard's Cairn was named after the LRDG navigator who had erected it. Itself in the U of the Sand Sea, it was hidden and protected by minor dunes. Later in the year Paddy Mayne and Sandy Scratchley used it as a base for their operations between Fuka and Derna at the time of the Battle of Alamein. It was as secure and remote as any hideout. From it they crossed the 'sea' and raided aerodromes or blew the railway lines. No enemy ground patrols dared to make the crossing; few enemy aircraft would attempt the flight.

On the afternoon of the 21st we continued south. The going was good. At midday on the 22nd we came to a disused well, near which were built some tiny stone huts. Round about lay huge Ali Baba water jars, many of which were broken, but there were a few intact, two of which we took back to Kufra. Starting early on the morning of 23 September, we reached the outer oases. From here we could see the Kufra Fort, where we arrived at eleven in the morning, seven days after leaving The Seat of Learning.

The Spell of Kufra

We spent almost two weeks at Kufra. They were the last days of September and we watched the duck flight. They settled on the salt marshes and upon the salt lakes. They must have come from the Sudan, a long and waterless flight. For a whole week we heard no news of David. The others had all arrived long ago, but the days went by and nothing came in from the north. We were all pretty confident, knowing David, that he would get back, even if he had to walk. But I for one was uneasy, feeling that if he did not return the unit would disintegrate and the many who had been willing to follow where David led would not be content to hazard their lives under a lesser chief.

As the days went by the restlessness grew, but we had plenty of leisure to explore, or to laze, or to swim. There was the concrete pool full of sweet fresh water, filled from a well by a wind pump. Into it one could take a shallow dive. Then there was the sapphire lake. It lay in the middle of the sand, fringed by date palms, on the western outskirts of the oasis. It was a deep, transparent blue and very saline. In the middle of the day one could lie floating on its buoyant surface, cool, while others baked and sweated. Once out of the water, one ran naked across the sand and was dry immediately, only having to brush one's body of the salt crystals, and from one's feet the dried sand.

West of our camp was a dried salt marsh, the surface composed of pink salt crystals. One could walk on its pink crust as on ice. Here Stephen and I chose a spot beneath an ancient palm whose branches bent beneath a load of ripening yellow dates. Here under the palm we slept. But in a few days the owner of the tree built us a palm-leaf house.

Two men weaved the palm-frond walls and roof and at the end of the day it was complete. Finding it would accommodate three, we invited Gordon Alston to join us. Inside we used the rubber dinghies (meant for Benghazi harbour) as beds. A goatskin, purchased in the local market, did for our water supply. When thirsty we only had to open the door and tilt up the goatskin where it hung to quench our thirst. When hungry, a clod of earth thrown up into the tree produced a harvest of golden dates.

The men were a few yards away on the other side of the track and had arranged shelters amongst the thick undergrowth. There were three cookhouse fires, and at the time of the evening meal the three fires would glow, each fire illuminating its circle of bending palms and its ring of silent men. The men in those strange shadows looked a rough crew, some with Arab headcloths, some with torn shirts, some with no shirt. It was at this hour that one would come to consider many strange things. One night we heard the voice of Stephen's father, Major Lewis Hastings, speaking on the BBC, of some faraway event. It was odd to think that we were perhaps the southernmost outpost of a fighting line of which the northern limit was the Arctic Ocean.

On the morning of our arrival out of the Sand Sea, much to our relief, we had found Stephen and Gordon already in Kufra. We exchanged enthusiastic greetings for there was much news to impart. They had been caught in Wadi Gamra and suffered the strafing. The air attack on our base at Wadi Gamra had been severe and had continued without ceasing all day on 17 September. Of all the vehicles with which we had arrived, of the 3-tonners only four were left and of the jeeps, only ten. The 100-odd men from 'Death Valley' as the men called it, were divided into two parties, one led by Paddy and the other by Sandy. They had driven towards Jalo to see what was happening there, but having neither theodolites nor other navigational instruments, one of the parties had lost their way. Thinking themselves towards Marada, they had happily stumbled on Jalo and luckily joined up with the SDF, for they were critically short of food and water.

Sandy's party had approached the oasis from the north and found themselves on the Italian side of a battle against the SDF. They lay low in a stone fort all day. Later the SDF told them that if it had not been for the strong point of the fort they could have happily captured the oasis. Bimbashi Stubbs was not amused when told that Sandy had been ensconced there all day! On the orders of Cairo the SDF then withdrew together with the two SAS parties.

Return via Wadi Halfa

David came in a week after we had arrived. He rolled in with his two jeeps like a hurricane, his head teeming with plans. His one object in returning to Kufra, it seemed, was to collect a party for a reprisal raid on Jalo. Later the plan was modified, but nevertheless a party of jeeps set out for Jalo on the following day. David flew off to Cairo, followed by Paddy and all the best men. The idea was that Paddy should return after a brief refit, base his squadron (a term new to our vocabulary) on Kufra, and raid coastal targets from Derna to Alamein. A new squadron was to be formed at Kabrit in the meantime, which we were to join. After the scorching test of this last raid a number of men were being returned to their units as unsuitable. These Steve and I would take back by land to Kabrit. The reward for this extra chore was that we were both being given extended leave in Kenya.

After ten days we were a diminished party left at Kufra. For our return overland we also had the French party, including Martin, Haron, and Lesec. Geoffrey Creed and Brian Dillon also joined us, a total of sixty men. Leaving the vehicles, relics of the raid, behind us, we were to catch the first SDF supply convoy of thirty 10-tonners, down to Wadi Halfa, thence passing down the Nile by river boat to Aswan, and then by train to Cairo.

The journey to the Nile took us five days. The convoy was in charge one RASC officer and his Technical Sergeant, with Sudanese drivers. His only navigational aid was one prismatic compass. Each week he made this monotonous journey away from the world and remote from the fighting front and one could not help admiring his courage. We held common views on the Bimbashis of the SDF and we would have nightly readings of Steve's poem 'Bimbashi Stubbs', which, after scorching days and frequent recitals, never ceased to entertain us.

After travelling for a thousand miles across a barren waterless plain it was no light experience to reach a broad, swiftly flowing river, the Nile, just below the second cataract. We each gave a huge sigh of relief and eagerly accepted the cool cans of beer that, while we waited for the ferry, were pressed upon us.

We arrived back in Cairo literally in rags, bearded and battle-stained. We were a dreadful sight as we de-trained at Cairo main railway station and went by lorry to Abbassia Barracks to be issued with new kit and clothing.

The results of the mass attacks on the various targets along the North African coast had been almost universally disastrous. In particular at Tobruk the naval back-up force had lost one cruiser, HMS *Coventry*, and two destroyers, HMS *Sikh* and HMS *Zulu* (both Hunt Class). Other naval craft had been badly damaged. John Haseldon, the leader of the land-party, had been killed. Other bad news reached us on arrival, the failure of the Dieppe Raid in France.

If the series of raids from which we had just returned were judged by normal criteria then the whole enterprise was a costly failure. If the ultimate object was, however, the destabilization of Rommel's position on the Alamein line then it was surely demonstrated that his position was very insecure and highly vulnerable, both his ports and airfields and his extended line of communications. This must have affected his decision to withdraw in the later stages of the coming battle.

Once back at Kabrit we prepared to go on leave. It was time to have a pause and to take a deep breath to assimilate all our varied experiences.

We had had some extraordinary adventures and our land-party was quite exhausted, but the natural resilience of youth came to the rescue. I had to remind myself that I had entered the war with my eyes open. There would be opportunities for pitting oneself against the elements and unknown forces, challenges which might never come our way again in a lifetime. There were no psychological hang-ups here, nor modern panaceas to relieve them. For most of us it was purely the culmination of night after night without sleep, and its compound interest, which some day would have to be repaid.

'Leave' in a tranquil environment would do the trick, and my mind began to dwell upon the several delectable alternatives.

Then a bombshell struck me. It was a signal from the Army Commander. It read:

'*Personal*
From Army Commander to Mather stop.
I have directed your leave be cancelled stop.
You are to report to me forthwith.'

This cryptic message sent my head spinning. What could it all be about?

PART VI
WITH MONTGOMERY AT ALAMEIN

21

FLASHBACK

Perhaps I should make use of this lull in affairs to explain how I came to receive such an abrupt demand. My knowledge of Montgomery began in Switzerland when I was quite a young boy. It was in the 1920s and my family was staying at Gstaad on a skiing holiday. We ski-ed over to Saanen Moser, a neighbouring village where a great friend of my mother's was staying. Betty Carver was recently widowed and was staying there with her two boys, John and Dick. Also staying at the same hotel was a Colonel Montgomery. My brother Bill, then aged 12, five years older than myself, took an instant dislike to this peppery colonel who was so bossy and who tried to organize everybody. However, the following year 'the Colonel' was staying at the same hotel, where Betty was again holidaying. It was shortly after that that they became engaged to be married.

Montgomery was everything one expected of a soldier, lean with steel grey eyes and a clipped military moustache. Yet there was a romantic aura about him which spoke of Kipling's India, of war in the trenches, so recently over, and of a spartan boyhood.

But even at that young age I must have struck up some kind of *rapport* with this prickly martinet. If I had looked at the palm of my hand and could have seen that his life-line crossed and recrossed my own, it would have been an alarming prospect.

The death of Betty, some ten years later, in tragic circumstances, was a great blow to Monty. Betty had been everything that he was not, a delightful person, bubbling over with charm, and humour. Vague, fey, artistic, she moved in a Bohemian circle which included such people as Augustus John. Monty took over all the arrangements of her life and was devoted to her. Following her death he lapsed into his last remaining interest, soldiering. At this time, in the late 'thirties, he was convinced that war was going to come and concentrated his entire life to this end. He shocked my mother by relishing the idea and looked forward to it as the consummation of his career.

In 1937, six months after Betty's death, Monty was in command of the 9th Infantry Brigade at Portsmouth. I had just left school and was sent down for a few days to keep him company. He was living at Ravelin House, the garrison comander's quarters, a typical redbrick army quarter of the period. Its interior was gloomy to a degree. In this spartan establishment all the staff appeared to be soldiers, adding another touch of austerity. Monty was still shattered by his loss, but beginning to come to terms with things, and in this rather awesome atmosphere I accompanied him on his daily rounds. He took a schoolboyish delight in all his new warlike toys, something which one could readily respond to.

A series of island forts in Portsmouth harbour, of Napoleonic origin, were part of his command. He was particularly proud of his quasi-naval responsibilities (as garrison commander he took precedence over the Royal Navy), and as such disposed of a handsome motor launch. In his company I visited these old Martello towers. Climbing up the seaweed-encrusted iron ladder from the rising and sinking vessel, he would inquire of the corporal in charge the state of readiness of his ancient seige gun.

'Now tell me Corporal, when was this gun last fired?' he demanded in his flat but rasping voice.

'Oo – don't rightly know sir. Not since I 'bin 'ere. I'm only supposed to keep it clean and oiled.'

'Oh, so you don't know when it was last fired!'

'Noo sir.'

'Very well,' ordered Monty, 'tell your commanding officer that I want to see it ready for firing, with five rounds of ammunition, next Tuesday at 11 o'clock.'

With very similar words he inspected all the forts in the harbour. I cannot imagine what consternation this caused in the higher echelons of the Ordnance Inspectorate, or the Naval Dockyards at Chatham whence these pieces most likely had their origin.

My next encounter was in 1938 when 9th Infantry Brigade were carrying out manoeuvres on Salisbury Plain. By this time I was at Cambridge University and had joined the University OTC Cavalry Squadron, still exercising on horses armed with swords and lances. Monty invited me down for a week to act as his 'galloper'. And in a motley collection of uniform I appeared. I was allotted a spacious tent to myself and a batman, and was thus plunged into the military life of the British Army in the late '30s as it was belatedly preparing for war.

The Brigade, consisting of the 2nd Queens, the 2nd Middlesex and the 1st KOSB, was encamped on the edge of Salisbury Plain near Tidworth. And a very fine sight it was with all the ordered confusion of a military encampment unchanged down the ages. The bell tents were dressed in serried ranks (a thing never possible in the war to come). Bugle calls sounded the passing hours, cookhouses steamed with strange brews; there was an atmosphere of good humour and self-assurance which I found wholly satisfying. The exercise upon which we were engaged was to test the measures necessary against attack by poison gas. This was a weapon which was being widely used by the Italians in their campaign against the Ethiopian tribesmen in Abyssinia. Their use of mustard gas shocked the world. It was thought to be a weapon which would certainly form part of any future war.

This must have been one of the last occasions that an infantry brigadier rode around 'the battlefield' mounted on 'a charger'. At the time its historical significance was lost upon me, although the following year my cavalry squadron said goodbye to its horses. I was only conscious of a sense of well-being as we rode across the plains, and of the evocative aroma of leather, saddle soap and horseflesh, a lost concomitant of war.

The exercise must have lasted the best part of a week, as Monty and I rode around inspecting the tactical situation. From time to time there was a low-flying aircraft attack, which greatly frightened the horses, when a horrible slob of yellow 'blancmange' was somehow ejected by the pilot and landed with a sickening smack on the ground nearby. This was a simulation of the dreaded 'mustard gas'.

Monty's report after the exercise was much applauded by the powers that be, for he gave a definite answer to each question posed, a rather unusual occurrence. He said that the menace of mustard gas must not be allowed to throw the Army off balance. 'It was necessary to have a sense of proportion and in war legitimate risks had to be accepted. And that probably better to be sprayed with gas than to be shelled or bombed with high explosive.'[1]

What impressed me most about my initiation into the impending world of war was Monty's open-air address to the assembled brigade, sitting in a grassy amphitheatre, after the exercise was over. It was a bravura performance. His talk was a mixture of admonition, humour and realism. At one moment the men appeared chastened, the next moment they were roaring with laughter, and it was at this point that he drove his lesson home. Little did I realize it at the time, but I was to witness repeat performances on two other occasions, first on the eve of the battle of Alamein and then at Southwick House before the Normandy landings, but the one that struck my imagination most was at the camp on Salisbury Plain.

22

'THE KILLING GROUNDS'

'All ranks must be told that this is probably the decisive battle of the war; if we win this battle and destroy the Panzer Army it will be the turning point of the war.'
                Montgomery, address to officers, eve of Alamein.

Eighth Army Tac HQ was located on the seashore at Burg el Arab, only 20 miles from Alexandria, from where the naval base had already been evacuated. My interview with Monty was brief and along these lines.

'I sent for you because there is going to be a terrific battle. I thought you would like to be here with me. As for your leave – there's plenty of bathing here on the seashore! I need a personal liaison officer to go around the battlefield to tell me what's happening!'

I could hardly refuse such a request. I was to report back in two days' time. It was altogether an unexpected and exciting prospect, and I hurried back to Cairo where I obtained the necessary leave of absence from David who was not altogether displeased at having one of his own people in the pocket of the Army Commander. Their relationship had not been too good and perhaps I could smooth things over.

The offensive was due to begin on 23 October, a fateful day in the history of the war. Meantime, with about a fortnight to go, I had masses to do. A new jeep and driver had been alloted to me. There were modifications to be seen to, maps and plans to be studied, briefings to attend. I had to familiarize myself with all the complicated routes through the minefields. There were divisions to be visited, generals to be met, so that when the balloon went up I should know and be known in this vast area. The SAS cap badge of a winged dagger, which I now wore, was a slight embarrassment. No one had ever seen it before! But at least it was better than the Welsh Guards leek – so suspect in Tobruk as the Afrika Corps emblem.

After a few days I started to drive Monty about in his open Humber staff car to address the troops and visit divisional commanders.

Two visits remain vividly in my memory, one to General Morshead's 9th Australian Division and the other to General Freyberg's 2nd New Zealand Division. It was a moot point how these 'tough' empire troops would receive the 'limey' Army Commander, whose knees were barely brown, but they took to him at once. Had he not already seen off Rommel at Alam Halfa? A commanding presence, combined with a professionalism that every one could see, exuded confidence, and thus was it imparted to others.

His talk to the troops went something like this:

'There will be no further retreats. I've taken your transport away! We stand here and fight. We fight *and* we die if need be! We will only win this war by killing Germans, and this is where it will be done. There will be a terrific dog-fight and it will last at least a week. Our tails are up! And we will hit Rommel for a six, right out of Africa!'

At the New Zealand Division he elaborated upon this theme with the classic words:

'Everyone must be imbued with a burning desire to kill Germans. Even the padres! One per weekday, and two on Sundays!'

This went down like a bomb and had the men roaring with laughter. They were even tickled to death with his exhortation to 'die if need be'. They had never heard anything like it before. In motorized warfare up till now it was very easy to do a tactical withdrawal and think nothing about it. There was always another position to defend. But now the acid test had come. There was nowhere else to go!

As Monty remarked at the time, 'I am not convinced that our soldiers are really fit and hard. They are sunburnt and brown and look well, but they seldom move anywhere on foot and have led a static life for many weeks.'[1]

At the New Zealand Division an open air concert had been arranged.

And a Kiwi soldier dressed as a little girl, thumb in mouth, sang a song of which the first line was 'A man came to our house – Ma says he very nice . . . '

And then the story unfolded about how the man's visits increased. He came to stay and became a second father. The New Zealanders all squatting in a huge circle in the sand evidently found this very amusing. But the irony of the words struck me, and I could not get the words, or the tune, out of my mind. I cannot even to this day forget the poignancy of that innocent ditty, sung a few days before the great battle, the turning point, was joined and in which many of the men here present, and far from home, were surely going to die. It will for ever remind me of Alamein.

It was a well known fact that before the arrival of Montgomery in Egypt the Alamein line was not considered the last stand. Parts of GHQ Cairo had already been evacuated to Palestine, including some base depots. Secret papers were being incinerated at the GHQ buildings in the heart of the city. Columns of smoke could not be disguised, either from the civilian population or the troops *en passage.* So confident had the Axis leaders become that Mussolini was already in North Africa, at Derna, not many miles away, preparing to make his triumphal entry into Cairo. SAS and LRDG raiding parties had been issued with maps of Palestine and the Sudan to cover a possible retreat, as I well remember. Some historians, in order to belittle Montgomery's impact on the situation, claim that there were no such plans and that the whole position was exaggerated. But this is simply not true. Regrettably, the feeling among senior commanders and staff, particularly at GHQ, was one of defeatism. Hence the remarkable achievement of Montgomery in turning the situation round, which led to such a dramatic improvement in morale.

The plans for the battle, to an old desert hand like myself, were entirely novel, encompassing a set-piece attack on a massive scale, the punching of two holes or channels through the enemy's defences, and the passage of the armour through those holes. It sounds simple enough but it was not to prove so. The first problem was mines. The Germans had laid extensive minefields in front of their positions, which became known as 'mine marshes'. Some of these were five miles deep. Any forward progress depended upon a narrow passage being cleared. This usually resulted in the bunching and congestion of transport in these passages which became a prime target for enemy artillery. The German mines were almost exclusively anti-tank mines. Anti-personnel mines had not yet really come into being. This meant that sappers and infantry could find the mines by prodding the ground they were clearing with a bayonet, then lift and defuse them. Progress by this method was painfully slow, and each cleared lane had to be unmistakably marked. A new invention was the flail tank or Scorpion which, by means of a forward revolving drum and heavy chains, beat the ground in front of it to explode the mines, but there were few of these. Meanwhile the artillery creeping barrage would move only yards ahead of the leading troops, a considerable feat of synchronization. Six lanes on the 30 Corps front had to be prepared to reach their Start Line beyond which the artillery would begin their creeping fire.

Vast amounts of stores, fuel, food, ammunition, water and medical supplies had to be stockpiled nearby, behind the battle line. This could only be moved into position by night and skilfully camouflaged to deceive the enemy. To complete the illusion of a false thrust to the south a dummy pipeline had been laid, section by section. Enemy reconaissance planes each day noted its progress and direction which was cunningly designed to indicate an attack some two weeks later than that planned, and in the wrong place.

The deception plan could not conceal the massive build-up of Eighth Army leading to an offensive, but it could conceal the direction of attack, the time and date. This was done by establishing the actual presence required for H-hour near the front and maintaining this by means of dummies, whilst the real troops withdrew for rest, training and refitting. They gradually moved back into position as D-Day approached, moving only under cover of darkness, so to the enemy there appeared to be no change. Naturally, in the area of the feint attack, in the far south, there was a considerable build-up of dummy tanks, vehicles and dumps. Thanks to this plan complete surprise was obtained. Even General Rommel was away on leave!

The other remarkable change was in the use of artillery which was now available in great strength. For the first time in the desert war proper divisional fire plans were made possible, making full use of the artillery arm and protecting our own infantry's advance with the deadly creeping barrage. The barrage laid down at H-hour, consisting of almost 1000 artillery pieces, was the biggest witnessed so far in this war. This was augmented by close support bombing by the RAF. As can be imagined this had a devastating effect on the enemy, but the Germans at least were tough fighters who took a lot of punishment.

Tac HQ 8th Army was, as I have said, located at Burg el Arab very near Alexandria, right on the seashore. A more healthy spot cannot be imagined, and the other HQ were near at hand. But the proximity of

Alexandria brought it home to one how vulnerable had become the whole of the Nile Valley, and the land bridge to the Levant.

At Burg el Arab they had established a carrier-pigeon loft, and to my surprise I was given a crate of pigeons to take out on my daily visits. Writing in minute letters on the tiny scroll of paper and rolling it up and inserting it into the capsule was a nightmare. I do not know who was responsible for this mad idea, but as soon as we moved camp 'the chickens' lost their sense of direction!

I kept an intermittent diary, but I had to use circumspection in what I said and tried to confine myself to the atmosphere of the thing, casual conversations and the days events.

Montgomery had established a Tactical Headquarters for this battle, a system which he was to develop as time went on. He was insulated against the scores of visitors which otherwise might have plagued him, and this gave him 'time to think'. Much of this thinking was done 'in the caravan' before a portrait of his opponent Rommel. Monty's dog later was called Rommel, all of which perhaps put his opponent into proper perspective.

At Tac HQ Montgomery maintained only a small personal staff, most of them very young, among whom he found his relaxation. In his mess tent in the evenings he would make a series of provocative remarks goading his embarrassed aides into unwise responses. Sometimes the subject was women, or sex, or love, or the military art; sometimes he would make incautious criticisms of his predecessors, sometimes it would be night life in Cairo. Surprising to some, he had a well-developed sense of humour and there could be uproarious occasions, even in the heat of battle. There were a series of honorary members who sometimes drifted in: the Air Officer Commanding Desert Airforce, 'Maori' Coningham[2], Monty's Chief of Staff, Freddy de Guingand[3], 8th Army Chief Administrative Officer Brian Robertson[4] and the head of the I Branch, Bill Williams[5]. On these occasions the conversation could be very stimulating. But I never remember Alexander dining in our mess. This was 'Monty's show' and Alex let him get on with it.

John Poston, an 11th Hussar officer and already a veteran of desert warfare, was his leading ADC. He and I shared the duties of conducting the Chief, as we called him, about the battlefield, sometimes being loosed on separate missions to key areas of the fight. One at least would report to him each evening, having marked up his report in the map lorry. Here one would squat alone with Montgomery giving an eye-witness account of all one had seen and done that day, and any personal messages from the appropriate commander. He would ask a few questions. One quickly learnt how much he came to rely upon our reports, once confidence had been established.

So the attack was to be launched on 23 October to take advantage of the full moon. Winston had been pressing for an earlier date because of the Torch landings in Algeria early in November, but Montgomery insisted on the later date. Not until then would he be ready.

23

ALAMEIN DIARY

'These precise co-ordinates: there can be no other place and moment in the world like this. Thus the theme is the uniqueness, the once-onliness of experience.'
    Laurence Whistler, *Pictures on Glass*, describing his engraving entitled 'Exact Time, appointed Place'.

The night of 23 October was a starry one, and very soon the full moon appeared. We were at our new campsite nearer the front. John Poston was in Monty's caravan receiving his instructions for 'tonight and tomorrow'. I was due in next. I noted in my diary:

'Full moon, quietness, silvery sea and peace – one could almost hear the distant music, so romantic was the scene.'

Tonight the music is yet to come – in a few hours time. Earlier in the day my brother Bill had called in and we had swum in the translucent blue of a Mediterranean inlet. He was with General Lumsden of the 10th Armoured Corps, the *Corps de Chasse* as Monty had named it.I was to have a rather fateful encounter with Lumsden later in the battle.
    At 9.40 p.m. precisely the barrage began. Never had such concentrated firepower been seen in the desert, let alone anywhere else. It was a spectacular firework display. Shells pounded the enemy forward positions. The whole length of their front lit up; it put great heart into our side. Montgomery, as was his usual wont, was in bed by 10 p.m. He ignored the barrage. It had all been laid on and there was nothing more to do. Having watched the gunfire I crept into my sleeping bag under Monty's caravan; it kept me out of the heavy dew that was then falling, and I was soon fast asleep.

'The Armour Seems to be Stuck'

At dawn on 24 October I crawled out of my sleeping bag and was ready for the day. Early reports coming in gave a decided success to the infantry night attack. I was sent off to the southern funnel in the morning to see General Freyberg of the New Zealanders, and General Alec Gatehouse, (my former brigade commander), now commanding 10th Armoured Division, to report on the progress of the armoured advance. In the afternoon I had to visit the northern funnel and make contact with General Wimberley's 51st Highland Division and General Briggs (nicknamed 'the umbrella man', or as some would have it 'the black pirate') who commanded 1st Armoured Division. My final task was to visit his forward armoured brigade. As can be imagined there was a good deal of confusion with smoke, shot and shell. The cresendo of noise from our own artillery and ack-ack guns, from RAF fighters and bombers and the enemy's own efforts all added to the fun. A cryptic note in my diary reports,

> 'I reported to the Army Commander this evening "Fairly heavy casualties in the infantry. No tank to tank battles yet. The armour seems to be stuck".'

I marked up, in the usual way, our latest dispositions in the map lorry before he came in. He asked a few questions and out I went to report my information to the ops tent.

Monty seemed moderately pleased with how things were going, but was worried about the armour. The tanks should be winning through to open desert so that the infantry, protected by the armour, could begin to roll up the enemy front, an operation which Monty called 'the crumbling process'. Very deep minefields prevented this, any tanks bunched in the narrow funnels being an easy target for the deadly German 88mm anti-tank guns. I got a whiff of trouble brewing up between the infantry and armour. Freyberg in particular was sceptical about the tankmen's offensive spirit. I passed this on, but it was early days yet, I thought.

A Crisis in the Caravan

However, that night a crisis began to develop. De Guingand became seriously worried at the lack of progress of the armour and there were rumours that they might even be planning to pull back, to the dismay of the infantry. De Guingand decided on the exceptional measure of waking the Army Commander at 3.30 a.m., thus breaking the golden rule, and summoning Leese and Lumsden, the two corps commanders concerned, to a conference at Monty's HQ. I was blissfully unaware of what was going on above my head and only heard about it next morning.

As De Guingand described it, Monty was in his map lorry when the generals arrived 'seated on a stool examining a map fixed to the wall. He greeted us most cheerfully . . . and then asked each Corps Commander to tell his story . . . There was a certain "atmosphere"; Lumsden was not happy. As the situation was being described I looked out of the map lorry and saw the placid Mediterranean at our feet twinkling in the moonlight. In contrast to the peaceful scene was the constant fire of AA guns, the droning of aircraft overhead, and every now and again the vicious whistle and crump of a bomb nearby.'[1]

Monty was apparently unrelenting in his plan to drive the armour through, even though heavy casualties might be expected. This was the beginning of an increasingly bad relationship between Lumsden and Montgomery.

'My Job is Very Soft'

The next day I set out before dawn to visit the Australian sector in the north, with their right flank resting on the sea. They had been engaged in a night attack.

26 October
> 'Visited Aussies first light this morning, took Monty's Humber. Attack a success, and one bn. claims 80+ [Germans] killed. Passed a long line of prisoners, about 130 mostly *boche*, marching back along road in first light.'

This reference to taking Monty's Humber rather surprises me now. How extraordinarily trusting he must have been! When I got back it was still early morning,

> 'Sitting outside caravan just now over-looking sea, beautiful cool morning. Two 109s have just passed, chased by a 'Spit' skimming the water. 'Spit' firing like mad, and all whisked away across desert – makes one envious! Shortly after, a large flight of duck flew past.'

Three days later the battle is still undecided but I have time to collect my thoughts:

28 October
'My job is really very soft. I usually take Monty in the mornings to a division, come back for lunch, and then maybe out by myself in the afternoon to find out some particular piece of information about the front. It isn't dangerous as no real information can be gained right up in the fighting line, except from an Armoured Brigade. The most one suffers from is a few stray shells. It is quite amusing driving a great open Humber, with the AC alongside, being saluted by everyone, but one feels rather a stooge. And one cannot attend personally all the conferences. But still, in this static fighting it is interesting to see how an AC works. And one is pretty well in the picture the whole time. And it is restful, which I enjoy. Although I am just beginning to feel now that I need a little hard work and excitement, which is a good sign.'

The Unknown Soldier
This day I was to visit the South Africans under General Pieaar who were located on the south-eastern end of the Miteirya Ridge just south of the southern funnel. I wended my way along the maze of tracks which criss-crossed the battlefield, each cross-tracks being clearly marked with its code-name, 'Piccadilly', 'Knightsbridge', etc. The dust upon these tracks was suffocating; being of the consistency of talcum powder, the slightest movement would send clouds into the air. Dull thuds marked the artillery exchange and small mushroom clouds intermittently arose as enemy shells hit the dust. A yellowish fog hung over the battlefield.

At one of these cross-tracks, within a barbed-wire enclosure, lay a dead Highlander. Each day I passed he was still there. Why was he not removed? Was the body booby-trapped, I wondered, for him to be left so callously unburied. And then day by day more layers of dust accumulated and he was as if turned to stone. In my mind he became a monument to the unknown soldier of Alamein.

A Bad Omen
28 October (continued)
'Today I went and arranged Monty's visit to Dan Pienaar. "Come 'een and sit down," [said the South African commander].
['I did so. He was a very quiet mild-looking little man with a very unfrightening-looking face, and a quiet rather soothing voice which was fascinating to hear. I said my piece and he was very

pleased. Then he went on to talk about the battle and drew a map in the sand of his dugout. I could not follow a word of his plan, his voice having an hypnotic effect which trailed away and sent me off to sleep. "Not that I'm creeticising the Army Commander's plan," he murmured, as his finger moved across the sand putting a Corps here an infantry division there. I noticed one of his fingers was missing.'

Did he expect me, I wondered, to relay all this back to the Army Commander. Monty did expect his orders to be carried out and hated belly-aching. Pienaar was showing little belly for the fight and was 'excessively casualty conscious', which I thought a bad omen at the very beginning of this campaign.[2] My session was interrupted by the arrival of Pienaar's Corps Commander, Oliver Leese. Pienaar's last remark was that 'he never thought that we could destroy the German army by this attack'.

However, Monty soon arrived and emerged from Dan Pienaar's dugout apparently cock-a-hoop, for he declared, 'He's tremendously keen and says that he will kill all the Germans.' (!)

It was on this day that Monty changed the axis of attack, at a conference with his northern corps commander, Axis armour having been drawn up to the northern funnel. We would never get the armour out there. So the main thrust was moved to the coast along the road and rail axis in the Australian Sector.

Later that evening at Tac HQ I received my orders for the following day.

> 'Tonight the Aussies are making an attack to clear the northern coastal area and I shall be leaving here at 5.30 a.m. tomorrow morning to get the results of the battle. No good pretending one is in the battle really, but there is no doubt it is interesting meeting all the generals. Also, keeping the AC informed of the fighting one feels is fairly important.'

These somewhat diffident remarks do not take account of the historic nature of the campaign, only later to be realized. So often in war one sees only what is in front of one's nose. I added,

> 'The front line is about 7 miles from here, and there is a continual fog over the field of battle. This is caused by vehicles and guns moving, bombs falling, and vehicles burning. As you get up to the

coast road you can see it on your left and forward. In the early mornings it is a dull grey heavy mist, and in the middle of the day it is a layer of drifting sand and smoke.'

'You Might Tell Those Damned Tanks to do a Little Work!'

29 October

'I left at about 5.45 and put on my British Warm. It was very cold motoring along the coast road in my jeep. Got to division well before light and crawled down into their dugout. "I've come from the Army Commander," I began. "Any news about the battle?"

"Can we see your identity card?" they answered. The badge on my cap was already causing trouble, I supposed. The attack had been half successful. I sat and listened to the telephone conversations [reporting back from the bns]. A young lieutenant suddenly came in with a tommy-gun, having just come back from 15th Bn, which had gained their objective. He was saying that the Eyeties were terrified and came running out surrendering when they [the Aussies] appeared.

'It was getting light and I hopped into my jeep and went to 20 Bde. I followed a track through a lot of minefields where one vehicle had been blown up that night. One shell dropped about 30 yards away and we both ducked. There was quite a lot of spasmodic shelling – just enough to make you look round to see where the last one had gone. The ground was pock-marked with small craters which had been caused by our 25 pndr barrage the night before. Found the Brigadier [of 20 Aust. Bde] asleep, and the Bde Major lying on the dugout floor looking very tired. I said who I was and what I wanted. "Couldn't you get that at Div?" he drawled. "No, I couldn't," I replied. "Can you tell me the Bn dispositions and how many prisoners you've taken?"'

I gradually got the things I wanted.

'"Now if you've come from 'Army' (used as a term of contempt) you might tell those damn tanks to do a little work! Why can't they get out here?" he said, pointing to the place we'd been trying to get them to since the battle began. There seems to be a continual battle between the tanks and the infantry, each seem unable to understand eath other's point of view, – when really the whole thing boils down to the enemy minefields.'

Freyberg

Although increasingly concerned about the course of the battle, Monty found his relaxation in the company of his young aides who were members of his small mess. Contrary to the legend that his life-style was austere and humourless, he loved goading his young staff into indiscretions and embarrassing revelations, and the flapping or sagging tent was loud with the jollity of these occasions.

On one occasion General Horrocks came for lunch. As he was commanding 13 Corps in the south we had not seen much of him. He was an old friend of Monty's and on this occasion provoked the Army Commander into recounting his story about 'the officer who had too many women'! Monty claimed that he came to an agreement with this officer (his MG platoon commander in Alexandria before the war) that he should lay off for six months. But whilst out dining in Alexandria he receives a telephone call from his Adjutant to say that Nicholson (for that was his name) begs leave to break his vow. 'Is it absolutely necessary?' demands Monty. The answer was 'Yes'. Monty orders his Adjutant to tell Nicholson that 'he may have one woman, once, and back by 10'. These hilarious occasions were spiced with more penetrating character assessments of his subordinates. As was this one which my diary records, on Freyberg.

30 October

'At dinner AC spoke about Freyberg.

"Amazing fellow Freyberg," he said. "An absolutely first class divisional commander. You know what he said [to his division], "We will advance through the enemy minefield – and I will lead you", and he did, went through the minefields and Freyberg led. A little bit slow up here you know [tapping his head], but a first class leader.

"I asked him what his plan actually was," said Monty, "and he told me."

"Quite simple," he said. A regiment of Shermans leading. Myself with them, and the infantry following on the left, and on the right a squadron of tanks, the two brigadiers with them, and their brigades following them. All they do is to advance straight forward, of course a bit of a gamble you know. A bit of a gamble, and my chaps aren't properly trained. But I shall lead them!"

"And how shall I find your headquarters?" asked Monty.

"Red lamp on top of a huge pole by night, and a large flag by day."

Monty ruminated. "Oh, old Freyberg is worth a whole division in himself. A bit slow up here, but give him the ideas and he's first class".'

The Crumbling Process

But first the Aussies are to make another attack, to pinch out the enemy on the coast, against the strong points of Barrel Hill and Thompson's Post. This has been described as 'one of the most complicated small operations in the history of warfare'.

30/31 October

'The Aussies tonight are doing a night attack and joining their peak up to the coast, hoping to cut off a large number of enemy. If they are wise [the enemy] they will have beat it already. A concentrated and terrific barrage is now going on, and the flashes light up the sky. At 5.30 tomorrow morning I leave for the Aussie brigades to bring the picture back to Monty. It is now after ten, so I must go to bed. I think the attack will be successful, although I think they are a little tired.' I add later, 'The result was mostly successful, 540 prisoners and the thrust through to the coast, but not a permanent join.'

1 November

'It is quite chilly this evening. Tonight a full scale attack is being put in by the NZs, and followed up by the armour, which will surpass in intensity the attack on D 1 (at any rate the barrage will). I shall leave here at 8 p.m. with Monty to go up to the NZ div.'

Slowly but surely the enemy armour was being worn down, although we could only suspect it at the time. It was about now that some very good news came through, that an enemy petrol tanker, the *Louisano*, bound for Tobruk with vital fuel supplies for the panzer army, had been sunk. A few days now elapse in my diary, presumably caused by frantic activity.

What had happened was this. The enemy armour had now been drawn up to the coastal sector, reacting to the weight of our attack. Montgomery perceived a gap just north of the northern funnel at the German/Italian junction point. Freyberg's New Zealanders, assisted by the British 9th Armoured Brigade, would advance westwards and blow a gap, 6,000 yards deep and 4,000 yards wide, through the enemy defences. Through this gap would pass Lumsden's *Corps de Chasse*, consisting of three British armoured divisions and two armoured car regiments. They would pass out into the open desert and engage the enemy armour. This was named 'Operation Supercharge'. Montgomery made it clear that, should the New Zealanders fail to gain their objectives, the armoured divisions were to fight their way through. In the event 9th Armoured Brigade reached its objective on the Sidi Abd el Rahman track, the enemy's lateral supply line (upon which I had been targeted a few months before). They hit a tough anti-tank screen, sustaining 75 per cent casualties, but held their ground, thus holding open the door of the bridgehead. As Briggs' 1st Armoured Division came up, fierce tank to tank fighting broke out about Tel el Aqqaqir. 51st Highland Division then expanded the bridgehead to the south.

On the night of 4/5 November Freyberg halts at midnight at Sidi Ibeid. He is clear of the enemy defences and has broken through into open country beyond. At the same time Rommel orders a general retreat to the Fuka line.

'A Pantaloon Show'
The Army Commander is seriously disenchanted with the activities of the commander of the *Corps de Chasse*, General Herbert Lumsden, who will not keep in touch.

Monty and I set out in a jeep and staff car in pursuit of Lumsden to meet him at a pre-arranged rendezvous in the open desert. The RV is the usual six-figure map reference and I am navigating. By means of a prismatic compass and the vehicle's milometer I arrive at the spot, cheerfully announcing to Monty that this is where we are supposed to meet Lumsden. It is wide open desert with not a sign of life on any horizon. We have no escort just the two drivers and ourselves.

'Are you sure this is the spot?' demands Monty.

'Absolutely certain, Sir,' I reply, Monty still believing that I am a wizard at navigation.

'Very well then. But Herbert's not here!'

'Perhaps his navigator isn't very experienced,' I hazard.

'Very likely not!'

Monty paces up and down, stops from time to time and mutters, 'Pantaloon Show! Pantaloon Show!'

I returned a frustrated and furious Montgomery to his Main HQ. He is breathing fire and slaughter against Lumsden, and I am loosed off in my jeep to find Lumsden come what may. It was not till years later that I discovered that my brother Bill was in the party navigating Lumsden!

The desert is a big place. How am I to find Lumsden? I now turn to Bill Mather's version of this cat and mouse game as he told me quite recently.

> 'Lumsden was meticulous in dress. Tall, smart and elegant, even in battle. I had been put in his HQ by the Army Commander to keep an eye on him. Therefore I was a bit of a "gooseberry" and Lumsden knew this. After the breakout we set off in two jeeps, into the open desert. Lumsden, driven by Douglas Darling, was supposed to keep Monty informed and report regularly his situation. Whenever I put up the Wyndham Aerial to contact HQ, Lumsden would say, "Whips out!" and we would move on, egged on, I may say, by Darling who was a very dashing soldier. We never did report. Then suddenly out of the blue one of Monty's LOs turns up! It was you! You told him that he must report to the Army Commander at Main Army HQ forthwith. You went off, and we returned to 10 Corps HQ "to think things over". It was quite clear that he was going to get a real bollocking and possibly the sack.
>
> 'He finally reported to Monty at Main Army HQ and those near Monty's tent heard a tremendous row going on. Nearby in the command centre of the HQ complex some staff officers (former stockbrokers it was said) had set up a large board showing how the desert generals were running in the leadership stakes. When the row was heard next door, Lumsden's star plummeted and was marked down in a steep dive. Lumsden, who had never entered the complex before, suddenly appeared. An army blanket covered the board, on which was pinned a notice, MOST SECRET. He ripped off the blanket, and all was revealed – he hardly needed it rubbing in.'[3]

Very shortly afterwards Lumsden got the sack, and was never allowed in any of Monty's commands again. So he was posted to the Far East where, it is said, he was killed by a shell on the bridge of a battleship. So ended the career of a gallant but unfortunate soldier.

24

THE BREAKOUT

The armour is now streaming out through the gaps, but not as fast as Monty would like. He visits 10th Armoured Division to see Gatehouse and 'apply ginger'. My diary brings some dramatic news. The commander of the German Afrika Corps (DAK), deputising for Rommel in his absence on sick leave, is taken prisoner.

5th November
   'Yesterday General von Thoma was captured in his tank by "a 10th Hussar", and was immediately sent to Tac Army to see Monty. He commands the DAK. Geoffrey Keating was in charge of getting him washed and shaved and showing him his tent.[1] Von Thoma regarded the bivy and exclaimed, '*Ah Vikend*!' Monty was in great form during dinner and the general sat on his right hand. He was one of the better types of Germans, lean face and good-looking and very polite and not at all surly or arrogant and answered all questions as best he could. He did not speak English so we had an interpreter as a go-between.
   "Now tell the General," said Monty, "that I have enjoyed the battle very much."
   'The interpreter translated this, Monty all the while turned facing the German to watch his reaction. The latter gave a sort of sickly smile. "Now ask the General if Rommel is any better? I heard he had some kind of stomach trouble." "No," came the answer back. "He asked to have a holiday in Germany as he was very tired." After this revelation the German General was asked how he was captured. He had apparently gone forward to do a recce as reports had come through about tanks getting through his southern flank. He had first sent a message back to Rommel

[who had now returned], saying that 150 tanks were advancing towards him, and that he was going to evacuate the position. [In the confusion of the moment his position was overrun and he found himself a prisoner.]

'One of the more extraordinary things was that Mike Alexander who had been captured in the commando raid [see p. 107] a few months back, had been to dinner with Von Thoma the evening of his capture. I asked Von Thoma how Mike Alexander was and how he was captured.

'"The General says," answered the interpreter, "that he was looking very well and that he was driving about in a captured British vehicle. But then the General says – he has so many of them!"

'At this stage Monty got down on the table, with pencil and pepper pots, to the battles of Alamein 1 and 2. Great sweeps were made across the oilcloth with pencils.

'"The pivot of Egypt is Alamein," declared Von Thoma.

'"No it is here on this high ground here – the Miteirya Ridge", Monty contradicted him.

'"Tell the General that I met Rommel once in August and I beat him; and I have met him again now, and I shall do the same thing!"

'"It is your turn," Von Thoma replied. "You have the short lines of communication and we the long ones; the German people will not worry if we go back to El Agheila again. We have been there before!"'

These incongrous conversations took place exactly as I recorded them at the time in my diary, and now unearthed like so many pots and sherds, 53 years later, add further fragments to the jigsaw puzzle of this moment in history.

'"Now," said the Victor, warming to this moment and about to enjoy it, "tell the General that I have captured Fuka!" Monty was watching Von Thoma closely.

'"The Army Commander says that he has taken Fuka," said the interpreter leaning across to Von Thoma.

'"Fuka? Fuka!"

'"I have Fuka!"

'"Fuka – yetz?"

'"Yes – tell the General I have my troops in Fuka."

'Von Thoma was astonished. Monty was visibly enjoying himself.'

A message came in and Monty read it, and then, pointing to the tablecloth, south of his Daba mark, said,

'"I have a division here!"
'"*So!*" exclaims Von Thoma.
'"Yes, that's where it is."
'"*Das ist zer kritisch.*"
'"Yes, very critical" replied Monty.'

Somewhat shaken by this news Von Thoma went on to tell the Commander of British Eighth Army,

'"In the German army they have a character sketch of you."
"Oh do they? Do they now? How interesting. And what do they say?" asked Monty.
"They say that you are a very hard and ruthless man." ('*hart und rücksichtsloser Mann*')
"Oh," said Monty clearly pleased, "hard and ruthless? Not a bit of it!"
"They also say that when you are not fighting the battle, you live in Cairo!"
This got Monty on the raw.
"Oh, ho ho, ha ha. Only ever been to Alexandria, and that was once to have a bath! But my ADCs here have girlfriends and spend all their time there or on the beach."'

My diary picks up once more the threads of events.

6 November
'Since the 1st November when we had a kind of second offensive [Supercharge] I have been kept busy. First during the hard fighting following that night attack, when I used to make two journeys a day up to a Tac Brigade, along those "talcum-powder" tracks in the smothering sand. That lasted 4 days, and after the first day I gave up my jeep because of the shelling, and took to an armoured scout car. It was quite interesting but most unpleasant, and very tiring.
'Then came the great breakout, when the Germans could

withstand the pressure no longer, and their line crumbled, with the capture of many prisoners, and a lot of material. That was the night that Von Thoma came to dinner. The next day I was sent out along the coastal road in the late afternoon – to see how far I could get without meeting the enemy, and to find out where the main enemy concentrations were. There was very little information. It was nose to tail with vehicles all the way to Daba. Six miles outside Daba it began to get dark. The road was not empty, and no one knew what was happening in front – was it us or the enemy? So I turned back and had the most unpleasant drive in the dark, was bombed, and arrived back at 8.30 p.m.

7 November
'The next day Monty, John and I set out in the open Humber with my jeep following, with armoured car protection up the road. We got as far as Fuka in the pouring rain, and here I was set loose to find out again how far forward we had got up the road. And where the NZs were, and enemy etc. It was pelting with rain [and seriously holding up our advance], and the road was flooded in parts. I passed the Notts Yeomanry and they had no information further forward. So I pushed on slowly, and when I got to Sidi Baguish I halted. There were some quite fresh fires, and a rather unpleasant smell about the place. Then on the left coming slowly down the escarpment I saw some tanks. They turned out to be the NZ's 9th Armoured Brigade and had just reached the road to cut it – a bit late! I was glad I did not push on any farther, having stopped at Sidi Haneish [the very place on which we had launched the aerodrome mass attack]. I drove back fast to Daba and then to Army HQ to give the news.

'The next day, John, Monty and I again – and along the Daba road, past an immense quantity of abandoned and destroyed enemy transport, guns and tanks. We went up as far as 3 miles outside Matruh, and then we halted. The advance was being held up by some guns still firmly lodged inside the strong defences.'

Next morning I was sent back to Mersa Matruh to report on the situation.

8 November

'Left at 5.30 a.m. for fighting outside Matruh. Saw Alec Gatehouse [Commander of 10th Armoured Division], who gave me a large breakfast. Heard over the Rear Link reports coming in from the fighting line.

'"First tank of right-hand regiment through the wire, Sir!"

'"Left-hand regiment (3 RTR) reports itself on main road west out of Matruh, and now probing defences!"

'"Three tanks of right-hand regiment over A/T ditch, Sir, and no opposition."

'"3 RTR past aerodrome and inside defences, and see no enemy, Sir!"

'And so Mersa fell. I went back to 'Army', only half an hour away and reported the news. Had a second breakfast and a shave, and then back again and into Mersa this time, to report on harbour, aerodrome and roads. Not much changed in Mersa but most of the stuff destroyed.'[2]

These were exciting days. Enemy-held towns were falling like ninepins, the Germans and Eyeties leaving everything in their flight.

'After lunch John [Poston] and I located a food dump. Came back the richer for 2 cases Chianti, 2 cases red wine, 1 barrel Chianti, 1 case Suchard's chocolate, 1 case sardines, tomatoes, potatoes and M and V – not bad for one haul!'

My diary entry for 10 November reports my going over to the RAF Mess to have a drink with Maori Coningham's PA, John Lancaster. I got so tight on Chianti that I did not dare return to Monty's Mess for dinner. There was a squadron leader who had the Shark Squadron, with a DFC and bar and looked terribly young – only 23?

When I got back to our camp I was handed a note by John Poston. Everyone had apparently been searching all over the camp for me.

The message read,

'Monty wants you to leave camp at 6.00 a.m., and go and visit the NZ's and see Freyberg. Then go to 10 Corps [Lumsden's] and find out their complete situation, also find out the state and situation of 7th Armoured Division, 4th South African Armoured Cars, the 11th Hussars and 9th Armoured Brigade. Also any other news you can find out. You must be back as soon as you can.'

At the time this hardly registered, but nevertheless I was up at 6.00 a.m. and pounding up the coast road.³

10 November
'Traffic on the one road was quite awful. After a few searchings I found the NZs and Freyberg, two and a half hours later. I was told to jump up on his Honey [tank] and my jeep to follow, as we bowled down the road – until we met any resistance. Freyberg believed in leading his troops, so all his soldiers were behind him! In front was 4th Light Armoured Brigade. His Div HQ consisted of two tanks.'

I was enjoying bumping down the road perched on this vantage point, only myself and the ADC clinging on to the turret of Freyberg's tank. And Freyberg chatting away about the progress of battle, which I was drinking in to relay to my lord and master.

It was exhilarating riding shotgun to the leader of the British advance. One town after another was falling. This was worth all the travail of the past months.

'Presently we came to 'Barrani and passed the ruins, exactly as they had been left after Wavell's advance. In the early morning sun they looked mellow and the piles of rubble had grown into mounds. "Sidi Barrani, Sidi Barrani," I thought. How much we have heard that name in the last two years. There will be headlines at home saying "Barrani captured!" And it was done with no more than the breath of a tank's exhaust!'

We rumbled on quite happily for another 10 miles.

'Freyberg sitting in the turret, and "Jack" the ADC and myself clinging on to the side. We passed an aerodrome with a lot of planes parked on it, and we all had a look through our glasses but nothing stirred. I kept looking behind to see if my jeep was following OK. Presently the troops in front [4th Light armoured Brigade] stopped. They had come across a strongpoint which required removing. F said that he hoped to be through Buq Buq by the afternoon and Sollum the next morning [across the old frontier wire]. I had all I wanted. It was midday so I set off back again – 110 miles. Traffic again awful. Arrived back at 5.00 p.m.'

25

A FATEFUL DECISION

The next day David Stirling arrives at Monty's HQ and he tells me about his future plans. He is mounting a major expedition into Tripolitania to cut the enemy's supply lines at several different points. It will involve a journey of some 2,000 miles.

11 November
   'Saw David last night. All rather disturbing. Don't feel quite ready for another long desert journey, and was very much looking forward to Syria [my promised leave] and ski-ing.[1] However, my conscience said, "You cannot miss this one, of them all". David at first said, "Impossible, I'm giving you a long rest. Quite out of the question." However, I didn't allow him to go on for long, and he agreed. It's a pity it's going to happen so soon, as I was enjoying my present job very much, and it is a complete change. Wonder if I'll be able to fix Monty? Left with the AC at 7.00 a.m. this morning. Humber, jeep and armoured cars. We soon left the A/C's behind. Roads much clearer and we bowled along at great speed – how I hate these bloody jeeps! My mind kept on revolving upon the Expedition. Of course I could say that Monty refused to let me go, and stay where I was. A pity to leave such an interesting job so soon. But what a journey to have done, the reason for one's existence in the Middle East. Pity it is taking place so soon – no time to get kit together.'

I spent several days agonizing upon this decision. Was I right to do it or not? But the die was cast. I had made the proposal to David, and he had accepted it. Monty made no difficulties, as it turned out. He was very good about that kind of thing. However, that moment had not yet arrived, I was still Personal Liaison Officer to the Army Commander.

11 November (continued)
'We eventually arrived at Halfaya Pass and Sollum, and met Lumsden and Freyberg. Monty was being congratulated as he has just become a full General and a 'Sir'. He addressed his commanders thus:
"Now from what I have been told by my reliable sources, the *boche* is almost finished. He's got lots of bits of units, but nothing that can fight as a unit. He is really finished." Douglas Darling, Lumsden's GSO1, meantime reported that the important Water Point at Buq Buq was okay. The AC now turned to Lumsden. They were both being excessively polite.

'"Now Herbert, for the next three days we must have a halt. I want you to get your armoured cars right up, and everything else back here for maintenance."

'Lumsden indicated that he had got the 11th Hussars, and tomorrow the KDGs right up front. Turning to Freyberg the AC said, "Now my dear fellow – tell your chaps that I'm, extremely pleased with them – they've done a first class show during the past few days."

Freyberg modestly demurred and claimed the credit for the 4th Light Armoured Brigade. Monty was in an expansive mood and turning to his ADC said, "John, give General Freyberg some chocolate."

'Lumsden obsequiously observed how pleased he was at Monty's promotion. But he did not get offered any chocolate!'[2]

An arrangement was made to meet Lumsden the following afternoon on Sollum Hill. Sollum itself was on the sea, and at the foot of the hill up which winds the narrow Halfaya Pass ('Hellfire pass' in common parlance). Sollum Hill is in a commanding position looking over the terrain we had traversed and that yet to come.

11 November (continued)
'Back to Tac Army. a 2-hour drive, very dusty. Very charming camp site. I had a swim – very cold.'

At dinner that night Bill had come to visit. There was just him, Monty, Freddie de Guingand, John Poston and myself. The discussion turned on War. Particularly the recent calamities in the Middle East.

'"There's one man to blame and one man only," declared Montgomery. "Auchinleck – he was responsible for the whole thing! Good soldier in India – fighting against savages – one brigade going up one valley – one up another and meeting at the top. Good polo player, but no good for war – proper war!"'

Warming to his subject he went on,

'"You see he wouldn't get good chaps out from England – was offered anyone he wanted but wouldn't have them. He wanted small chaps under him, not big ones. Look at his Chief of Staff! Ivory from the neck upwards – and downwards – complete ivory!"'[3]

Monty then had a crack at the desert warriors, the so-called Desert Rats, in his view stubborn-minded romantics fighting yesterday's war, although the table consisted almost entirely of that specimen. Perhaps he was a little jealous!

'"These people who surround themselves with chaps who are supposed 'to *know*' the desert – desert experts, don't know how to make war! War is the same anywhere – whatever the country. If you know how to make war you can do it anywhere – anywhere, and make adaptions for the climate and terrain – have your advisers – but *you* must *know* how to make war *yourself*."'
'"Well Sir," interjected de Guingand, "you have John and he's an original desert rat!" [Poston was with the 11th Hussars from the start.]
'"Ah," replied Monty, "he is *not* my military adviser – definitely not! No, all those chaps, all those desert rats will have to be thinking of something else soon. Have to forget all about the desert; the desert will be out of date soon. All the fighting will be in *Europe – Europe!*"'

12 November
'Left at first light for the 7th Armoured Division at Sidi Azeiz north-west of Capuzzo. Saw John Harding[4] [its commander] who gave me lunch, and got his complete story off him. He reckoned he had seen the remnants of the 21st and 15th Panzers in two columns, one of 29 and the other of 18 tanks. He was very keen for his division to be sent to El Ageilha to try and cut off the enemy. The drive [back] was long and tiring.

13 November

'Left at 8.30 with Monty, driving him in the Humber, and my jeep following, for 10 Corps to see Herbert Lumsden. Beautiful morning. Got there just as everyone was moving and just caught Lumsden in an armoured car before he left.

'"Ah Herbert," said Monty with a touch of menace in his voice, "now tell me your complete situation."'

Lumsden was able to tell him that early that morning they had taken Tobruk with no resistance [Tobruk was the German's front line port] and that 4th Light Armoured was round behind, with 7th Armoured Division on the high ground at El Adem, and the New Zealanders 'here' pointing to the map. Monty was delighted and no doubt relieved to be able to give Lumsden a word of praise.

'"Ah that's excellent, excellent. So we've got Tobruk! Good. We must get that information right back as soon as possible. Excellent propaganda for the people at home – buck 'em all up tremendously."'

Then he gave Lumsden his new orders:

'"Now what I want you to do is this. We must have the aerodrome at Martuba by the evening of the 15th to give the Malta Convoy air protection until dark, and then they can get as far as this and be met by the Malta chaps [air cover]. If we don't do it then Malta will fall – vital food and ammunition! So I want you to get that aerodrome, and be prepared to hold it for 24 hours. The airforce are flying in supplies so all we have to worry about is the protection of it."

'"I shall get a 12th Lancer Group up there," replied Lumsden. "They know the country, were there last April."

"Good, then we simply sit on the Gazala line for a day or two and reorganize. Get our maintenance done and supplies up. I don't want to go charging on. Supply position very acute as it is – very acute."

Turning to me he said, "Carol, just get out your glasses and see if Sollum Hill is open yet?"

'I could see the traffic slowly winding up the road. We went home.'

17 November

'Been driving Monty about during the last few days to visit various people and places. "Army" has also moved to Gambut, a horrid place full of dust and dirtiness. Actually it has been raining continually since we got here [Gambut]. Yesterday I took Monty into Tobruk. He was very interested. We were taken immediately to the Albergo Tobruk [the Tobruk Inn] by the temporary garrison commander. As we entered the doors I looked back to June, 1941, when George and I had lived in the shattered wreck for a month under seige, planning our attack on the Gazala aerodromes and waiting a favourable opportunity. Little did I think then that I should be entering the Albergo with the Army Commander 18 months later!

'Yesterday the bells of Tobruk church rang all day, as they were doing for the first time in England.'

My diary records 'an appalling downpour of rain' that night. It ran through the mess like a river. The continual rain was a great hindrance to our advance and thwarted our attempts to cut off the enemy.

'That night a desultory conversation took place in the Mess between the AOC (Coningham), the AOA (Tommy Elmhirst) and the AC (Monty) about the American landings in North Africa and the German situation.

AOA: "My bet with General Strickland is that we will be in Tunis and Bizerta in eight days from now. And my bet is a pukka champagne dinner in the first civilized hotel!"

AOC: "Eight days – nonsense! With the Americans completely untrained. Now either the Germans have realized that this is a continental threat, the equivalent of a continental landing, or they have not. If they have you can be sure that they will shove everything into it – absolutely everything."

AC: "Either the Germans will decide to cut their losses, or they will put up a damn good show here."

AOA: "Well I don't think we can have been such fools this time, after all our experience, not properly to have assessed what the Germans can put in the field against us. If we haven't done that, then we don't deserve to win."

"But we *don't* deserve to win the war!" concluded Monty.'

18 November
'Walked to the sea this morning on my own, a two-hour walk. Sat down there for half an hour to try and sort out my ideas. There is no battle going on now, as there has been for the past week, just follow-up operations. Therefore apart from driving Monty from place to place I have no intelligence to gain. Today was my first day in for a week, and this afternoon I persuaded John Lancaster to take me up in a Lizzie [Lysander]. We went to Gazala, half an hour's flight, and back in a Lodestar. What fun to get up in the air again, and watch in a kind of detached way all the pettiness on earth. We flew over the defences of Tobruk.'

19 November
'Last night a telegram came from Winston for Monty, congratulating him on his successes, but urging him on to try and cut off the remnants of the German forces.

'Monty sent back this morning a message saying that many people had urged him to various and different things, and if he had taken their advice he would not be in his present position, and that it was only by doing what he believed was right that he had arrived where he was! Therefore he was not going to endanger his position by extending his army. But instead was going to form, and work from, a firm base, and advance methodically forward. This position could only be appreciated by the man on the spot – himself!'

This exchange with Churchill foreshadowed others to come, but Churchill, who would try bullying tactics, respected those who stood up to him and was sometimes disarmingly contrite.

My Alamein ended with this entry. The next day, 10 November, 1942, I made my way back to Cairo en route for Tripolitania.

PART VII
CAPTURE AND ESCAPE

26

JOURNEY'S END

'YOU MUST LIVE OFF YOUR FINGERNAILS'

Eighth Army HQ was camped on the edge of the Jebel country near Derna, and when I left Eighth Army had just captured Benghazi. I flew back to Cairo and made straight for David's flat. Time for a quick bath and then onto Shepheard's Hotel where we were to meet for dinner before departure. No time to get any kit together. All I had was what I stood up in plus a bedding roll.

David's plans were always unpredictable, but usually involved some huge and impossible adventure. This time it was to strafe soft-skinned vehicles behind the lines over a 500-mile stretch of road between El Agheila (our new front line), and the town of Tripoli, the enemy base. For each fifteen miles of road there would be a patrol of three jeeps lying in wait. To strafe the road, we would operate only by night, thus forcing the traffic onto the road by day when the RAF would be responsible. At any rate that was the plan. For the purpose of this exercise we disposed of two SAS squadrons – one 'the originals' – the other a body of newly-trained men which I was to join. Those at the Tripoli end (which included myself) might have to survive for a month before relief by the advance of Eighth Army. It was a one-way journey – there was only enough petrol for the outward trip!

But for our immediate plans David and I were to meet the main body at the familiar Ain El Gazala, just west of Tobruk.

The new 'squadron' consisted of some forty jeeps and fifteen 3-tonners. For this expedition the average load per jeep was made up of:

70 gallons of petrol in containers;
2 gallons of oil;
4 Vickers (K) guns;

2000 rounds of ammunition;
100 lbs. of explosive;
a case of 10 mines;
10 gallons of water and food for a week!

With this top-heavy burden we were to start our journey.

Meantime, having finished our meal, we left Shepheard's Hotel at 9 p.m. and raced for the desert. Our two lightly-laden vehicles, one jeep and David's Blitz buggy would speed us on our way. One backward glance at the familiar outline of Shepheard's Hotel, with its broad verandah on which were seated assorted members of the Short-Range Shepheard's Group (as GHQ staff officers were laughingly known) sipping their John Collins's and no doubt muttering 'there but for the grace of God go I'. And in long white galabias, red belt and red tarboosh, the sufragis were dancing attendance. On the pavement at the foot of the steps stood the Turkish-pantalooned grand dragoman who seemed to control all the taxi and gharry drivers in Cairo. Half shading the terrace was the gnarled tree under which one of Napoleon's generals had concluded an important victory. When would I see all this again? We were going farther and farther away from home – 1000, 2000, even 3000 miles it might prove to be.

David and I slept that night in the desert near Half Way House, a spot midway between Cairo and Alexandria. In two days we were at Gazala. We found the new squadron scattered in the scrub below the escarpment.

Most of the faces were new to me, except Gordon Alston with whom I was to share a jeep for the first leg of the journey. Just before we left, a travel-stained jeep came rattling down the escarpment. In it were three bearded and muffled figures. They had been operating from Kufra, 800 miles to the south, all that was left of a patrol which had occupied Martuba aerodrome. The others had run into minefields.[1]

Passing Army HQ, I called in and showed Monty our operation in his caravan. By this time relations between the two men were restored. On their previous meeting, before the battle, a row had broken out between Montgomery and Stirling. Stirling had become a law unto himself and Monty would not accept this, even though the SAS were under GHQ orders and not his. He considered that Stirling was a spoilt boy, 'Baby boy' he used to call him. Others might put up with his gasconading, but Monty would not. Stirling had gone to demand more volunteers from Eighth Army. Monty cut him short with a 'in what way do you think you can use my trained soldiers better than I can?'

And he was sent away with a flea in his ear. He then had to scour the base areas for recruits, of which I was to feel the results shortly thereafter. It was about the time of my visit that Monty's changed opinion of Stirling manifested itself with the following remark. 'The boy Stirling is mad. Quite, quite mad. However, in war there is often a place for mad people!'

I said goodbye to my friends at Tac HQ. I had been very happy there, and as a parting present John Poston loaded on some of the loot we had collected together at the German dump.

David and I drove along the coast road. Past Benghazi and Agedabia, (fateful names!) and south of El Ageilha, where Rommel had made his stand, we took to the desert and rendezvous'd with the old squadron 200 miles south of the coast, in the neighbourhood of Bir Zalten. Three days were spent reorganizing and planning the operation, it was good cover and there were no enemy aircraft to spy upon us. From here the squadrons separated, Paddy remaining in command of the old one ('A' Squadron), and David the new ('B' Squadron). The new squadron set off on its longer journey towards Tripoli, always remaining 100–200 miles south of the coast, for we were now in enemy territory. It was bitterly cold travelling, especially during the long nights. I wore an outsize troop's greatcoat, with a Hebron fleece coat fitted inside, and under that a leather jerkin.

We continued driving for ten days, night and day, sleeping from dawn till about 10 a.m., halting an hour for lunch and an hour for dinner. At first we used headlights, but nearer the objective we drove in the dark. The going was as bad as we had ever experienced, wadis with cliff-like sides interspersed by soft sand. These wadis, curling northways towards the sea, were shallower at their heads; even so we had to build tracks to get the vehicles up and down.

The puncture situation soon became acute for the inner tube would only bear a limited number of repairs. However, after about seven days we had passed the worst. We had completed the first vehicle crossing in that part of the desert.

South of Misurata, a coastal town, we had to cross a main north-south road, where there was a bottleneck of Italian posts. We sighted the road about 2 o'clock in the afternoon and drew up behind a low ridge. Everyone looked through their glasses. We could see an Italian post on a hill, but it look deserted. While David led our remaining thirty jeeps towards the road I concentrated on locating a rattling biscuit-tin somewhere on my jeep. Others seemed to be behaving in the same way, until we realized that we were under fire. Our intention was to avoid a fight, so we increased speed a little and altered direction. Each vehicle was like a mobile time-bomb for we were packed with gelignite, gun cotton and detonators. Now we became the target for quite a lot of mortar fire and some armoured cars appeared quite close, so we reluctantly engaged them with our 0.5 gauge machine guns and had quite a little shooting match, losing three of our jeeps in the process.

My party was to consist of three jeeps each manned by two men. They were mostly inexperienced in desert ways, as a result of Monty's dictat; some had been AA gunners in Syria – good chaps but clueless about the desert. My driver was only 20 and too young. My Sergeant came from Glasgow and had no control over the men. Another man from the RASC claimed to be a former gamekeeper, which I thought promising but I was to be disappointed. I had one old hand, Walster, from a yeomanry regiment, a first class man, but one who could not conceal his contempt for the others, including the Sergeant! I managed to change the latter for a regular sapper whose knowledge of explosives would mean that we could operate in two parties.

Our final RV was in a deep and scrubby wadi near El Fascia with plenty of acacias growing which gave us good protection. It was raining heavily. Here we did our final planning. Scattered about the wadi were some of the officers recently enrolled, but all experienced desert hands: Vivian Street, who had now taken over 'B' Squadron, and Pat Hore-Ruthven, both of the Rifle Brigade, Brian Franks of the Middlesex Yeomanry, Wilfrid Thesiger, our Arabist, and of course David Stirling himself.[2]

The strip of road I was responsible for was 60 miles east of Tripoli and 15 miles in length. It took in the town of Homs with its port and aerodrome. Its eastern boundary included the ancient Roman city of Leptis Magna, the ruins of one of the oldest and most flourishing of the Phoenician *emporia* on the coast of North Africa. From the air photographs it looked good cover, but there were scattered settlements and the depth of the wadis was hard to judge.

'Right,' said David in a breezy way, 'You'd better be off now!'

'David,' I said, 'we must stay "on target" for at least a month and we've got food only for ten days. What do we do then?'

'Oh,' replied David rather vaguely, 'you'll just have to live off your fingernails. Forage around and see what you can pick up in the Italian settlements. They're bound to have hams and that kind of thing!'[3]

The idea of raiding a farmhouse and snatching a ham while the family was at dinner was occupying my mind as we drove off.

Happy-go-lucky as we were, it gradually began to dawn on me that this indeed was a one-way ticket with no return! Another immediate problem was water. We had used up our limited supply on the march and we would have to find both food and water. We had not fully taken into account the fact that the local arabs were not the friendly Senussi of the Libyan desert, but untried Tripolitanian villagers. We assumed that their hatred of the Italians would make them co-operative. The inadequate Italian maps told us little of the terrain; colonial settlements and Arab villages were frequently missing.

Andy Hough, a captain in the Rifle Brigade, was my immediate next door neighbour. His sector began at the ruins of Leptis Magna. To begin with our party of six jeeps travelled in one body. Our milometers were showing just under 3000 miles since we had left the Delta, and we had been travelling for just under a month. It was becoming increasingly close country with a lot of Arab encampments. The first night we collected quite a lot of rainwater out of puddles, several gallons, enough to last us a good week. To the north we could hear the traffic on the road near Misurata. The first night we slept in the rain in a ploughed field, an unwelcome sign of civilization. Andy had lost all his kit in our encounter with the armoured cars, so I lent him my outsize greatcoat.

Two days later Andy and I parted, he to his own area of operations and I to mine. By this time my party had crossed over a range of hills dissected by streams. We could average only two miles a day; one vehicle turned a somersault but we managed to recover it. By now it was dark. We could not find the right track so we slept where we were. We reckoned we were fifteen miles away from the main road at Homs.

The next morning we crept cautiously on. We could see Italian farms, Arab houses and olive trees, the first settlements since we had left the Delta. Suddenly my Sergeant said, looking through his glasses,

'Down there Sir, look! Can you see them?'

'What is it?' I asked in some alarm.

'Hens,' he replied. 'About a dozen of them!'

27

CAPTURE

The chickens were now coming home to roost. But at least here was our chance for some eggs! We drove into a nearby olive grove. We did not know what attitude those Arabs would adopt for we had left the Senussi area far behind. We bought a dozen eggs. The Arabs squatted around us watching, and accepting our cigarettes.

'*Tedeschi*'? [German] they enquired. We nodded.

'*Englese*'? (English) they questioned again; we nodded again.

This was risky but we had heard so much about the Italian ill-treatment of these people that we thought it might gain their sympathy.

'*Italiani*'! one thrust the stump of an arm towards us.

'*Italiani*'! he said again, pointing to his amputated limb. They were eyeing us curiously; their attitude seemed friendly but reserved.

We moved on very slowly, encouraged even to ask at houses how far the village of Cussabat lay, for there was a main road running through the village which we must avoid in daylight hours. From this village the main coastal road was only six miles away. After a few miles, following a dusty track, we halted in a thick olive grove. I told the others to sort out the ammunition and food into three loads, one for this week to be carried, and two further weeks' supply to be hidden and buried.

I took Walster and we walked a mile, climbed a knob and lay flat on top among the rocks. Cussabat lay less than a mile away, part hidden by a fort. It looked like a big Arab village. Walster whispered, 'Look'! and below us only 200 yards away rumbled three Italian 10-tonners on a road we had not seen. We watched the traffic pass for an hour. We could see a big camp a mile away with soldiers moving about. Then we returned to our jeeps in the olive grove. An Arab came up and he asked us who we were, so we sat down and told him 'Tedeschi'. We gave him a cigarette and he held it between the two stumps where his hands had been. He told us, whilst glowering suspiciously, that the Italians had cut off his hands ten years ago. He stayed for an hour and then he left. It was proving quite impossible to move around this country unseen, an experience that was quite new to us and which confounded the very essence of our operations – hit and run. This was going to be very difficult, for once we had plunged into this country we could not get out.

The evening light faded slowly and we had no more visitors. We were able to eat our evening meal in peace. After this we dismantled one jeep, for jeeps were no use without petrol, and as best we could, hid and buried the parts. As the moon rose we started up the remaining two jeeps and pulled out onto the track. We had decided to drive through the village, 'When in enemy country do as the enemy do' was a good motto, for a detour across country would take us across plough and impassable wadis, and arouse suspicion.

Once on the track we switched off our engines and listened. Ahead of us was likely to be a garrisoned fort and a road block. It was quite eerie. Had the Arabs informed the Italians of our presence? Of the three strange vehicles hidden in an olive grove? Several Arabs passed us coming from the village, '*Salaam Alekum*' was the usual greeting. '*Alekum Salaam*' the reply. A man on a donkey overtook us heading towards the village, and when a cloud obscured the moon we overtook him. We did not want his news to reach the village before our arrival.

> 'Driving very slowly we reached the fort, towering above us. By now we were on a tarmac road. Nothing stirred in the fort. We went faster and before we knew it had passed three tank transporters fully laden. Their crews were standing by on the side of the road.'

This was the moment for split second decisions for we were still on our approach march and could not risk an affray. We drove on.

> 'Then we found ourselves in the village, with an avenue of trees and shops, with a mosque on the right. Immediately we were into a square with a fountain and a road block with a large red light barring our path. I just caught sight of a road on the left. We swung our wheels over to the left, passing within a few yards of the soldiers and *carabinieri* guarding the block, who let out piercing cries. They failed to shoot, so we sped on for a mile into

the countryside, slipped into an olive grove and switched off our engines. No sooner had we stopped than two cars roared by. But we had given them the slip.'

So far so good! But the following day we could expect a hue and cry. It was no good thinking we could melt into the desert. There was none. Any movement was tortuous and slow. In any case we had to reach our objective, for even one night's operation would partially justify the trip.

Later that night we found a good deep wadi with palm trees and good cover. For eight hours we worked by the light of the moon hiding the explosives in caves which were plentiful in those limestone escarpments. We hid the jeeps as best as we could, for they were of no more use to us; henceforth we would be on our feet. We found a cave for ourselves a little way away from the scene of our labours and at 4.00 a.m. lay down to sleep.

> 'Leaving the others sleeping I stole out at 5.00 a.m. I had to walk five miles and then I only "heard" the traffic on the main coast road. I could not see it. I lost the way and talked to several Arabs but reached the cave at 9.00 a.m.'

When I returned I found a sentry correctly posted on a knoll above the cave, but down below they all seemed drugged with sleep. It was not long before we had a curious crowd at the mouth of our cave chattering away to themselves. It was market day and this proved to be a main Arab thoroughfare with camels and donkeys laden with all the produce for the *souk*. The situation was laughable, so we began to cook some breakfast. As I was about to eat my first mouthful of scrambled egg, quite suddenly our visitors disappeared.

> 'There was a cry from the lookout above! He came clattering down the hill shouting "There's an Eyetie patrol coming down the wadi!" Silly fool! He'd been told to shoot first, to hold them up, so that we might have time to evacuate. As we had discovered, the cave was not in a very strategic position. The Italians had spotted our sentry's movement and were now approaching fairly fast. Grabbing our weapons and anything else we could lay our hands on we scrambled up the wadi side, luckily under cover, and lay behind a low earth wall on the ridge at the top.'

As they came down the wadi we could see about twenty of them armed with rifles and machine guns. Still unaware of our presence, now above them on the opposite side of the wadi, they entered the cave cautiously. When they saw our campfire with the unconsumed breakfast, the blankets, explosive and ammunition they crowded round in an excited group. This was our chance. From our elevated position we fired down into the midst of the group, hoping we might hit some explosive which would bring the roof down. There was a scene of confusion, some fled, others, evidently wounded, lay on the floor of the cave. A few took up their weapons and fired wildly in every direction. Our second fusillade brought down some fire upon us, and we again evacuated our position.

Where were we? What were we going to do? There was no time to decide; our pursuers were after us. We were armed only with rifles and what ammunition we had about us. We were, ironically enough, moving westwards away from home and in the direction of Tripoli. Always moving, we managed to keep our pursuers at bay through most of that day by dint of superior marksmanship, but it was now only a question of time; the game would soon be up. We tried to break contact with them, but, being tired, we could not shake them off. And we had to move carefully, for some of their wild shots came uncomfortably near.

It seemed they had Arab trackers with them, and as our bedraggled group (we had been reduced to five as the gamekeeper had disappeared!) passed by villages all the children screamed and the men jumped onto the roof of their houses and pointed out the fugitives.

'By 4.00 p.m. a lot more Arabs seemed to have joined in the chase. Still two hours till darkness and a possible escape. Soon we became aware that we were surrounded. We had fired off our remaining ammunition and could no longer move in any direction. We waited, recognizing our fate was sealed, first up an olive tree, and then, when they ranged their machine gun, in a shallow ditch. They closed in and when the grenades started landing we got out and put up our hands. They all came rushing across, very excited, jabbering away in a mixture of Italian and Arabic. A moment of confusion followed as the leading corporal lined us up against a wall and prepared to shoot. A fierce argument followed in which we enthusiastically joined, demonstrating what might happen to them when the Allies arrived.'

The anger had arisen, one could only believe, because our shots had found their mark in the cave. But as subsequent experience showed we were extremely lucky to get away with our lives. It was all over in a couple of minutes. We were now prisoners of war.

28

THE ITALIAN SUBMARINE

We were taken prisoner on 20 December, only two days after arriving in our area of operations.

> 'After these last weeks of strain, a strange kind of relaxation came over me. I was feeling much too tired to think of escaping, and they guarded us like lynxes. I managed to save my book, Thackeray's *Henry Esmond*, my pipe and tobacco which was a great solace. We were taken away in a big truck. We were treated well that night; interrogated by some decent Eyties who asked nervously if more of our friends were coming and were given a good dinner.'

Next morning we were moved to a camp and put in a cell. Someone had been ill in it and it was filthy. The walls were covered in inscriptions by previous inmates complaining bitterly of the bread and water régime. Sample menus were written on the wall 'Monday – bread and water. Tuesday – hot water tasting of rice'. One unfortunate had spent fifty days on such a menu. That night we had our trousers removed, presumably to stop us escaping. It was bitterly cold.

This camp, Tarhuna, happened to be in the area of operations of my nextdoor neighbour to the west. He had been briefed about the existence of a PoW camp at Tarhuna, but had been expressly told that on no account should he attempt to release the prisoners as that might endanger the success of the operation.

The next day, when I was still turning over in my mind the prospects of his ignoring this injuction and mounting an operation to release us, I was taken into the next cell where my hopes were dashed, for there he lay, picked up as we had been the day before. In the same room was an RAF pilot who was a bit of a chatterbox.

'No need to ask who you fellows are. I met your crowd down at Kufra. As a matter of fact I took Paddy Mayne back to Cairo in my old crate. How's old so and so?'

He started talking about escaping. No, he could not join us because he had a bad leg, evidence of which was a tear in his battledress trousers. He seemed to be well up on the latest news, and said blandly, 'Have you a map? I'll show you'. Unwisely I produced my silk handkerchief map of the North African coast.

'We RAF types all carry these. Lost mine when I got pranged at Homs! Funny,' he drawled on, 'I was taken to have dinner with old General ——. [He mentioned a high-ranking Italian general] He's the chap I've been trying to get for the last year. Never thought I'd be having dinner with him!'

Later that evening an Italian guard came in and led him away.

'Ta ta for now,' he said cheerily as he left the cell.

The next day I was searched and all my clothes, into which silk maps and button compasses had been concealed, were removed even down to my boots and socks. I was thrown an Italian private soldier's uniform to wear, short grey jacket and pantaloons, but no puttees. For my feet I was given an iron-hard pair of Italian issue boots, and the Italian army version of socks which was a canvas square which one wrapped round one's naked foot.

The message was quite clear: our fellow prisoner had been an impostor, a stool-pigeon planted by Italian intelligence to spy on us.[1] Later that night some genuine RAF pilots were brought in, including an old school friend of mine. After a day or two we were moved to Tripoli into a large camp with a few officers and a lot of Tobruk South Africans, all in a very weak state. Each day we had soup and a roll of bread for sustenance. From here we were taken to Tripoli town, from whose port, much to our surprise, we were embarked upon an Italian submarine. It gradually dawned upon us that the Axis were in a far worse state than we had imagined. Surface ships no longer dared cross the Mediterranean because of allied bombing. Essential supplies and interesting prisoners all went by submarine.

Just before we departed, much to my dismay, Andy Hough was brought on board, captured in much the same way. This spelt the collapse of the Tripoli end of our operation.

Fifteen officers were put in the submarine hold, the torpedo storage compartment. It was 4 feet by 4 feet, about 20 feet in length. We could neither stand up nor stretch out. As soon as we left the harbour we quickly submerged, or so it seemed to us. Later this was followed by a commotion on board and the sound of dull thuds. Evidently the British were depth-charging. It was an eerie experience; we could not tell how near they were.

For four days we crept along the bottom of the sea bed. The food was minimal and the officers none too friendly. On Christmas Day, 1942, they threw us a few scraps from the wardroom table. But on the fifth day we were brought up one by one into the conning tower to get a breath of fresh air. We had surfaced and could see the coast of Sicily.

Having hours simply to contemplate the wall opposite one's thoughts inevitably ran back over the past weeks, months and even years. I was now in a netherworld, neither a combatant officer nor a fully accredited PoW, bound goodness knows where, with no possessions, not even one's own clothes, clad in the enemy's uniform, with hair shorn and barely enough to eat. But there was one last saving grace – it was still in the nature of an adventure! One did not know where it would lead. A story to tell in years to come maybe. Naturally one's thoughts ran back over the events leading to one's capture. Were we foolish to have acted in the way we had? Should we have attacked the first target we saw, that is the tank transporters in the village of Cussabat? But our orders were to disrupt traffic on the main coast road 5 miles away and to stay there, not to attack an opportunity target on our uncompleted approach march. Should we have stayed in our cave with all our supplies of ammunition, etc? The cave was indefensible. Should we have somehow eked out our ammunition while on the run, to have warded off our attackers till nightfall? It might have won us a short reprieve. But could we have removed ourselves out of this hostile country by night, with all the villages, and the dogs barking throughout the neighbourhood? The nub of the matter was that we were in hostile territory, 500 miles away from any hope of rescue. And the Tripolitanian Arabs were not yet prepared for a reversal of fortune for the Axis powers; the severed hands bore mute witness what might happen to them if they sided with 'the enemy'. It was some comfort to think this matter over logically and coolly assess our position. Escape was the last thing in one's mind at that moment for we were soon to realize that an escape plan was like a military operation; it had to be planned in the minutest detail.

We were landed at the port of Taranto and shipped off to a PoW transit camp near Bari. Here we were to reach the depths of our present degradation: a hutted camp in the driving December rain surrounded by watch towers, a group of prisoners huddled round the only stove, from which 'new boys' were excluded. Near starvation rations, skilly or prison soup twice a day plus one roll of bread. This was the low point. From here on it could not get worse; it might even get better! After several days 800 Yugoslav prisoners were brought into Bari Camp, in the last stages of starvation. They were separated from us by a wire fence. About this experience I wrote,

> 'I have never seen people looking like living skeletons before. For the last six months they had lived off nothing but soup. Ten of them died immediately they arrived.'

These were Yugoslav Royalists who wore the distinctive strawberry-coloured uniform, or the remnants of it. Their lives were of no value to the Fascists, for Yugoslavia was a broken nation, whereas our lives were of more consequence – we still might win!

We could converse with them through the wire. For two rolls of bread a former tailor was willing to make me a suit of battledress out of an army blanket. This gave a tremendous boost to morale, for some silly English prisoners had thought my Italian uniform marked me as a man to be avoided!

Another bonus was the company of my running-mate, Andy Hough. We began to 'case the joint' and consider our situation as our training had taught us. We had noticed that every day, sometimes twice a day, a horse-drawn dead-cart came to collect the coffins of those unfortunate Yugoslavs who had died. We also discovered that the Yugoslav prisoners themselves prepared the dead for burial and nailed up the coffins, loading them on to the wagons. Would not it be easy therefore to replace the corpses with two live escapees, who on the lonely road to the cemetery could rise out of their wooden boxes and overpower the coachman? Possibly seizing the reins and making away with the wagon and all! Our imaginations were now beginning to run away with us, but the more we thought about it the more we were persuaded of its practical possibilities. The first thing to be done was to approach the Yugoslavs. And for this purpose my tailor was the intermediary. The message came back. 'We are Allies; yes, of course we can fix it! No problem!' – or words to that effect. The next question was getting through the wire into their camp. The guarding of this joint wire between the camps was rather slack and we did not anticipate any major difficulties. The one important factor was our trust in the Yugoslavs. We did not need an absent-minded Slav at the last moment to nail the coffins down with us inside!

Planning the escape occupied our every waking hour. It was the best antidote to 'prisoner-of-war-blues'. We had shaken off all our lethargy. But of course we had to keep it a deadly secret and go about our work in a circumspect manner. At any moment we might get a message over the wire that two Yugoslavs had died.

Needless to say, the best-laid plans . . . yes, at short notice we were moved out of that camp and that was the end of the story. And yet it had had the mark of originality, the *sine qua non* of any successful escape. As to what we would do when we had overpowered the undertaker we had taken no thought. For this was in the nature of a glorious practical joke upon our captors.

29

LIFE AS A PRISONER OF WAR

In order to follow the proper sequence of events I will recount what happened to the rest of our companions in that ill-fated raid into western Tripolitania.

Pat Hore-Ruthven, my fellow patrol leader, had been reported missing, believed wounded. He sadly died of wounds as it was subsequently discovered, following an attack on enemy transport. I hardly had time to get to know him. Humourous, with a long lugubrious face, he loved horses but had an aesthetic streak which manifested itself in poetry. He was a loss to his friends and to his generation, and a book in his memory testifies to this.[1]

My two neighbouring patrols were rounded up and put in the bag, as already recounted.

Vivian Street, whom David had placed in command of the fragmented squadron, but actually operating a patrol like myself, was to have an extraordinary adventure. He too had fallen into an ambush and had trodden the same path ending with a submarine voyage across the Mediterranean. During the course of the voyage a British bomber dropped some depth charges and brought the vessel to the surface. Inside the submarine there was total chaos. Like us, they were confined to the torpedo storage compartment – American pilots, South Africans and two British. After the initial explosion, when all the lights went out, they were trapped by the watertight doors which closed with an ominous clang. Water began to seep in, causing a chemical reaction releasing a cloud of ammonia.

No more claustrophobic situation can be imagined, but there was no panic amongst the prisoners, unlike the crew. A dim torchlight led them to an adjoining chamber where two Italian Army officers and some guards were also trapped. Imagining their last moment had come they could not believe it when the bulkhead door was slowly unclamped. Guards and crew scrambled up the companion ladder into the conning tower where the vessel was seen to be awash. The prisoners were last and did not move until many an 'after you', an amusing commentary on national characteristics! A British plane circled overhead and was seen signalling to some unseen ships. Shortly after two British destroyers appeared and proceeded to bombard the crippled submarine. This was the moment for Vivian and others to slide off into the icy water, without the aid of lifebelts of course, and strike away from the stricken vessel. Vivian soon got into difficulties but he was prevented from drowning by a fellow swimmer, an American pilot who happened to have been a professional life saver! A British boat put out from the destroyers to pick up the survivors, first a South African then two Americans, and an Italian and finally Vivian who gasped 'English!' as he was dragged on board. The crew were horrified to think that it might have been 'one of ours'.[2]

Paddy Mayne's squadron fared better than we did, being in more open country, and carried out successful raids. But David Stirling himself came to grief at the end of January, and this visionary and gallant leader was to spend the rest of the war, in between escapes, in the notorious Colditz camp in Germany.

But the dream that David dreamed in such unpropitious circumstances many months before had come to pass. The SAS was born, and to this day lives on, gathering ever fresh renown.

One thing David Stirling did bring to the face of modern war, by this time so entrenched and mechanized, was an erstwhile spirit of chivalry in the very gaiety and dare-devilry of his operations. In the self-sacrifice which he demanded of his companions, and the selflessness which in the early days envisaged no awards for acts of bravery. His operations often had that touch of humour about them which mystified our enemy, not least our own high command. And the perfect exemplar was this *beau sabreur* himself. But the spirit of invincibility this built was to prove our downfall in Tripolitania.

Now we must return to the sombre march of events in Italy. We left the Bari Transit Camp after a stay of two months, much thinner and physically worse for wear than when we had arrived. On the train journey north, to the Chieti Camp which lay on the Pescara river, Andy Hough and I had made our preparations for a possible train jump, and had managed to acquire enough food for a week, a map and a compass. The guards were drunk and sleepy, and by great good fortune both of us sat next to an open window. We planned to leave the train at night as we drew away from Termoli station. We arrived there at one o'clock in the morning but failed to leave till six, by which time it was daylight. Once again our plans had miscarried.

Chieti – Learning the Ropes

The gates to *Campo Concentramente Prigonieri di Guerra No 21* at Chieti opened on to a bleak compound with wooden huts in serried ranks on either side. This was to be our home for the next few months. The *Commandante* was a well known Fascist and the interpreter, named Croce (our main contact), was of the same mind. The camp housed 1,500 officer prisoners of war, many of whom were the casualties of Tobruk. The diet was of the same starvation levels of soup and one bread roll a day. We began to crave for fat, a sign of serious deficiencies, ameliorated a month or two later by the arrival of Red Cross food parcels.

There was a lively camp organization consisting of a Senior British Officer, who did all the negotiating with the Italian Staff, an 'escape committee' which vetted and co-ordinated all escape plans, a library for the circulation of books and a very effective amateur dramatic group and orchestra. Shortly after my arrival I was invited to address the assembled company on the Battle of Alamein, an event of which they had little knowledge. The whole camp assembled in one of the long huts with our sentries posted to warn of the unwelcome arrival of camp guards. The news of a great British victory put fresh heart in everyone and I was fortunate to be the harbinger of such good tidings.

At this camp escape was in everyone's mind, so soul-destroying were the conditions of life. Some elaborate schemes were devised. In one a tunnel was dug under the stage of the theatre where crucial activity was concealed by the staging of concerts. In another a mass breakout was planned, with bedboards being used as scaling ladders. Having fused the electricity system, an assault over the high wire was to take place at several different points. The scheme was, I believe, finally vetoed by the SBO as likely to lead to unacceptable loss of life. Another cunning tunnel was constructed in the open playground, the entrance to which was disguised by an open air lecture, under cover of which diggers got to work and a lid was fashioned imperceptible to the passer-by. The ingenuity and skill which went into escape plans was remarkable.

The officer population of the camp were adjusting themselves to a whole new way of life. Ostensibly languishing in captivity, in fact a busy industry was in progress. Many were finding hidden talents and skills, either to improve their living conditions or to enhance their chances of escape. All sorts of arts and crafts flourished. There were master-forgers, for escape into enemy territory was impossible without documents; there were self-taught tailors and masters of disguise; language teachers; tinsmiths, for tin was our basic raw material; joiners and welders, only using the heat of a candle as their power supply; stove and lamp-makers; entrepreneurs and traders; air-conditioning engineers, so essential to work in a tunnel. Waste-disposal was another speciality, for quantities of spoil had to be disposed of without arousing curiousity. All the trades and crafts were carried on with the most primitive of stone age tools. Intellectual life was not neglected for there were lecture courses on almost every conceivable subject.

The camp guards were either unaware of or frowned on many of these activities. Frequent searches took place without any warning and hiding places had to be found for all these artefacts. Nevertheless, apart from our self-provided work, we were still prisoners, deprived of our liberty and without a finite end in sight. It had occurred to me that such escape attempts had very little chance of success given that it was virtually impossible to reach allied lines (then still in North Africa) from the Italian peninsula, surrounded as it was by sea.

I decided to head north with the aim of reaching Switzerland. For this purpose I enlisted the aid of the Italians to transport me to within 60 miles of the Swiss frontier. It happened like this. A draft was due to depart for a camp in the north, PG49 at Fontanellato, near Parma in the Plain of Lombardy. A fellow-prisoner, warned for the draft, wished to remain at Chieti. I wished to go to Parma. We simply exchanged identities but so completely that it took months to disentangle. I assumed his regimental identity, army number and badges of rank, and he mine. We changed names. He wrote home to my parents and I to his, which caused considerable surprise and confusion on the home front. Remarkable to say, I have completely forgotten the false name with which my partner so generously provided me, and the other alibis which we also exchanged.

I duly paraded with the new draft and nothing was said. I was not sorry to say goodbye to Chieti Camp. Although I left many friends behind, it was Fascist dominated, was too large, and had bad vibes. Our train journey was by daylight and an RAF officer who tried to jump the train as it pulled out of a station was cornered and brutally clubbed to death by Italian guards with rifle butts. This was a horrible scene, as it took place on the side of the track in our full view. Thereafter the train murmured with mutinous discontent as we drew away from the scene. At this the guards became trigger-happy and we were lucky not have another such incident. Sometime after midnight we arrived at a ghostly station called Castel Guelfo. There was no transport and we stood waiting in the pouring rain. Morale, having been high when we set out from Chieti, was now at its lowest ebb.

The Tunnel – Fontanellato
But Fontanellato, when we got there, we found altogether different from Chieti Camp. It was guarded by the Alpini Regiment, crack mountain troops then out of the line, and the Commandant, also an Alpini, turned out to be a civilized human being.

The building was a former orphanage on three floors and the Nunnery, to which it had been attached, was just across the road. The nuns used to do our washing and we carried on a clandestine traffic with them in the form of bars of soap and other goodies which were then being received in Red Cross parcels. There were only 500 officers in this camp; we slept on beds instead of wooden bunks; we had fruit and vegetables, and were able to purchase a daily ration of 'vino'.

Nevertheless, when my alibi was eventually discovered I was made to do a week's 'solitary', which I considered a small payment for my good fortune. Of course a state of armed neutrality existed between the prisoners, who by devious means were trying to escape, and the camp guards, jealous of their reputation in trying to forestall any such happening. But the prisoners in this camp fell roughly into two categories. One were the traditional 'escapers', the other a more intellectual group who had become accustomed to a monastic life of books, learning and artistic endeavour. They held the opinion that 'escapees' were simply on an ego-trip and ruined the life of everyone else who were inevitably penalized.

I was not of the lotus-eating school as I had not yet become institutionalized, being a very recent casualty. I was therefore involved in two escape attempts which were classics of their kind, and very ingenious they were too.

The first was a straightforward tunnel, dug from within the building, which was intended to surface on the far side of the wire, of about some 80 yards in length. The convenience of this particular tunnel was its entrance. We had managed to gain access from the basement dining hall into the space beneath the main external steps. This space was highly commodious and enabled us to store all our gear here unseen; we had a haulage system to extract the spoil, string for signalling to the 'working' face, and a receptacle for the soil, initially a wooden sledge. As time went on the tunnel became more sophisticated. From an electric point in the dining hall we were able to introduce an electric light into the cavity. This was a great boon and shed some light into the tunnel itself, previously illuminated by olive oil and a wick. An elaborate air-conditioning system was also constructed because it became more and more airless at the working face the further one went. The flue which supplied fresh air by means of home-made bellows was made of tin. As far as I can remember it consisted of a series of Klim (or powdered milk) tins obtainable from Red Cross parcels. The tunnel had to be revetted and shored up throughout its length, so quantities of wood to make pit-props were required. One of the biggest problems was the disposal of soil or spoil. The cavity enabled a working party to stuff the spoil into grey army socks. This could be concealed 'on the person' in case of passing an officer or camp guard. We had discovered a flue-hatch from an internal chimney at the top of the building, so a team of porters carried the spoil-filled socks to the top of the building and simply emptied the contents down the chimney.

Each stint at the working face lasted about an hour and a half. It took about five minutes crawling on stomach and elbows to reach the face and rather longer crawling backwards, and props had to be placed as one dug. It was a very claustrophobic experience with the danger of an imminent collapse of the roof, which was far from stable.

All these activities had to be concealed, not only from the camp guards but from other prisoners in case of careless talk.

The tunnel was making progress. We had been at it for about two months and were approaching the wire. Those who were privy to the scheme and who had a place on the escape plan knew that we could only release about four a night, my turn coming up about the fourth night. We began to feel our tunnel was foolproof. We had our escape kits ready – documents, civilian clothes or replica uniforms, food, maps – with the object of taking the train, a high-risk policy, to the nearest point to the Swiss border.

Then the inevitable happened. Someone left the light on! As it grew dark the camp guard patrolling outside noticed a chink of light coming from between the stone steps. His reaction was not very quick but he became suspicious and reported the matter. There was an immediate hue and cry. They soon discovered the entrance in the dining room and excited soldiers began digging everywhere. I do not think that the culprits were exposed but a collective punishment was imposed which affected everyone.

The rationale of these attempts was that every prisoner of war was expected to escape if he could. It was therefore the duty of the SBO to facilitate such efforts through the medium of an 'Escape Committee' which rigourously vetted, co-ordinated and authorized escape plans. Some, of course, were vetoed. Once in Switzerland escapees, from whichever direction they had come, were automatically interned but were allowed to move about freely. An onward escape route existed through France and Spain, and those with particular qualifications, such as RAF pilots who were then in short supply, were fed into this route and many rejoined the war effort, so that the policy was justified in practice.

So, very shortly after the collapse of this tunnel and the restoration of normal privileges by the Italian authorities, a new scheme was evolved. The beauty of this plan was its simplicity.

The orphanage was surrounded by a close wire fence so there was little room to exercise. The Italian authorities therefore opened a field, which abutted on to the wire in front of the building, about the size of a football pitch. By day, when this field was open for exercise, the watchtowers surrounding it were manned, but at dusk, when the field was closed, the watchtowers were unmanned. Of course the guards did a sweep of the field before closure, but it was as flat as a pancake with hardly a blade of grass.

During the day the field was a scene of activity, with PoWs walking round the perimeter, playing games, or settling down to a lecture. It was now high summer and the weather was hot and dry. The idea was to use the group surrounding the lecturer to conceal work on a shallow grave with space enough for two people lying down. A cunning wooden lid was constructed with an earth top which could be easily opened from inside. Into this top was introduced a pipe for breathing purposes. In the evening before the evacuation of the field two men were hidden in the grave. The sentry posts were then withdrawn and, during a moonless night, they lifted the lid, clambered out and made for the unguarded wire. As far as I can remember this worked perfectly for the first two nights. We concealed the absence of the four men with dummies, and my own turn was within sight. How the disaster happened I cannot now recall. Either the escapees' absence was detected or they were caught on the run. However, the game was up. The privilege of the field and guarded walks was withdrawn, combined with a stricter régime and more hostile guards.

In the orphanage we read the Italian newspapers every day. From this it was possible to detect, but only just, that war for the Italians was not going too well! The papers were full of braggadocio.

'*Uno dei sommergible ha affondate tutte le navi da guerra Inglesi nel "nostro mare"'* ('One of our submarines has sunk all the English Navy in "our sea"') was a typical headline. The censor was unable to deny the landing of allied troops in Sicily, but our world was unaffected by these distant rumblings. A huge bell in the campanile of the nunnery told the passing hours. The routine continued untroubled. Summer foliage and dusty farm workers continued to enliven the landscape. Would summer turn into winter before we saw any sign of release?

30

ESCAPE
THE LONG WALK HOME

Summer turned to autumn. Through our window on the outside world we watched the *contadini* carrying out their immemorial tasks. Nothing seemed to have changed. The big bass bell tolled the passing hours calling the nuns to prayer. Then one day in September it happened.

On 8 September, 1943, the Italians agreed to an Armistice. Unusual activity was observed on the camp perimeter. Soldiers were talking in groups (always a good sign!) Cycles were whizzing past and officers were striding about in a purposeful way. The SBO addressed us and told us not to get too excited. But excitement was in the air. Rumours were rife. German troops were in the vicinity. Italian scouts were out and would warn us of their approach, in which case the English alarm would be sounded when we were to form up and march out in our allotted companies. From then on we were at five minutes' notice to move. Rumours multiplied. The British 'had landed at Pisa' and the Germans 'were attacking the Italians in Parma'. The Italian camp staff bravely declared that they would defend the camp against all comers!

At midday the camp guards suddenly jumped down from their posts and into the big ditch. Five got into the pigsty with a machine gun. There was much shouting. The alarm sounded and we formed up and marched out into the countryside, having cut our way through the wire. A fellow-prisoner, Eric Newby, who had a bad leg, was riding on a pony.[1] A German plane came over us flying very low. We all scattered and lay flat.

We had now stepped through 'the window' and shattered the picture we had been gazing upon for so long. But we were not quite free, for we were to stay in our formed bodies in case rescue was at hand. As we lay hiding in the vineyard the SBO insisted on these rigid and unrealistic instructions, on pain of court martial! On hearing this two of us decided to leave immediately! Why wait to be rounded up by Germans, a fate reserved, alas, for many of our companions? Without a word to anyone, Archie Hubbard, a fellow officer, and myself slipped away from this doomed encampment.[2] It was every man for himself! Just before we left we heard that the Italian *Commandante* had been taken prisoner by the Germans.

Later that night we started upon our journey, free and unencumbered. Our sole possessions were the clothes we stood up in, peasant clothing of the Italian *contadini*, well-worn trousers, a shirt, a threadbare jacket and a billycock hat. That same evening a kindly farmer had taken us in and received our battledress in exchange for his cast-off clothing. But we still had our strong army boots which proved to be a godsend.[3] Round the kitchen table we planned our night's march. We must cross the Apennine foothills and head for La Spezia on the Gulf of Genoa where rumours told of an Allied landing. Once we had reached the foothills of the Apennines we would be within 80 miles of the Gulf.

These *contadini* bore no ill-will against the English. The old wife went to the chimney-piece and removed two Madonna ikons which she pressed upon us 'for the journey', adding two eggs and a loaf of bread.

'Which way is west?' I asked the old man.

'There, towards the moon,' he pointed.

'But remember – *sempre in campagna – niente strada – sempre in campagna.*' (Always in the country – never roads.)*

This was good advice as we were to learn later.

There was enough visibility by the light of the moon to be able to steer past farmhouses, where the dogs would start barking, a painful lesson already learnt in Tripolitania, and keep on our bearing towards the west. We had one main obstacle to negotiate before we reached the foothills, the Via Emilia, the main road which bisects the Lombardy plain, and its accompanying railway line. Our farmer friend had insisted that the German traffic would be travelling north, pulling out of Italy. At about one o'clock in the morning we came to a railway line which we crossed without difficulty. Only a hedge separated us from the main road. We were heartened to see that the German convoys, consisting of heavy lorries and guns, were indeed going north and apparently away from Italy. We were in a ditch and the traffic rumbled

---

* The Italian is as I wrote it at the time. I have not corrected it.

and whined above our heads; a crossing might be difficult. No self-respecting peasant would be out at that time of night and, if spotted, we would arouse suspicion. However, a lull enabled us to slip across the road; another railway line quickly followed and then we were out in open country again.

We sat down and helped ourselves to a bunch of grapes from a convenient vineyard and took stock of the situation. As can be expected we were in a state of euphoria. We were now free men able at last to exercise our own free will, freely to choose our route and destination, to stretch our limbs in this new-found environment. We believed that we were almost home already, whispering, 'Home in three days!'

'Maybe sooner – thank God we left the others – no regrets!'

At 3 a.m. we reached the foothills. The moon had now disappeared. We had made excellent going across the flat plain, only causing a few dogs to bark, which was the countryside's alarm signal. In the balmy air we lay down by a small stream and slept till dawn.

When we woke we were indeed on the edge of the hills. We wandered up tracks and came to a farmhouse. Here we were excitedly greeted by an Italian soldier returning home, who embarrassed us by his disregard for safety. Here we managed to listen to a BBC bulletin. There was no mention of an allied landing anywhere near, only in the distant south. Somewhat crestfallen, we accompanied our friend to another farmhouse where we were taken in and fed. That night we sat with the peasants, the ancient ones and some buxom young lassies, for the men were all away, peeling the *grano turco* (Indian corn) under the full moon. We joined in their song *Fiori in del Prato* (the flowers of the field), the haunting melody – I can remember it to this day – echoing across the valley as we peeled the provocative seed-pods. Traveller beware of such moments of euphoria! Think of Ulysses and the temptations which delayed his journey to the Isle of Ithaca! That night we slept in a barn, in the hay, well out of harm's way.

Our soldier-companion left early next morning, saying that he was going to get news. By this time we had become a little apprehensive about his easy ways. Could he be a Fascist? As a precaution we crept out of the barn and up the hillside where we lay, waiting on events. Sure enough he came back in suspicious company. We were now certain he intended to betray us.

As it turned out this was a timely warning, and the words of our first farmer friend came back to us, '*Sempre in campagna – niente strada.*'

But first we had an important decision to make. Should we go north and try to cross the Swiss frontier, a mere 60 miles away, but a notoriously difficult border to cross, or shold we go south towards Naples? We decided upon the latter. We would keep in the high mountains of the Apennines as far as we could, avoiding centres of civilization. At 20 miles a day it might take us two months to reach our objective, the allied lines, the precise whereabouts of which we did not know. But our assumption was that the allied armies would have occupied Italy very much quicker than they actually did, and this determined our decision.

As for disguise, my travelling companion was dark and could pass quite easily as an Italian. I was fair and I gave my provenance as the Sud-Tyrol in northern Italy, former Austrian-occupied territory where inhabitants spoke the German tongue. This worked, up to a point, with casual encounters, but we very soon found that among the peasants there was much sympathy for us fugitives. Many of their sons were doing the same thing, former soldiers keeping out of the way of the Germans. It was summed up with a knowing look and an *'Eh girare, girare'*! (going round and round), and usually followed by *'Pauvre ragazzi'* (poor boys) *'Quando finire la guerra?'* (when will the war finish?)

After a week of walking we dropped down one evening to a remote village. We were invited into the house of an old woman with one eye whose granddaughters called her 'Nona'. She gave us the last of everything as we sat down to a meal of eggs, tomatoes and onions, and a bottle of raw country wine.

'Tonight,' chuckled the old woman, 'you will sleep with these fine young girls, one with one, eh?' she croaked. 'Is that not right? Is that not as it should be? One with one, *uno con uno* – e bene – e vero?'

What sense of modesty prevented our accepting this siren call I cannot now tell, but this second temptation had to be resisted if we were to accomplish our journey and escape the clutches of our enemies, as others were to find to their cost. We slept in a barn that night and stayed all next day, attended by the girls, resting our aching feet and blisters. That evening whilst Nona was feeding us, a local cobbler who had heard we were there presented us with a beautiful folding road map of the whole of Italy and planned a route for us. This proved a tremendous boon and put an end to our aimless wandering.

A day or two later we found ourselves in the village of Cerredolo, still on the eastern slope of the Appennine ridge. Here the bells were ringing for Matins. We sat and rested under the shade of a vine. Then all of a sudden out of the church came running hundreds of little black figures. They crowded round like a swarm of ants, all talking at once.

'Oh you are English!' they exclaimed.

'They are two Englishmen.' ('*duo Inglesi*')

'You are fugitives escaping from the Germans ('*sone fugitivi dai tedeschi*'), they said one to another.

'Look how fair one is, the other is dark like an Italian!' ('*con Italiano*')

'Come. You must come with us and we will hide you in a wood.'

'It is too dangerous for you to go to Naples.' ('*Sono molto periculoso viagare verso Napoli. Impossibile*')

'You must stay for a week, or two weeks, in our wood, and we will feed you!'

'We are all friends of the English. We are to be missionaries in China after the war. In China there are plenty of English.'

'Brother Pietro, some water'. (*Fratello Pietro acqua fresco*).

'Pietro will get you some water. We have no wine but water is better. Now you must eat!'

In their white sun hats and black habits with young beards just sprouting these novices resembled a swarm of black beetles. When we were safely hidden in the wood they returned almost immediately bearing plates of meat, salad, fruit and bread.

'Now eat, eat and we will talk.'

'They are tired. We must go away, but two of us will stay.'

They watched us silently as we ate. They brought us eiderdowns and pillows and said we must now lie down. We reluctantly did so, for we were still fresh and wished to continue our journey. It was now early afternoon and putting frustration aside we had to admit it was peaceful as we lay in the dappled shade of the wood.

Then at four o'clock sixteen black figures came scrambling up the hillside, sweating and breathless.

'Oh! we have such bad news for you,' they cried. 'The Germans say on the radio that anyone who helps English prisoners will be shot! English and Italian soldiers must report to them in twenty-four hours otherwise they will be declared outlaws and may also be shot. We have fear for you. It is better for you to go. Go to the high mountains where you may live as shepherds ('*pastorelli*').

All day you must watch sheep. You must go by way of Castelnuovo, Firenzuola, Santa Maria and San Benedetto in Alpe. Then in the mountain you must live the pastoral life.'

Their faces, as they anxiously regarded us, were open and kind. Did I recognize in them the faces of friends known long ago? Or was it a sudden impression brought on by the tenseness of the situation and so strange an encounter?

It was incredible to think that here we were in the Italian mountains in the middle of the war, being succoured by former enemies upon whom we had poured unsparing scorn. What extraordinary combination of circumstances had brought us to this point? It was sobering to think that human kindness transcended the mightiest affairs of nations.

'Now you must go,' they said. 'We will pray for you every day, and you must pray also. You must pray for us. We may be taken by the Germans. We don't know. But Brother Gregory will accompany you to the first village.'

And so it was that we learnt that there was a price on our heads, and that this price would have to be paid by anyone who helped us.

31

ESCAPE
CROSSING THE LINES

Many Italian soldiers were now walking towards their homes or hiding in the hills, so fugitives were not an unusual sight to the peasants. Although we spoke only broken Italian many of the *contadini* were prepared to accept us as Italians from another part of Italy, with different dialects. It was only after we had joined them in their simple evening meal (usually polenta poured onto a scrubbed wooden table where it solidified and the mass was carved into by each member of the family) that it began to dawn upon them that we might be English.

Then credulous questions followed in quick succession,

'You came from Egypt? But is *Inghilterra* the same country as *Egitto*?'

'But where are your *casa* – your homes?'

'How long on foot to *Inghilterra*? Two months or more! *Pauvre ragazzi*' (poor boys).

Often there would be a hurried consultation and a nodding of heads that perhaps we had become a little 'foolish' on account of the *bruto tempo* (bad times).

'But have you mammas and papas? Three years since you last saw them? *Quel miseria*! (what misery).'

Often the Nona of the house would conclude, 'We are all Christians, all God's children, So what does it matter?'

The resignation of these incredibly poor people was heartrending to see. With very little food they lacked the basic necessities of life, but were always willing to share with those they considered worse off than themselves. They looked at their feet and exclaimed '*Scarpe Mussolini*' (Mussolini shoes) as they showed us the cut-up motor tyres they were using as footwear. We had brought with us some spare pieces of soap and a tin or two of tobacco from Red Cross parcels. They had not seen real soap for years and we were able to provide some; likewise an odd fill or two of tobacco worked wonders.

Every two days we might have a fairly main road to cross, the warning ('*sempre in campagna niente strada*') still ringing in our ears. Sometimes a river or a railway provided the obstacle. By now always walking by day, we usually made these crossings in the early hours of the morning about dawn when there was little traffic about. In September the rivers proved no problem, and we were able to wade most knee-deep, at first bare-footed, but after cuts and bruises, with our boots on!

Soon we struck a belt of miserable country, not high mountains but a series of precipitous ridges rising to some 3000 feet. It meant traversing three or four of the ridges a day to keep up our average mileage. Here the *casa* were few and far between. The farmers, none too friendly, extracted their livelihood from a few acres of chestnut trees (*castinia*) and enough maize to produce a coarse bread. We lived on bread and water; we were never very welcome guests and had to ask for what we got. In the chestnut forests were to be found the sinister and taciturn charcoal-burners whose company we mostly avoided, although the umbrageous chestnut woods were a delight to walk in after so many weeks exposure to the sun. Climbing one of the ridges I strained a tendon, whilst Archie was stricken with neuralgia, but still we plodded on.

Then one day, after we had been walking for three weeks, we sighted more open country in front and that evening we dropped down into a beautiful valley full of grape vines. We had picked out our *casa* from a few miles away and it proved a lucky choice. We got gloriously drunk that night on the vino generously provided, together with a rare meal of meat and potatoes. Next morning we woke up in a barn full of sweet-smelling hay.

Up till then we had had fine sunny days. Walking was hot but the going was firm. However, during our drunken slumber at the farm in the valley of the grapes it had rained cats and dogs, for October was approaching and walking after the rain became a slither and a slide. This was a timely warning so we quickened our pace.

In our progress down Italy life was simple but rewarding. We had no worries except the fulfilment of our mission – survival and escape. We had no responsibilities for anyone else. Nor had we any possessions except the clothes we stood up in. This was indeed travelling light. The evident contradictions between our clandestine journey and the complete freedom which we felt gave a vicarious thrill to the experience. Nor was I unlucky in my choice of companion. Archie Hubbard had qualitites well adapted for such a time. We never had a quarrel or dispute as far as I can remember. Of tough and wiry physique, he could well withstand the rigours of the pace. His chosen profession after the war was that of hop-farmer and his reaction to events was that of the placid countryman with a countryman's instincts. Humour was never far from the surface and his initial dubbing of my sense of direction as 'uncanny' became a standing joke, particularly when I led him astray, as often happened. It was almost impossible to distinguish him from the real *contadini* so convincing was his appearance, particularly with his gift for picking up the local dialect. What bound us together was our itchy feet and our determination to keep going come what may.

One day was much like another with minor incidents to relieve the tedium. A swarm of wasps settled on my head. Removing my hat to swat them they settled in my hair and I was badly stung, giving me a cracking headache. Archie lost his hat. I lost my watch. But we gradually crept along (*sempre in campagna!*) avoiding if we could other escapees (two was quite enough), Italian soldiers, *carabinieri* – the para-military police, priests and villagers. But one day sheltering from the rain in a small hamlet I looked through the window and saw two armed *carabinieri* coming down the road past the house in which we were sheltering. I pointed this out to the owner. He told us to be quick and follow him, and he rushed us down to the cellar but opened a door at the bottom and before we knew it we were out on the road with the man crying '*Via! Via!*' (away, away!). The door slammed and the *carabinieri* turned the corner about 15 yards away from where we stood. We walked away with feigned nonchalance, whistling as we went. The price on our heads would have made a tempting capture for an alert *carabinieri*, for they were still under the orders of the Germans. Another lucky escape.

On another occasion, having walked some 35 miles in one day, from one blue ridge to another, we came to rest at a farmhouse, where we shared a stall for the night with the great white oxen – the motive-power for all farm work since the days of the Romans. In that part of Italy, the Abruzzi, the oxen were kept under the living room, a primitive but effective form of central heating. But I do not recommend them as bed-fellows. The noise was truly catastrophic as they performed their nightly ablutions! The great white oxen, so common then over all parts of Italy, have now vanished, like their masters, the former *contadini*. In retrospect we were indeed fortunate to witness this way of life, for it had served the peninsula for well over a thousand years. Soon it was to be swept away for ever.

After four weeks we had done over half the distance to the fighting line, or where we supposed it to be. Then we began to climb the mountains leading to the grandest feature of them all, the Gran Sasso d'Italia, a massif some 10,000 feet high which dominated all the country to the south-west. Once we had crossed this obstacle we reckoned we would be within 100 miles of the fighting. In these parts we heard of a lot of former PoWs lying up or walking about but we tended to avoid them as we were confident in our own painfully gathered local lore and did not need to be encumbered with 'passengers'. At this time of year the shepherds were still in those high pasture regions and many a friendly greeting we received, but to our surprise we were addressed in broad Yankee slang for many of these same shepherds had done a spell in America, from whence they had sent back remittances to their families at home. All this had happened in the period before the war, since when they had returned quite happily to their former pastoral life. My journal of this journey written a few weeks after these events records that

> 'The morning we crossed the Gran Sasso we had only managed to get three potatoes to eat, but after climbing for five hours we passed over the watershed at about 9,000 ft in a swirling mist. Once clear of this we sat down on the far side with a shepherd lad, equipped with the universal black umbrella, and discussed with him the fine panorama which now opened up to the south-west. There was the town of Aquila with the long valley cutting down Italy, which held the road and railway and no doubt many Germans. There was the village of San Stephano, way below us and the route we planned to take, following just inside the Gran Sasso range as it curled down towards the south-west and my former prison camp of Chieti.'

It was certainly curious being perched on these ranges which we had gazed at so longingly from the confines of Campo 21. After we had dropped down to San Stephano later that night we were guided by villagers to a cave where we found two British soldiers.

> 'We ate a huge meal with them and curled up under their warm blankets. The etiquette was that Archie would share Mac's bed and I should share Jim's. According to their rules of hospitality,

the guests were not allowed to sleep under the same blanket. The next morning before it was light we splashed in the stream in the woods and, having stuffed ourselves with as much cold macaroni as we could, we were off into the hills as dawn came.'

We spent most of that day crossing a high plateau. We had now moved into country with no isolated farmhouses, and the villages were occupied by Germans. It would be dangerous to seek help there, so we found a convenient cave, and collected a plentiful supply of grapes, nuts and tomatoes and lay eating on the grass outside our cave by the light of a young moon. Then we raided a wood pile and built a large fire inside the cave and slept curled up around the embers. This was only the second night that we had had to spend out during the whole of our progress so far.

The following evening we were given shelter in a farm just above the Rome-Pescara road, the ancient Via Tiburtina. The old *padrone*, or master of the house, aged 78, was demonstrating to us a negro dance which he had seen in America fifty years before. We however, had our thoughts, concentrated upon the road below us. It was the main German lateral communication between the two fighting fronts split by the Apennines. Besides the road there was a railway and a deep and swiftly-flowing river, the Pescara, so it was a very likely fall-back position for the Germans. For us, the sooner we were across this obstacle the better. Once beyond this line, it was about a week's march to Campobasso which we believed to be in Allied hands. The obstacles ahead, quite apart from defensive positions, included five rivers, including the Sangro, several roads and one big range of mountains, the Maiella, which rose to 8,000 feet.

> '"The road ahead is dangerous," said our hosts. "*Aspett* – wait, wait for only two days and then your friends will be here. Only wait and we will feed you in a cave; otherwise you will be taken by the Germans." We had heard this kindly advice so often that we were almost tempted to stay, but we also knew that once winter had set in, and our troops had not advanced, we would be stuck in a very dangerous area.'

Always we were warned of the dangers ahead, but so often they did not materialize. Thus from a high wooded eminence, we lay and watched the German transport crawl by. Where the railway bridge crossed the river we could see no German guards, so we would try and cross there, then follow the river bank for 200 yards and move towards the road where a fold in the ground gave us some cover. I would cross the river first and wait for Archie on the far bank. All went according to plan. We crossed the river, railway and road without any trouble and took shelter from the rain in a *casa* on the far side, barely 300 yards away from the road, and congratulated ourselves on this feat. The inhabitants were very friendly and fed us, and, as it was still raining, invited us to spend the night, although it was only late afternoon. Disregarding one of our principal rules, we agreed to do so. Not only that but we slept in a bed in the farmhouse!

Archie and I and the son of the house, a goatherd, were put in a large double bed next to the *salone*. We went to bed early and soon the watchdog started barking. The *padrone* ran out and said to two figures in the dark, 'No fear; there are no Germans here!'

The figures were two German soldiers, who demanded entry into the room next to ours, loudly asking for olive oil. We could not move for fear the house was surrounded. We just lay doggo. To placate them our host offered them a meal, which seemed to last an age. We could hear every word they said. They demanded olive oil again and were about to search the house when they suddenly decided to clear off.

The goatherd led us up the hill. We were glad to shake the dust off our feet for we were in a very exposed position. Then began a series of improbable events which followed in quick succession. We were near the fighting line for we could now hear the guns. None of the locals had a clue as to exactly where it was, but they were only too ready to help.

On the 37th day of continuous walking we called in at a farm for directions. All the women were in tears,

'There are Germans everywhere!' they said. 'They take everything. From here one hour ago they took a sheep. They are now at the farm below. What ugly times! *Momma mia. Quando finire la guerra?* (when will the war finish) *Madonna, madonna – pauvre noi, pauvre noi*' (poor us).

Later in the day we were directed to a farm said to contain an English woman. In our carefully rehearsed Italian we knocked at the door and said, '*Abbiamo sentito que in questa casa abita una donna qui parla Englesi*'. (We have heard that in this house lives a women who speaks English.) The woman at the door answered in peasant's dialect, and then broke into English and said in a strong American accent, 'Careful, kids! Don't look now but there are twelve Germans on my left by the river. This is the last zone of operations before they take up their new line. Do not look, but walk slowly up the hill. Go now or they will see you!'

We did not take her warning seriously, but we left the house and followed her instructions. Truth to tell, we had hardly seen a German all day.

> 'As we turned a corner, in the track we were following, Archie suddenly whispered, "Stop!" There, ten yards in front of us were two German soldiers on horseback. We turned abruptly and slouched down the hill, not knowing if they had seen us, only to hear footsteps quite close behind. We dodged behind a hedge and lay flat. Two infantrymen passed within a few yards. We lay still for half an hour, then made across an exposed hill towards some cover beyond. As we reached the middle of the exposed patch, there was a great deal of shouting behind. Three Eyeties were running after us and yelling at us to stop.'

We were exasperated by this folly as we were apparently now surrounded by Germans.

We dived into some rushes and lay flat as the first one came running up.

'*Kamerad! Kamerad!*' He embraced us.

'*Ich bin Deutsch, ich Deutsch!*'

'*Aspett! Aspett!*' shouted the other two as they came crashing over the skyline.

'*Abbiamo qui-un soldato tedesche!*' (We have here a German soldier) they exploded.

'I'm an Austrian from Vienna,' he explained breathlessly.

'My father owns a farm. My brother is in London. I must come with you to the English!'

'Yes,' said the Italians, 'we must all come with you to the English. They are only two kilometres away. It will take only one night. We know the way – we have a friend who knows the way.'

Archie quickly sized up the situation. He told the German deserter he was a fool. Didn't he realize that his compatriots occupied every vantage point. That if re-captured he would be shot. No, we would have nothing to do with him, and he must leave us at once. 'But,' answered the German, 'I know where all the positions are.' We now began to wonder whether we were right to dismiss these intruders. It might be as well to question them first. They seemed genuine enough.

The German said that he knew all the enemy dispositions. The long wooded ridge above us was the German front line. On it we would find only fifty armed men with nothing larger than LMGs. They would be scattered in twos and threes on the tracks through the woods. Beyond that we would find no Germans, and after that a two-hour walk would bring us to the River Biferno and our own lines. The two Italians said that at their uncle's house was a man who knew the country intimately who would be prepared to guide us across. We began to ponder this offer. It might be worth risking. At any rate we might talk to the guide. One of them and the deserter would stay with us in the rushes while the other departed to fetch the guide. We said we would wait one hour. We waited and waited. No one came. Three hours after darkness fell we heard a faint shout from below.

'Oyee-ee-e!' shouted back our Italian. Then followed shouts and cries concerning uncles, deserters and Englishmen. This was madness, the German front line was apparently only two kilometres away. We had come all this way unscathed only to be at the mercy of lunatics. We trailed down to the faint voice in the valley below which grew in volume as we approached. When the unknown voice was reached, the owner suddenly broke into a whisper: '*Tacete!*' (Be quiet). Sshh. Germans are everywhere! Don't say a word or they will hear you. It is impossible for you to move tonight.'

By this time we were quite hysterical. Even the German saw the humour of it. So, taking the deserter with us, we left. We really could not be embarrassed by his presence much longer, but we would first test his knowledge and sense of direction. Soon he began to veer too far to the right, away from our supposed direction. We corrected him. He did it again.

'Right,' we said to the deserter, 'it is better for you now to continue alone. We will wait here until the moon rises.'

He embraced us again, was pathetically grateful for the note of identification which we had scrawled for him on a dirty piece of paper with a burnt-out match head, and disappeared into the darkness.

What would be our next encounter in this Alice-in-Wonderland progress? It was a particularly dark night. Soon we stumbled upon a farmhouse and invited ourselves to dinner. Here we were given eggs, wine and macaroni. An old man who was there offered to lead us by an unknown track through the woods to the top of the ridge. Here all the old phrases which we knew so well were trotted out by our kind hosts for the last time.

'*Quel miseria.*'
'*Bruto tempo.*'

'*Pauvre ragazzi – pauvre noi;*' the final despairing cry '*Quando finire la guerra?*', and the reply, '*Speriamo presto*' (I hope soon).

The old woman who was stoking the fire looked down at her feet wrapped round with old motor tyres, and spat out '*Scarpe Mussolini.*'

'When we get home,' we said, 'we will send you shoes, soap and wool.' (So easy to say but how difficult to do, to locate even one of these remote farmhouses whose names and location we never committed to paper in case of recapture.)

The old man, a leprechaun-like figure, led us well and we passed swiftly through the trees. Over the top of the ridge there was a clearing and here he told us that we must walk towards the flashes of the guns we saw firing, for they were ours. We gave him our tobacco and bade him goodnight.

It was by now a soft moonlit night. We carefully avoided the bridges and villages he had told us about. This was only our second walk in the dark. We could hear the familiar noises of military activity but we saw not a thing, nor did we stumble across gun emplacements, barbed wire or mines.

At three in the morning we waded across our thirtieth and last river, the Biferno. Once over the other side we sat down under a clump of poplars and ate some bread. Ten miles further on, we reckoned, was the Termoli-Campobasso road which we intended to cross before daylight.

At a farm on the river bank we saw three men standing talking. Odd at that hour in the morning. Perhaps it was a German outpost. We decided to investigate. Carefully stalking up to their position we began to overhear their conversation. They were speaking in a very excited way and they were clearly Italians. We stood up and declared ourselves to be British prisoners of war escaped from the Germans. They said the Germans had gone: '*Scaparti!*' One of them said he would lead us to an English gun. He was a little man in a long cloak and a billycock hat. Halfway up the track he stopped, hopped round and declared, 'You are free! No more Germans! *Tedeschi Finito!* Have no more fear!'

He pointed to the British position and disappeared. Were we at the end of our long, long, trail? Or was this another false rumour or even ambush? We were soon to know.

32

END OF STORY

It was a good long climb to find the gun. We thought we saw a camouflaged truck right in the middle of the track. No sooner had we seen it than we were challenged.

A voice cried, 'Alt!' We froze in our tracks and our hearts sank. Was this to be the ignominious end of our month-long trek? And then, 'Oo goes there?'

'Friends', we called out feeling we looked anything but it.

'Ad-vance one and be recognized!'

The familiar, homely, north-country tones were now unmistakeable. I stepped forward, in ragged shirt and torn trousers with boots bleached white in fording innumerable rivers, and said in as nonchalant a voice as I could command, "Escaped Prisoners-of-war".

The Gunner Corporal, for this was he whose voice we heard, was in charge of an anti-tank gun which we could now see pointing in the direction we had come. He accepted us immediately at face-value, despite our appearance, asked no further questions and pointed us in the direction of his HQ. Here we were given cigarettes and, as the officer was still asleep, we walked on to Brigade HQ.

Even though it was still only five o'clock in the morning we expected some kind of reception committee. Instead we were arrested.

Everyone, including the duty officer, appeared to be asleep. We hung about on a railway siding until a kind soldier took pity on us and gave us a bed in a railway wagon until daylight. We were made to feel that our arrival at this hour in the morning was most inconvenient, and it was only after a lengthy interrogation by the brigade major that we were finally invited into the officers' mess where we ate an enormous breakfast, a breakfast such as we had dreamed of every morning of our captivity and escape.

We got a lift down to 8th Army HQ and were greeted by many old friends, but the transformation from *contadino* to British officer was only half complete. Even after we had bathed and changed we had not yet crossed the psychological barrier.

At Tac HQ we found that Monty was away in England for a conference. But his ADC, Johnny Henderson, looked after us. For our first night of freedom Archie was put in Monty's caravan captured from the Italians. I found him the next morning lying in what had been General Messe's bed, with the plan of campaign on his knees sipping early morning tea! I had left Monty's HQ in November, 1942; it was now mid-October 1943, almost a year later. During our walk down Italy we reckoned to have covered twice the distance 'as the crow flies', in fact about 1000 kilometres or over 600 miles. But this was pure guesswork; who could say the distance we had actually walked? However, our relentless progress had saved us from a terrible winter, probably snow-bound sheltering in a cave, ending in almost certain re-capture and internment in Germany.

After a frustrating few days in a transit camp we were flown over to Algiers, from whence we took a troopship homeward bound. After a circuitous voyage via the mid-Atlantic, avoiding enemy submarine packs, we arrived safely back home at the beginning of November, 1943. Here Archie Hubbard and I parted company; it had been a most successful partnership. We landed in Liverpool. My family, then in Cheshire, had just received official notification of my passing through the lines. In fact it arrived the same day, much to my parents astonishment, that I walked through the front door. All was then revealed concerning the mysterious writer who had been posing as their son (see p.217), but the ruse which got me out of Chieti Camp turned out to be a blessing in disguise, for very few from Chieti managed to cross the lines.

Ten years later, in 1953, I was motoring down Italy with Philippa, my wife, to take up a military attaché post at the British Embassy, Athens. It seemed a golden opportunity to look up and, hopefully, repay some of the hospitality and shelter that we had received during our escape down Italy. The problem was how should we find these people? No names had been written down, nor sketch maps kept. Most of the *casa* had been well off the beaten track. It would be like looking for a needle in a haystack. There was only one *casa* of which I could positively fix a position. This farmhouse was near where the railway line crosses the River Pescara, the house where we encountered the German patrol and had been surprised in bed. Philippa and I had now left Rome and were motoring along the road to Pescara, the very road above which Archie and I had lain in wait watching the German traffic. Suddenly it all came back to me and I jammed on the brakes. We had passed the railway bridge and there was the track up which we must have gone. We parked the car, full of our belongings being transported to Greece, as best we could by the narrow roadway.

Philippa and I scrambled up the track – 200 – 300 – 400 yards and I began to think I was mistaken. Then, suddenly, there it was, the old farmhouse just as delapidated as when I had last seen it. We knocked at the door, it creaked open. I began my long-rehearsed speech, '*Ecco! Prigoniori di guerra . . . , quarante-tre!*'

The door flew open! Looks of disbelief! Arms were flung round us. Embraces all round. They remembered! It was the same family, but our goatherd boy had emigrated to Australia. We were dragged inside and there by the familiar hearthside we were entertained to a feast. Then the whole family accompanied us down the track again, talking and laughing excitedly. When we got to the car we wondered what we could possibly give them. Our brand new travelling rugs, a recent wedding present, was the answer, and these we pressed upon them, more as a souvenir than a reward. They were overcome. And that moment made it all worthwhile.

Memories crowded back . . . the Italian submarine . . . the Yugoslav death-camp at Bari . . . the ghostly station at Castel Guelfo . . . the big bass bell at Fontanellato . . . hiding in the vineyard . . . 'escape a court-martial offence' . . . '*sempre in campagna*' . . . the betrayal . . . the young novices at Cerredolo . . . a price on our heads . . . the sinister charcoal burners in the chestnut woods . . . the German deserter . . . one more river to cross – safe at last.

In retrospect all worthwhile. But now more like a dream than reality.

PART VIII
THE SECOND FRONT

I REJOIN MONTGOMERY

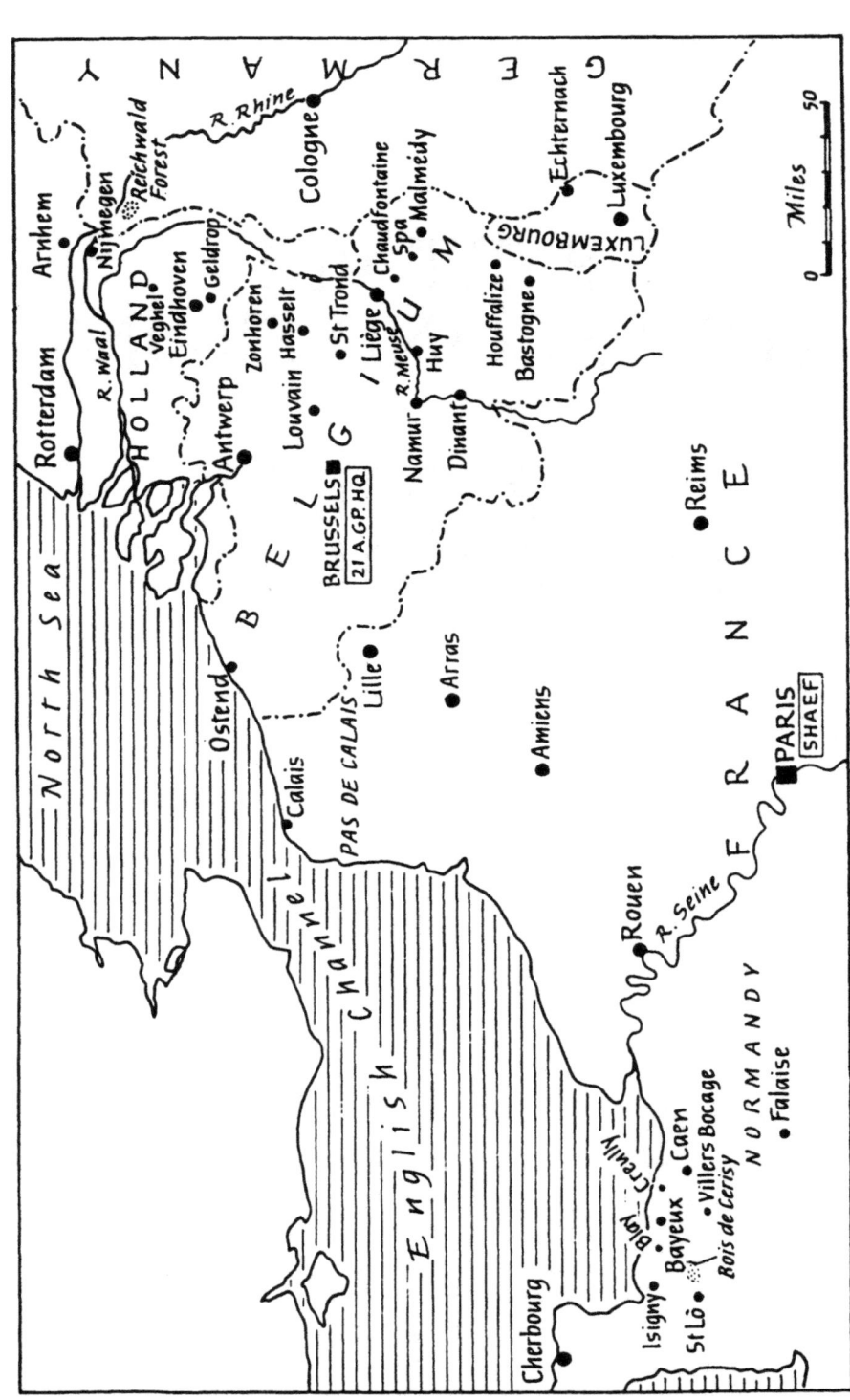

33

PREPARING FOR D-DAY

'ITS GOING TO BE QUITE A PARTY'

Poor England was very badly battered. London had become a ghost town, but how beautiful on a moonlight night to walk down those silent streets, the buildings, those still standing, being perfectly illuminated by the light of the moon, in one harmonious whole. And how romantic, I might add, for one who had been deprived of romance for so long. There was no special treatment of returned prisoners-of-war, no latter-day 'counselling' except that administered by the current girl friend. Often of an admonitary kind!

I had not witnessed an English spring since 1940 and, after a lapse of four years, the spring of 1944 was a revelation. This was my real homecoming. I saw the first signs of spring at Pickering Camp in Yorkshire where I had joined 2nd (Armoured) Bn, Welsh Guards. I felt it was high time I got back to my regiment after all this swanning about the world. It was part of the Guards Armoured Division which was training on the Yorkshire Wolds. I met many old friends. They were a delightful crowd and the men of the regiment with their Welsh lilt and whimsical sense of humour were a joy to be with again.

David Stirling was still languishing in Colditz and I could not face rejoining the SAS without his leadership and egregious sense of fun. The Commanding Officer of 2 WG, Jim Windsor-Lewis, another of the hard-riding set, made up for this loss, for Jim was a swashbuckling charmer who the men would have followed anywhere. The steadiness and high morale of all those people who had been for so long out of the mainstream of the war was truly remarkable and, for someone as jaundiced as myself, most refreshing. John Spencer was my Squadron Commander; he was considerably older than us but he had a way with his young officers. To him they were known as 'the bears', and the bears were always getting into trouble, either absconding over a weekend, having too much to drink, or dabbling in black market petrol. The tank park would, of course, have been a temptation, but the authorities had thoughtfully dyed tank fuel red, so woe betide anyone found with that in their petrol tank.[1] But there were a series of black market sources which were kept a deadly secret except to those in the know.

The most notorious was that of 'the Governor', a big fat chap who kept a workshop under the railway arches at Hammersmith Broadway, some way distant from Pickering, Yorkshire, it must be said, but handy for a quick flip to London in the old banger to see the girlfriend, switching off and free-wheeling down every hill in order to save the precious fluid. The password which inevitably produced the goods went as follows:

'Morning, Gov. Fill me up with the usual please.'

Then he would scowl and oblige for the outrageous sum of £10.

On one occasion I was lucky enough to be attached to a destroyer, HMS *Cossack*, in passage from Hull to the south coast for an invasion practice. It was commanded by Lt-Commander 'Hughie' Hodgkinson (DSC and Bar)[2] whose brother Reggie served in our battalion. The voyage entailed passing through the English Channel by night, with occupied France only a few miles away. The Commander was on the bridge all night wearing his emblem, a cossack hat, and peering into the fog which had then descended. We were clearly lost and none of those lovely new instruments such as asdics seemed to help us find our way. 'If we hit the coast of France tell them up front to shove us off again!' he exclaimed at one moment. We eventually made it to Studland Bay in Dorset where we were to bombard the coast with live shells in a mock landing. Our little party of Welsh Guardsmen were eventually put ashore at Portsmouth, and then began a dreamlike train journey through the heart of England – but oh how slowly! The spring had blossomed to its full glory. I could not believe it! The birds screamed, primroses crowded the banks and a distant haze of blue smudged the woodland floor signifying the arrival of the first bluebells.

About this time I was sent for by Montgomery. He invited me to become one of his LOs for the invasion of Europe. Loth as I was to leave my new-found friends it was an invitation I could not turn down. I went to see him at Claridge's Hotel, a rather unusual campsite for one so contemptuous of the comforts of life.

His words, as ever, were short and to the point: 'This is going to be quite a party!' Adding ruefully, 'If you come with me your chances of survival are not very good!' I did not realize at the time how true those words might become.

The Guards Armoured Division moved south to their assembly area for the invasion, to Brighton, now a fortified salient. All the tanks were camouflaged up under trees or other cover, in our case the municipal gardens in the centre of Brighton. My parting memory was of inspecting the half-completed picture by Rex Whistler on the wall in the parlour of his billet nearby, entitled 'The Spirit of Brighton'.

Southwick House outside Portsmouth was the headquarters of Montgomery, who was in command of all the Land Forces, British, American and Canadian. Eisenhower, as Supreme Commander, had his headquarters there too. The number of LOs for the coming battle had now expanded to some seven or eight in number, including two Americans. Walking through the tented camp in the park at Southwick it was as if I was back again in the Western Desert, the headquarters all laid out according to plan, with many familiar faces.

'20 May, 1944

I arrived down here a few days ago and this evening had dinner with the CinC. Broomfield House is a white house in the country surrounded by oak trees and lawns. Monty's caravans are out on the lawn, and the ADCs and various other dog's bodies are in Nissen huts. I was presently called in to the great man. Seated in his study he asked me to "sit down or remain standing". This rhetorical invitation left me standing on my feet! He showed me a pair of engraved binoculars "Look what I've been given", he said proudly.

'The room was full of photographs and pictures and together we walked round and looked at them. On a table were Eisenhower, Tedder, Coningham and Ramsay. On the wall between the two windows was a large photograph of himself underneath which hung the coloured photograph of Rommel, which we had captured at Matruh and which he had hanging in his caravan ever since.

'"Perhaps," I suggested "you will have him to dine one night as you did Von Thoma?" "I hope so," he replied giving me a sharp look.'

'On the wall nearest the door was the photograph of himself standing in the ruins of a church at Ortona [in Italy], looking up rather wistfully at the shattered roof.

'"Yes, rather a good picture," he said as he paused in front of it. "I didn't know it was being taken".'

Now I was to hear the third great eve-of-battle oration that Monty made. My mind went back to the first on Salisbury Plain, the second on the eve of Alamein, and now here at Southwick House, before the great invasion.

On 2 June all the staff officers of 21st Army Group were gathered together and addressed by Monty on the lawn at Southwick House. We were sitting on green tarpaulins on the former tennis court. There was an air of expectancy among those gathered there. Officers of various ranks and even generals were squatting cross-legged on the ground.

Before us was a simple jeep with some mounting steps up to the flat bonnet. Behind this podium was a wood of tall chestnut trees in its fresh green livery. At our backs was the valley separating us from Portsdown Hill. It was a beautiful fresh sunny morning.

These occasions were carefully stage-managed, for Monty was by now a pastmaster at the art. The CinC's Rolls drew up behind us and, accompanied by an ADC, he walked slowly towards us. He paused to greet an American general. We all clambered to our feet and he motioned us to sit down again. He began in his usual undramatic way with a 'Now tell me if you can hear me at the back!' And this was the gist of what he had to say:

> 'I have gathered you together, all the officers of my staff, because I think it is a very good thing at such a time for us to have a talk. What I am going to do now is to "check up on" the war – to see how it's going, and where we stand. We will divide it into three phases, past, present and future . . . '

He then proceeded to give a *tour d'horizon* of the present state of the world and our part in it. It may be a surprise that Monty addressed his very intelligent staff officers in such simplistic terms, but the essence of his technique was clarity. Everyone knew exactly where they stood, where they were going and their part in the proceedings. The 'fog of war' was for a moment dispelled and the curtain lifted on future events. Those seated on the ground eagerly drank in his words. He spoke about the bad times that both we and the Americans (after they had come in) had been through. Of our four major objectives, one had been to drive the Germans out of Africa, two, to knock the Italians out of the war, three, to bring Turkey into the war, and four, to beat the Germans on their own soil.

He forecast that we would be in Berlin by the end of the year and that Japan would be out of the war six months thereafter. He concluded by giving five points to remember in the coming battle:

First, solidarity with our allies.

Second, fitness in body and mind, together with a belief in the righteousness of the cause.

Third, confidence. 'I may say that never in the history of the world had a better trained army left this country.'

Fourth, enthusiasm for the cause for which we are fighting.

Fifth, all-out effort and relentless pursuit, particularly in the initial stages of the landing.

For a moment, after he had finished speaking, time stood still as minds dwelt on the enormity of the task, whilst Monty intoned the words of Montrose.

'He either fears his fate too much,
Or his deserts are small,
That will not put it to the touch,
To win or lose it all.'

Then everyone burst out cheering and we knew we were going to win.[3]

It was now 2 June and we were within two or three days of D-Day. In the previous ten days we were occupied in familiarizing ourselves with plans and order of battle, but a plot emerged for the LOs to make a lightning tour of the south coast to visit commanders and staff we should have to deal with once we had landed. This was the cunning plan of John Poston. But it was 'a cover plan', for the real plan was to give us time for a final visit to families and girlfriends. In retrospect, I must say it was a most hair-raising proceeding for we were by now fully briefed and, following this process, everyone was supposed to be incarcerated in 'cages' – secure areas from which they could not escape!

The ostensible plan was to take three jeeps the length of the south coast to British and Canadian HQ on the basis of a carefully contrived time-table, to be completed in about sixty hours. The real plan was to complete this process in thirty hours, thus giving thirty hours of freedom to ourselves. All was quiet and carefully camouflaged in southern England, but the noise of jeep engines must have shattered the still air as we hurtled through the countryside to complete our visits and keep our trysts. We were to RV again at the Anchor Hotel at Liphook and thence to Brighton to spend the night before returning to Portsmouth. All went according to plan. For the night we found rooms in the Norfolk Hotel on Brighton's embattled seafront, and whilst the others were preparing for dinner I paid a last visit to my old Squadron where I had left it in the leafy suburbs. Being pressed for time on return I left my jeep outside the hotel and during dinner it was promptly pinched. It contained all John Poston's operational kit and mementos from his lady friend. Ah well – such are the hazards of love and war!

SPRING 1944

Earth like a hammered anvil shakes:
Quiet in the woods the bluebell wakes.

Vaster the cold seas's catacombs:
On western cliffs the sea-pink blooms.

Ten thousand deaths shriek down from Heaven:
Twitters the lark in the hush of even.

The dawn of the judgement reds the sky:
From her tomb twinkles the butterfly.

F.L. Lucas

34

THE NORMANDY LANDINGS

We loaded the Landing Ship Tank (LST) with our headquarters vehicles on 4 June, after some delay, owing to the storms at sea. I noted in my diary:

'We are sailing out of Gosport Hard in breezy weather, past the *Victory* and the old dockside at Portsmouth. Now we are lying in the Solent at anchor. Shipping is massed at Spithead in an immense quantity. I only hope this wind does not last and we can get moving tomorrow.

'5 June

'Yesterday was Sunday and as we drove through the old wharfside at Gosport the church bells were ringing. It all seemed so unreal and peaceful. I do not think a quarter of the men taking part in this great invasion realize its true significance, the liberation of Europe, the greatest seaborne invasion that has ever, in the history of the world, left these shores. The Second Army, comprising all Britain's manhood (apart from those fighting in Italy and Burma) about to make a seaborne invasion of France.'

My thoughts went back to the last time I had sailed away to war, in 1941, that glad morning so long ago it now seemed. And what had become of all my fine companions of those days, George Jellicoe, Gavin Astor, David Stirling, Frank Usher and Dermot Daly, Ian Collins, Randolph Churchill and Evelyn Waugh?

'Four years ago – we were certainly fresh then – and on the brink of a fine adventure. We were a compact society of soldiers, ready to do anything, and we were all such friends. Now they are all scattered,' I added nostalgically.

My diary which I now hold in my hand, and which was written on that very deck as I surveyed the scene, has a salt-sea tang as I turn its pages.

> 'But on this second time we leave England, we are all completely calm and stoic, hardly a glimmer of excitement as we go through the motions. (We must be tired.)
>
> 'Yesterday I was so amused by the men. They were being briefed by the Colonel (Leo Russell) as to where they were going to in France. They all sat spellbound as the maps were unfurled and the full story came out. As it came to an end, like an ENSA show, they all suddenly burst into loud clapping! It must have been the best and most exciting news for years. Up till now the complete lack of emotion and matter-of-factness which has attended all our moves has, I think, been a good sign.'

I add in my diary that 'today' (5 June) we had been due to land in France, but owing to the wind it had been put off for 24 hours,

> 'Now the powers-that-be are determined that, if possible, we shall do it tomorrow. But still the gale blows, the first real wind that we have had for a month. Surely the Almighty has some control of the weather on such an important occasion?'

It was well-nigh impossible, with the invasion fleet fully loaded with men and equipment, to delay any further. To keep the men cooped up in incredibly cramped and uncomfortable conditions for another 24 hours would have had a serious effect on their fighting capability. So, whatever the weather, the armada had to sail and Eisenhower knew this when he took the decision.

One's thoughts now began to turn upon the hours ahead and the fate that might await each one of us.

> 'It is always curious to think, before these great battles, that here we are – whole and alive and healthy – and in a few days' time that many of our's and the enemy's side will be dead. I remember thinking the same as I sat in the shade of a lean-to beneath Monty's caravan the day before Alamein, and it is the same again now – nothing can be more certain.'[1]

I keep on reminding myself of who I am and where I am going to provide a little dutch courage.

> 'It is now 18 months since I have taken part in any battle – a long time, and I am immensely thrilled. As we passed the *Victory* yesterday one of the men cried,
> "Look Joe – there's the *Victory*."
> "What the bluddy 'ell is that!"
> "That's the 'owd *Victory*," the first one repeated. Now they sit composed and quiet waiting patiently for the wind to drop. They know how to wait. They have done it for four years!'

We slid past Nelson's flagship (chequerboard sides, no camouflage there) to take up our position in the Solent.

> 'On this LST we have a third of the CinC's Tac HQ. The officers being John Poston, 'Smithy' the MT officer and three Americans. The rest lie quite close to us. If we attempt to land in this gale, or even in calm weather we are going to have a few very anxious days trying to maintain ourselves with supplies before the rest can land. A few hours ago we heard over the BBC that Rome had fallen – our first capital in Europe! Tomorrow equally momentous news will be passed over the BBC. For we are to land in France tomorrow morning – D-Day. We have heard that our ship is due in some time in the afternoon. The wind has luckily abated and the first flight has already left the Solent. We sail about midnight.'

The terrific news about Rome had been broadcast aboard our ship with special recordings from the capitol. We heard the bells of St Peter's mingled with the sound of tanks and guns, the cheers of the Romans, delirious with happiness. Liberation after twenty-one years of Mussolini rule. The BBC man said that never had there been such a Roman Holiday. "*Spero che in Roma ero eggi*," I thought in bastard Italian.

And yet, during all this the officers in the wardroom were content to sit stolidly over their cards. Only one spoke. "What a bloody awful noise!"

> '6 *June [D-Day]*
> We are now in open sea, sailing along accompanied by a vast fleet of many assorted craft. HMS *Rodney* [the British battleship]

is on our port beam. It is now just before lunch, and a glorious day – quite a swell so far. I am sitting on the deck with my feet over the side and my back against the wheel of a truck, secured to the deck. A destroyer has just raced past. We should land about 5 p.m. A message has just been intercepted from the beaches saying that vehicles have been landed and they are busy destroying mines and obstructions.

'It is very peaceful on deck now. Lunch is over, pork, sweetcorn and tinned pears. I am smoking a pipe and reading intermittently *Testament of Youth*. The sea is blue with small white horses, purple in patches where the clouds cast shadows. The BBC News has just announced the landings, and the Germans say there is heavy fighting near Caen, which is ten miles inland from where we are landing. I cannot see the coast of France yet – but we are told that some 9,000 bombers are pounding the coast and the beach landing areas, but very few planes have passed over us except for our fighter cover.'

'The coast of France is now quite clearly visible. From the top of the car [on the deck of the ship] in which I am riding I can see the Cherbourg Peninsula. The American Sector is quite clearly on the starboard bow. From the direction of Cherbourg port is a long continuous line of ships, returning to England for a second load. The line is unbroken from horizon to horizon. As far as I can see through my glasses none of them are damaged. I can see trees and fields on the coast and smoke – white smoke not black as one would have expected. But the coast is still about ten miles off so everything is rather a blur. I can hear no noise yet at all, and can see no aircraft in the air. Yes, now I can hear a noise, a deep thudding quite close [probably the naval bombardment]. The men have just gone down to get their tea. We should land in about 1½ hours. From the intercepts that are coming through we are apparently doing quite well. 30 Corps have reached Bonville.'

There was to be no landing that day. As I remark laconically in my diary 'the usual form! Twenty-four hours lying off the beaches because we were unable to unload – sea too rough and not enough beach exits.'

'7 June
An amazing 24 hours; not a single enemy aircraft seen, and a vast armada of ships lying off the coast – almost 7,000 I should say of all types – a fantastic sight, and no shelling from the shore.

Admittedly there were air raids last night, but very poor attempts, and as far as I know nothing damaged.'

The Allied deception plan had evidently been a huge success. This gave the impression that the landings were to take place in the Pas de Calais area. The Germans deployed only a thin screen covering the Normandy beachheads.

'At low tide this afternoon (7 June) we stuck fast a few hundred yards from the shore. So we will have to wait until the tide rises. We should get off late tonight.'

The situation was unreal. Here we are, at the outset of the great invasion, stuck within a few hundred yards of the enemy coast unable to move. To a shore battery we would have been a sitting duck, but the shore batteries, such as they were were silent, themselves the victims of superior fire-power. This enforced idleness gave me time for a few philosophical thoughts. I had just finished the wartime chapters of *Testament of Youth*.[2]

'I am ruminating on the passages in Vera Brittain's classic about the Great War and the enormous casualties sustained in France, a mere thirty years ago. What would be our fate? Only time would tell.'

Our Chief, the CinC, was aboard a destroyer, which had its own adventures, but by this time he had landed. But we had all his transport. It was therefore imperative that we land as soon as possible. Water-proofing and, upon landing, de-water-proofing of vehicles was a time-consuming part of the enterprise which added to the hazards of an opposed landing and the gaining of a lodgement area ashore.

'8 June
Yesterday evening, just after I had finished writing, a 'Rhino' ferry came alongside our ship. And into that we loaded all our seventy vehicles. The few Ducks (DUKWS) which we had aboard swam off the LST and waited in the water until we were ready to move. It was eleven o'clock at night when we pulled away from our mother-ship and almost dark. Our Rhino splashed across a mile of sea until we reached an open space on shore. The 'Queen Mary' staff car I was riding in with Smithy was to be first off. The

soldier acting as lookout and leadsman on the ferry stood at the side and shouted, "Six foot!" as he shoved his pole down.

"Fukin 'ell!" said the soldiers as we slowly glided in.

"Four and a half foot!"

"Come on chum, do the job proper," they jeered.

"Three foot!"

"That's the way lads!"

"One and a half foot!"

"Just the job!" came the cry.

We then slid onto the shore with a grinding, scraping sound.'

We had landed, unopposed, in Normandy.

35

BIZARRE ENCOUNTERS

In the twilight I looked for the Beachmaster, who, I hoped, would tell us which way to go. Then I jumped onto the shore, but I could find nobody who knew the way to our assembly area. So I signalled to Smithy to drive off and the staff car splashed into the water and climbed steeply up the shore. We turned right and followed the shoreline.

'From the sea the land had looked green and peaceful with trees, old stone churches and villages undisturbed. Apart from the jam of boats on the shore, the columns of smoke and the distant thudding we might have been lying off Spithead. Then, once having set foot on shore, one became aware of the urgency of battle. There was the acrid, pungent smell of powder; of damp clinging dust thrown up from tracks and ruined buildings; then of evening earth and herbage, mingled with petrol fumes and tank exhausts; the incongruous scent of may and lilac drifted from inshore. All these confused the senses already purged by sea air.'

A few yards inland and we approached a cross-tracks. In the dim light I found a Redcap at his wit's end. He was trying to direct a series of convoys all converging on his spot. There were four columns of equal emergency.

'Our own had to be off the ferry and inland as soon as possible; a convoy of Ducks laden with wounded was trying to get to the sea; a vast ammunition column was trying to pass laterally to reach another sector of the front. Tired voices were heard in the darkness,

"I've got sixty wounded, Sarge, in them Ducks."
"Orders to get the ammo up before dark".
"Which way to 102 Beach Group, Sarge?"
"Seen anything of 74 Commando?"'

None of these voices sounded as if they expected an answer – and none came.

At length we found ourselves in a quiet country lane, thick with powdered dust, which cast a white shroud on the hedges. We headed inland past shattered houses and villages which still reeked of explosive. In the *Place* of one village we passed a '14–'18 war memorial with withered roses round its base. The next moment a small château loomed, standing virgin and white behind iron gates, with a garden full of scented flowers. Then followed an *Estaminet*, a *Manoir* and a farm half-hidden by clinging roses.

> 'Roses were everywhere, climbing cottage walls or clinging to broken masonry. It was one of the first things that I noticed, a sight which further confused the senses.'

After we had driven in this way for about five miles, we stopped by the side of the road, got out our bedding rolls and slept.

As morning dawned we shook ourselves awake. Rumour had it that our men were a good ten miles inland and had over-run Bayeux. This was unexpectedly good news. Not so with the American landings; they had encountered tough resistance, and as we heard later cost a lot of lives.

We held a council of war. John Poston and Smithy would stay with the column, Trumball Warren (Monty's Canadian PA) and myself would recce forward to find the planned location of Monty's Tac HQ.

At Creully we found the château of Cruellet where we expected Tac to be established. It was a fine house, simple but dignified. The gates were closed. Beyond the gates one could see the drive circle round an overgrown lawn in front of the house. Another drive led to the stables and retainers' quarters. On the other side of the house was a long ornamental lake with stone steps dropping down to the water. On each side of the lake were parklands containing great sycamore trees.

> 'It was a gorgeous morning, the air heavy with mist, through which the sun was shining weakly. Our surroundings had an air of peace and that, coupled with our dramatic arrival in a new

country, made one feel that this was not war at all but one was returning home late from a dance!'

The rusty gates swung open with a groan. We inched them wide enough for a jeep and, leaving tracks in the untrodden gravel, reached the front door. The head of a girl appeared at a top window.

> '"*Est-ce que vous avez les soldats ici?*" I called (meaning 'British') and she pointed to one of the outbuildings and laughed.
> "*C'est à qui cette maison?*"
> "*A L'Abbé de Douval*".

So we walked towards the stone terrace at the foot of the outbuildings. As we did so one of the doors opened and out walked some figures in grey.

> 'I did not realize at first that they were Germans. And the next moment I did not know if we were their prisoners or they ours.'

The confusion was resolved by Trum and I drawing our pistols and ordering them to walk down the drive. There were twelve of them and they seemed unarmed. With their hands up, Trum covered them with a revolver whilst I searched them. In the barn we found all their rifles, pistols and ammunition.

> 'The girl was still leaning out of the window laughing. So we put the prisoners on the road and said to an under-officer, in a mixture of French and German,
> "*Marche! Nach Crépon*".
> And they shambled off.'

After a few hours we returned to the château and met an elderly lady pottering around the flowerbeds. She was wearing a shabby tweed skirt and shoes down at heel, on her head a wide-brimmed straw hat with navy blue band. She carried a trowel and some gardening gloves. The details are indelibly printed on my mind.

> '"*Peut être dans le bois,*" she replied to our anxious enquiries about further Germans on the place. "If you speak slowly I can understand English," she added. "Of course," she went on, "for four years we have had Germans living here in our house. But

they are not as bad as the Russians – a whole regiment of 'mongols' in our field which you can see beyond the gate. And then they come into the garden and cut down all our beautiful trees. And when they go they leave some of their little wagons – there is one by the corner of the wood. But they were something barbarous – for each man three horses!"

"Did you know, or did the Germans know that we were coming?" we asked.

"The Germans said always that you would come. That they would go back, but return and drive you into the sea again. For myself I did not think that you would come. Yes, it is certainly a relief that you are here".'

The voice trailed on, then the garden was at peace again. Above the sound of war planes and the distant battle the birds were singing in the wood, a dark wood with ivy-covered floor. We found no Germans here, but in the centre of the wood was an ancient gateway, rose and ivy-covered. Round the roses clustered bees loudly going about their business. Like Madame De Doubal they seemed to be unaffected by the events of the last few days.

'The bombardment; the rush of tanks and guns had swept past the rusty iron gates of the château. Standing in front of the house, you could only tell that the greatest event of our day had taken place, by the scattered German equipment on the lawn and, a little earlier, this dejected group of German prisoners standing on the gravel drive and who had asked plaintively if they might retrieve some of their personal possessions from the barn.'

It was hard to tell what was going on in the mind of Madame De Douval – an intelligent woman. That she could say "It is certainly a relief" meant only that one invader was, to her, the same as another. So long as the interior of her house was undisturbed she did not care whether it was English or Germans, so it seemed. I could detect no hatred of our common enemy in her voice, as would have been the case in the immediate pre-war years, only a note of resignation. It is true that her husband, L'Abbé De Douval, had pedalled on his bicycle down to the village to inform the authorities of the presence of the Germans lying in his barn, as would have been expected from an ex-cavalry officer. He appeared a little later, a tall slightly bent old gentleman in a dark blue suit, a black hat and high-winged collar.

For a brief few hours the old couple were at the centre of events. Their permission was obtained for British soldiers to enter their grounds.

'Then with the suddenness of the invasion itself another world is superimposed on that of their own, and the two, although within each other's ambit, are as unconnected as life on two separate planets. First, the Commander-in-Chief establishes his battle headquarters on their lawn, in the dark green wood, and in the field. He himself lives in a complex of heavily camouflaged tents and caravans on the front lawn only a few yards from the house. The De Douvals do not yet know who he is. They do not know that two of his caravans have travelled with him from Alamein, in the Egyptian desert, to Central Italy. They do not know that in one of the caravans is a large map of the present campaign, and upon this map is depicted events which are to influence so profoundly the future of France and the remainder of their days.'

Then later, whilst the old gentleman sits in his study giving instructions to his one remaining retainer concerning the potatoes and tomatoes in his kitchen garden, the Commander-in-Chief sits a few yards away discussing the fateful and dramatic events with Churchill. In a procession the great men pass: General Eisenhower, General de Gaulle, General Smuts.

During these first few days of the allied landings one mysterious remark of Madame De Douval was made clear to me. I was scouting around in the neighbourhood of Cruelly and had ordered my driver to pull the jeep into a farmyard to study the map. We were against a high wall and some unusual noises were coming from the other side, which made me stand on the bonnet and beckon the driver up. I could not at first believe my eyes for there appeared to be a regiment of cavalrymen about to mount their horses. Which war was I in, I began to wonder. When they saw our berets poking over the top, hurried orders were given, and in some disarray they mounted and clattered away. At first glance it seemed they were German soldiers in the regulation grey-green. But something peculiar struck me about the boots and headgear of these stocky little men. And then I remembered the words of Madame De Douval,

'"*Horr les Mongols!* They were something barbarous – for each man three horses!"'

For these were indeed the 'barbarians' of which she had spoken who had desecrated her fine trees. This was the first occasion we came to realize that Russians were fighting on the German side. We came to capture them, or receive their surrender, in increasing numbers, much to the astonishment and embarrassment of our Soviet allies who could not believe these stories. These Cossacks had been recruited by the Germans on the eastern front and used as low-grade troops on the long exposed coastline of northern France. Their capture and subsequent disposal was a cause of deep acrimony between ourselves and the Soviets, for they were to appear on other German fronts as well. The dispute over their fate lasted until well after the end of the war.[1]

36

VISIT OF DE GAULLE

Visits by VIPs to Montgomery's headquarters in Normandy became a bit of a problem for they hindered his concentration on the battle.

Such distractions went against his philosophy of 'command in war', that a commander should have 'time to think', away from the bustle of a big headquarters. Hence his creation of a small battle or tactical headquarters. He was therefore not very pleased by the insistence that, following others, De Gaulle should be allowed to visit France. On the face of it not an unreasonable request.

Montgomery's views on De Gaulle were well known, best expressed in his announcement, the day after the visit, that 'a cat on heat would not be excited by General De Gaulle'! During our second week in Normandy we were precariously balanced trying to extend our lodgement area. Accordingly the visit was arranged on a strict timetable lasting only a few hours. Even so it caused quite a 'flutter in the dovecots' of Tac HQ. I wrote,

> '15 June
> The events of the day had followed each other in hilarious succession. Sticky cakes had been ordered for De Gaulle's lunch by one of the ADCs. It was explained to the Chief that this formed an indispensable part of a Frenchman's midday meal. It also formed a fourth course in the C-in-C's mess – the custom was normally three. With an "if three courses are enough for me they are good enough for De Gaulle," Monty banned the cakes which did not appear on the luncheon table, but were consumed for tea, after De Gaulle had departed.'

After the carefully planned luncheon De Gaulle was to be taken to

Bayeux, in a jeep, escorted by 'Fuzzy' Sanderson, a fellow LO. Here he was to address the citizenry, returning to his destroyer, *La Combattante*, by four in the afternoon.[1]

At 1.15 p.m., a quarter of an hour after lunch had been ordered, 'Fuzzy' rang up from the beaches in a flap to say that the General had decided not to land until after the midday meal. But this had no further consequences, for lunch had already started punctually at one!

When he eventually arrived the Chief advanced towards him with a "Welcome to France, mon General!" and shook him firmly by the hand. The greetings over, the General was to address a representative body of British and American soldiers at his request. The only handy representatives were soldiers from our own defence platoon. So they were gathered in a square about the person of the French General.

'De Gaulle spoke in a torrent of words lasting several minutes. The soldiers regarded him in wondering awe, with blank uncomprehending expressions. Blank, because the General spoke in French, a language which they could not comprehend. The speech ended as abruptly as it had begun. Then his ADC stepped forward and translated,

"The General thanks you for your gallant liberation of France."

The soldiers' response was a muttered, "Fukin' 'ell!" and left at that!'

Sanderson had been instructed to allow only three Frenchmen up to our HQ, but he had been overwhelmed by sheer numbers and seventeen eventually arrived clinging onto the three jeeps that had been alloted. The party included Admirals, Generals and senior airmen, with a few civilians as well, De Gaulle's object apparently being to overcome by weight of numbers any obstruction that might have been placed in his path!

'So the little party of three jeeps set off for Bayeux, 'Fuzzy' driving the leading jeep with De Gaulle, awkwardly crammed into the passenger seat, and the retinue clinging on to the jeeps behind. The civilian population evidently did not realize who they had in their midst, so the occupants of the second vehicle pointed to the first and shouted "De Gaulle!"'

The reception at Bayeux was very disappointing to the visitors. About

500 people gathered in the square, clapped and shouted, but it was not the kind of reception to be expected of one who had come to liberate his country after four years of oppression. An educated woman who needed a rest asked to be allowed to sit in 'Fuzzy's' jeep and murmured to him in an aside that De Gaulle would never get a good reception in these parts as they were all communist!

Above all the people of Bayeux (which suffered no war damage) were thoroughly bewildered. Here was a French expatriate announcing liberation by other French expatriates. But there were already three other potential governments, the German, the Vichy and the Allied, and German propaganda had not yet lost its grips on French minds. I wrote,

> 'I read in The Times today [15 June] a headline proclaiming "The silent tears of Bayeux and the cheers of Rome", which compared the difference between the two liberated lands. I cannot understand it. One would have thought that De Gaulle would have been proclaimed as a national hero.'

Back at Tac HQ the next thing we heard was that De Gaulle's retinue had been seen heading for Isigny, a town in the American Sector, still in the company of 'Fuzzy' Sanderson, whilst the French leader was by now expected to have re-embarked aboard his destroyer to cross the Channel again. Also that rooms had been booked that night in the Lion d'Or at Bayeux for De Gaulle and all his suite.

> 'I was in the Chief's map wagon at the time giving him a report on the situation on one of the divisional fronts, when Col. Russell came in and announced this news. This caused a good deal of consternation, for if De Gaulle had taken it into his head to proclaim a Provisional Government with himself as titular head, it would be very difficult to control or even arrest him! For he had been specifically warned against making political speeches whilst in France.'

Monty decided that, as this was clearly a political matter, he could make no arrests or other moves unless directed to by the PM. The man was clearly a menace and would upset all our plans for the orderly transfer of power.

Meantime John Poston, who, like the rest of us, should have been up in the battle area, was dispatched post haste to the Lion d'Or at

Bayeux to investigate the hotel bookings. After a record run he returned to confirm that "five singles and one double" had been booked in the name of De Gaulle.

De Gaulle had indeed slipped into Isigny, a location not on his itinerary, and delivered a similar speech. He then visited a number of villages on the Normandy coast in one of which the General had been repeatedly embraced by two drunken American GIs from whom he had great difficulty in freeing himself. However, he may not have realized the reason for this ardour. For he is reported to have remarked afterwards that his welcome by the Americans was extremely cordial!

Arriving back at the beach it appeared that the French party's intention had been to collect their baggage and return to the Lion d'Or.[2] But here De Gaulle encountered the British Naval Officer in Charge (NOIC) every bit as determined as himself.[3] From his long black beard to his open neck shirt and shorts, with grey issue socks turned down over his army boots, he was evidently a character to be reckoned with. It is said that De Gaulle was given a direct order to get into his jeep and drive down to the ferry awaiting on the beach.

> 'Fuzzy Sanderson arrived back dusty and jaded with a jeep-full of wilting roses. A day or two later when the King was presenting decorations at our HQ, Fuzzy Sanderson was in the line-up to receive an MC, won earlier at Termoli in Italy. The King, after asking where he had won it, then demanded, "And how did you get on with De Gaulle?"'[4]

A few days later, before we left the château, I went and visited Madame De Douval once again to thank her and her husband for their hospitality.

> '*17 June*
> We went into the drawing room of the 18th century château and asked her many questions. Lying on a sofa was an old map of the area. Across it ran a cat's cradle of string marking the reported positions of our advance. It was the old man's map, and I corrected his line in places bringing it down a little further south to include the Bois de Cerisy.
> "Here," pointed the old lady, "you must be very careful in this terrain – *sud de* Villers Bocage – there are guns and emplacements; for years the Germans have been working on them. *Prenez garde!*"

She continued, "In the village they were saying that your General was here, but we did not ask. Yes, of course I had heard of him from *Afrique. Et Monsieur Churchill – et le Roi*. I did not see the King but I knew afterwards that he was here. De Gaulle! *Pas!* We do not want him. He is not the man for France. All the people here you know are very conservative. They do not like change. He is ambitious and unscrupulous. Poor old Pétain. He is an old man, you know, and he has had a very difficult job. But he has only one thought – for France! And during these four years he has done a lot for the poor French people. He has also helped England by not collaborating with the Germans as he might and refusing to raise the army again."[5]

She believed, although she was only speaking for a small Department, that this feeling was reflected over the whole of France. And then there were the prisoners – a million French prisoners in Germany, young people who were 'very active in their minds'. She paused.

'Poor France; for me it is easy to see that there will be civil war if De Gaulle is put in. Ah! But De Gaulle – you would have thought that he would have called into our house when he was here to see my husband, who is an ex-officer, a contemporary of the last war!'

I could not make out whether it was this slight which was responsible for the scorn for De Gaulle or whether it was the effect of insidious German propaganda. But clearly there was a problem here, and some truth in what she said. One could see how France had been divided into three blocs.

First the Fighting French, small in numbers but powerful, believing that their leader should (with our support) control the country.

Then the million French prisoners held in Germany, with leisure enough to study the causes of France's downfall, full of ideas for future action, believing that they, martyred, had the right to impose a solution.

Lastly, the people of France itself. Having suffered four years of German occupation, bewildered by the corrosive German propaganda, wanting a strong man, but wanting also peace.

All three blocs separated by the wide gulf of profound and varied experiences. There was a parallel in our own country.

'It is very easy to see. Our own soldiers returning from the Middle East after two or three years of active service. The soldiers at home bored and jealous – there was feeling between the two. To a major extent that will be true of France.'

Madame De Douval interrupted my thoughts.

'"The soldier who was killed by the shell," she asked at length, "is he buried by the Avenue? Because I can make some arrangements for him."'

We walked together to look for the grave in the avenue but could find no traces. We never found it.[6]

37

MOTORBIKES AND SNIPERS

Apart from the domestic life which characterized Monty's headquarters, as described in a previous chapter, there was no time lost in getting operational. The day after landing, LOs set out for the various salients where the fighting was taking place.

A major blow to our esteem was the decision that, after we had landed, LOs should be mounted on army motorcycles instead of jeeps. The 'loading manifests' of landing ships did not allow for any 'surplus' vehicles over and above what were required for the initial assault. Representation to the Chief had no effect. He had to set an example with his headquarters too. The country south of Bayeux was rather park-like, cornfields interspersed with clumps of tall trees. These trees, being in full leaf, were ideal cover for enemy 'stay behind' snipers. In the first few days snipers were a perfect menace and accounted for many casualties. The 'pop-pop-pop' of a motorbike made it impossible to hear the 'ping' of a sniper's bullet. Having not ridden an army motorcycle since my cadet days it took some getting used to! There were no road signs so one had to navigate by map insecurely held between one's handle bars. As one increased speed so the map-board began to rise in the air and then took off, inflicting a glancing blow about the head as it did so.

Once off the beaten track one was often riding, breast high, through fields of corn in a pristine landscape (as had the British cavalry in 1914), but probably with not a friend or foe in sight, not really sure where one was going. Halting on one occasion to get my bearings, I was conscious of the deadly crack of a sniper's bullet, somewhere uncomfortably close, as it zipped through the air. Seizing my machine I pumped the kick-start until it eventually sprang into life and leapt forward. One hidden ditch was enough to bring bike and rider crashing to the ground in a sprawling mass, sunk beneath the undulating corn as if swallowed up by the sea. No cries for help would avail; there was no one about – except the sniper! On this occasion no power on earth would move the infernal machine which lay panting gently on the ground. I crawled away leaving the motorbike, as it gave a last splutter, where it lay. In no way could I continue like this! I came to a road with an unattended jeep parked on the side, together with some other vehicles and their crews. I walked straight to the jeep, got in and drove away. There was no hue and cry! I did not stop until I reached Tac HQ workshops. Here they obligingly painted out the divisional signs identifying the vehicle and replaced them with our own. Thus ended my second day in the bridgehead.

On the third day I moved out at dawn, centaur-like, glued to my jeep, ready to defy anyone to remove me from my new mount. Soon I had acquired a driver and various other modifications were made. A discarded German holster neatly held a litre pot, from time to time replenished with Normandy cream. Another container was handy for eggs; basic cooking and sleeping materials made one completely self-contained, should one somehow be involuntarily detained.

Monty's technique of command had not changed much from the time of the desert campaign. Admittedly there were now seven of us LOs, whereas I was on my own at Alamein. The two Americans, Maurice Frary and Eddie Prisk, were alloted to the American bridgehead, and five of us worked the British and Canadian sectors. First thing in the morning we would attend a briefing by our small Ops group, run by Paul Odgers, to get the latest 'gen' on the battle fronts. We would then fan out, each to his alloted sector, which was usually done by mutual agreement among ourselves. Colonel Russell, who was ostensibly in charge, would try to interfere but as he himself had no battle experience and we were veterans, so to speak, we simply bypassed him and appealed to the Chief himself if there was any problem. The object of our journeys was to obtain an eye-witness account of the situation, which Monty would invariably treat as the authentic version if there was any variation from 'the usual channels'. These reports of course included a visit to the Divisional or other commander on the spot on whose front we were reporting. This led to a very close one-to-one relationship between Monty and his commanders in the field. Nothing was written down except the hieroglyphics upon one's map board (chinagraph crayon on talc), which could easily be rubbed out in an emergency. Having been de-briefed by Odgers for the Ops Room map, we then repaired to Monty's caravan to mark up his maps. At about 9.00 p.m. we reported in turn to Monty himself who would be sitting in his map caravan on a camp stool. He would listen intently to what one had to say, ask a few questions and then it was over. It was quite clear from his interest where we had to concentrate the next day.

The Allied Armies had landed on a 40-mile front, the Americans on the right towards the Cherbourg Peninsula, the British in the centre opposite Bayeux, the Canadians on the left facing Caen. Initially we had gained a ten-mile-deep lodgement area. At the end of the first week the Americans had swung right-handed towards the Cherbourg Peninsula whose port was vital for the build-up. British Commonwealth troops were probing southwards. We were now entering the mysterious 'Bocage' country. Resembling the sunken Devon roads, those lanes, worn by a millennium of droving and farm wagon traffic, were 10–20 feet deep; as we began to realize, each one was a tank-trap. No less of a hazard were the myriad of pocket-handkerchief-sized fields with high hedges which surrounded the lanes. This in effect was a defensive belt of immense value to the Germans akin to the 'mine marshes' laid around their positions at Alamein in the Egyptian desert. This country was 10–20 miles deep and the lanes could not be straddled by our newest tanks, the American Sherman and the British Cromwell. Only the lumbering British Churchill tank had a long enough chassis to surmount those obstacles, and I see from my notebook that I carried a message back from Brigadier Gerald Verney, commanding 6 Guards Tank Brigade, to Monty saying, 'Excellent co-operation between 6 Guards Tank and 15th Scottish Infantry. Churchills only tank that can make the country banks.'[1]

A very pressing problem in the lodgement area was the need for tactical airfields. At the end of the second week in the British sector we had only one established. This was an earthen strip bulldozed across open fields from which close-cover fighter support could operate. The dust from take-off and landings was appalling and every time the dust clouds rose the Germans shelled the airfield. There was much cudgelling of brains as to how this dust could be laid. The first recourse was to dousing the earthen strip with oil. This was worse than the dust, for the oil got sucked into the aircraft engines. The only solution was water. But water evaporated and we had no water carts. Then some bright spark had a brainwave. Why not harness the municipal water carts which ply in every fair-sized town in England? Many municipalities volunteered their water carts and civilian drivers, and these plied up and down the airstrip in a constant procession braving shot and shell. Emblazoned on their sides were such brave titles as Huddersfield UDC, Bexhill-on-Sea RDC.[2]

Equally serious was the vital need to provide a port. The port at Cherbourg when captured had been so badly damaged by the retreating Germans that it was unusable for months. The Channel ports in the Pas de Calais area were heavily defended, thanks to our deception plan. This was likely to continue for it was also the launching site for the deadly V1 and V2 rockets which were to pound London with such demoralizing effect. So *all* supplies had to come in over the beaches, greatly helped by the British-designed Mulberry Harbours and the life-saving Pluto fuel pipeline. But, when the storms raged, as they often did that summer, even these facilities were unusable, causing drastic delays to on-going operations. Believe it or not we were still supplying four armies in the field 'over the Normandy beaches' by the time we reached Brussels in September.

38

KNOCKING AT THE DOOR

'OPEN-AIR LIFE – MUST HAVE A DOG!'

Following the shelling and air attacks at Cruellet it was deemed sensible to evacuate the grounds of the château and move elsewhere. In addition we were only some three miles from an area where six or seven Panzer Divisions were concentrating. This information came from top secret intercepts codenamed Ultra which tapped communications between Hitler and his military leaders. Although Monty was receiving this information at a headquarters so small that 'everyone knew everything that was going on', nevertheless we knew nothing about Ultra. It was one of the best kept secrets of the war.

We next pitched camp near Blay in the Bocage country which was just inside the American zone, on a sloping field which I remember so well. From this campsite were fought some of the toughest battles of the whole European campaign. In the face of unremitting criticism from Eisenhower's headquarters, some of it emanating from the British Deputy, Air Marshal Tedder, and including Churchill himself, Monty stuck to his strategy of 'the hammer and the anvil'. By drawing the German armour on to the pivotal point of Caen, in the British zone, he would hold them there and enable Americans to break out in the west and, in a wide right hook, make for the River Seine and Paris.

Blay was also the site of the 'Pig Incident' which led to the sacking of Colonel Leo Russell. John Poston, with his cavalry attitude towards scavenging and 'living off the country', had come across a wounded pig which he brought back to Tac HQ (shades of our raiding the Italian dump in Cyrenacia!). Fried bacon for breakfast was keenly enjoyed by the three separate messes which inhabited Tac, the Chiefs, the Ops Staff and the ORs. Colonel Russell smelt a rat and accused John Poston of 'looting', subsequently accusing Monty of condoning looting, if not looting himself! This was preposterous and Russell had to go – forthwith. But this did not stop him from writing a long confidential report on the CinC's supposed proclivities (Monty must have been about the most important figure in the western world at that moment!) which somehow became attached to Montgomery's personal papers in the War Office. The sequel was that some years later, when he became CIGS, he sent for his papers, removed the offending document and burnt it!

My own liaison runs took me to the death-trap of Villers Bocage and in particular to Caen where some of the fiercest armoured fighting took place. The 7th Armoured Division (Desert Rats) got badly mauled at Villers Bocage. This was one of Monty's veteran divisions which had travelled with him from Alamein, across Italy and now to Normandy. Many of the original veterans were still with their regiments which had been cut up time and again since the early desert days. It was therefore understandable that they had become somewhat battle-weary as they entered their final campaign.

In writing of the Armoured Divisions some of the idiosyncracies of particular divisional commanders stand out. At General Alan Adair's Guards Armoured Divisions headquarters he was always to be found in his caravan smoking a thin-stemmed pipe and wreathed in the delicious aroma of Balkan Sobranie tobacco. This had the effect of lulling the senses into a delightful feeling of well-being and drowsiness, enhancing the 'reversal of rôles' from infantry to tanks of this remarkable division.

The commander of the Polish Armoured Division, General Matcek, the survivor of many a disaster, contented himself with the ownership of a beautiful chestnut mare which was to be found grazing near his caravan. Who knows whence it had come, for the Poles too were adept at 'living off the country'! I next saw them in a night attack south of Caen advancing on fixed lines under artificial moonlight.

At the end of June I had the misfortune to go down with a bout of asthma, an amalgam of hay fever and dust, and had to be evacuated back to the UK. But at this moment I recorded almost the last entry in my diary, before the breakout and pursuit put an end to the practice. Despite the enormous pressures on Montgomery at this particular time and quite apart from his own visits to his forward Commanders, the calm inner domestic life continued at Tac headquarters. On 27 June Kit Dawnay, Monty's long-serving personal assistant, his ADC Johnny Henderson, who had been with him since Alamein, and myself were sitting with the Chief at Blay having lunch. Montgomery expressed a wish that had evidently been maturing for some time, for he suddenly declared,

'"When you go to London, Kit, and take Carol, I should like you to buy me a dog – quite a small one that could fit into a caravan quite easily."'

He went on,

'"Of course, if I made a public announcement that I wanted a dog, I would get thousands, absolutely thousands. If Frank Gillard was to say on his BBC programme that General Montgomery wanted a dog there would be no difficulty at all! I bet Alan Moorehead could get me one." Turning to his ADC he said, "Johnny, go and see Frank Gillard and tell him that I want a dog – a wire-haired fox terrier, and will he put it on his programme. He could do it quite nicely, in the Children's Hour perhaps? All he'd have to say was that he was talking to General Montgomery the other day who was looking for a dog. He feels that leading an open air life he would like to have a small dog to take about with him. Open air life. Must have a dog!" concluded Monty.

"But what about expense?" asked the PA whose mind was still on the Harrods Pet Shop.

"Oh, won't have to worry about expense," rejoined the Chief, "it will be presented! In any case money is no object, no object at all! I get £300 a month, and my mess bill costs me £2. Money is absolutely no object. I want to get rid of it!"

"All dogs to the BBC by Tuesday next," he could say, and Kit, you could go and choose the best. Or they could come to your room at the Mayfair".'

So the matter was settled; the yearning for a dog was to be satisfied. As I watched Monty walk back to his caravans after lunch in a grey polo-nick sweater and corduroy trousers, he held a huge black umbrella over his head to keep off the rain. A small dog walked up. Both dog and Commander-in-Chief were lost for a moment beneath the billows of the umbrella from which issued endearing noises between man and dog.

I did not return to Normandy for the best part of three weeks, during which time Montgomery had been constantly knocking at the door of the bastion at Caen. Increasingly criticized and making little progress, he was in fact achieving his object and pinning down the German armour in the east at the vital hinge, thus freeing the Americans for a breakthrough.

By 10 July German tanks facing the American front numbered only 190, whereas 610 were now in front of the British/Canadian sector.[1]

This tells one all one needs to know about Montgomery's strategy in Normandy. His plans were paying off. I wrote my last diary entry just before the pursuit began.

'*26 July*

I have now been back three or four days. Three weeks has made a great difference to this part of France. I reached Normandy on the second day of the battle south of Caen [this was Operation GOODWOOD]. By the third day the line had stabilized again. It was the Guards Armoured's first battle; Rex Whistler in my Bn was killed – that is a great loss. I gathered that the Division did very well for their first battle. The following day I visited Caen. It can hardly be called a town; it is a frightful mess. I have never seen anything like it. It 'stenches' of broken things, the dust of centuries swirls and eddies round the trucks as they pass. The Cathedral stands, almost intact. The other churches, some very old, are broken and shattered, most with roofs missing. I went into one near the Orne bridges. A bomb had fallen through the roof down onto the altar. Débris, old beams, torn old paintings lay in a shambles on the floor. It was very quiet, and the sky showed blue through the roof.

7 August

'Now it is much later. The Caen attack has been, the American offensive [also], [and] the British attack south of Caumont. For the past week I have been working with Guards Armoured Div. south of Caumont. [Now] two days rest to get the red and yellow dust and the stench of dead cows out of our systems.'

By that time I had not taken in the thousands of dead horses and wagons (GS wagons in British Army parlance) which were the sole means of Infantry battalion transport in the German army, which lay scattered along the roadsides. It was not until our jeeps got into the Falaise Pocket, where much of the German army was trapped, that we saw the extent of the enemy disaster. Hundreds of dead German soldiers lay around, field upon field of them trapped by the joint pincers of the British and American armies. There was only one word to describe it – Armageddon. One could not linger at the scene for the smell was quite appalling, a sensation one seldom connects with the battlefields of history.

Once having dealt with the German forces in Normandy, we swept on almost unopposed, across the Seine to capture Paris and then on to Brussels. Lines of communication became very extended between Tac HQ and the forward troops, and so the LOs had to resort to Auster aircraft, a light recce plane, always keeping a jeep and driver up in the front line and using what airstrip we could. Many and hair-raising were the adventures we had with those new-found toys and their RAF pilots.

It has become the practice recently to decry the efforts of the British in the battle of Normandy, comparing them unfavourably with the Germans, the Americans or the Canadians. I have my own opinions on all these matters, but such comparisons, I believe, are entirely spurious and do a dishonour to those brave men, whoever they might be. But perhaps I may quote a comment by the swashbuckling American General, General 'Georgie' Patton who was addressing a staff college meeting back home shortly after the American *débâcle* at Kasserine Pass in North Africa. He was asked,

"But tell me General, how did our boys really do?"

"Well," said General Patton "I'll tell you. They were like a bunch of bananas. Some were yellow. Some were green. And the rest were plain rotten!"

Such an admission takes the wind out of any critic's sails! But one criticism we did have and that was for the American system of command. It was much more rigid than the British and much more hide-bound. They did not understand the 'Liaison Officer System' as used by Monty, and the very idea of a junior captain approaching a divisional commander on equal terms and demanding his battle state was anathema to the American *amour propre*. So the system did not work very well in that area. The Americans, like the Germans, would always commandeer the biggest castle or château in the district and seldom, like the British, have a tented camp for their headquarters. I once penetrated to an American headquarters on a snowbound day at the end of the year. So fierce was the heating in their château, then occupied by an American airborne division, that my chinagraph pencils began to melt!

It is estimated that for every day of the Normandy campaign 500 young men died on the British and Canadian front. Casualties were particularly heavy among the infantry. A crisis in manpower rapidly became apparent, with no more reserves at home to replace those lost in Normandy. The problem was even more acute with Canada which had so early thrown in its lot with us. By the winter of 1944/5 even the Americans were affected by a shortage of foot soldiers. We were dimly aware of these and other problems, but we still believed we were going to win the war.

39

THE ARNHEM OPERATION
'IF ONLY YOU HAD COME A WEEK BEFORE'

> '1st of September, 1944, was a climacteric of western history which would far transcend the events of the Second World War. It is never easy to set a precise date marking the decline of empires, but the demotion of Montgomery was certainly the moment when – definitively and most palpably – British predominance in the Western Alliance could be seen to pass to the United States.'
> Alistair Horne,
> *The Lonely Leader*, 1994

A pause had been expected between the fighting in Normandy and our arrival in Belgium. Owing to the disorganization of enemy resistance we were able to sweep through Belgium, and our lines of communication became stretched to breaking point. Second (British) Army had advanced 250 miles in six days, and our supply lines were some 300 miles long, stretching right back to Normandy. For bulk loads the emphasis was now on petrol to maintain the hot pursuit; ammunition was a secondary importance. Verbal links were also disrupted, for civil telephone lines were all down and normal field wireless communications were out of range. The only recourse was to the vulnerable dispatch rider who shouldered the burden of routine messages.

By use of the Auster aircraft Monty's Liaison Officers were able to report to him each evening, but it entailed a frantic chase in the jeep to reach the forward command posts and back again to the waiting aircraft. As we passed through Belgium there was an air of euphoria, the fighting vehicles were garlanded with flowers, and pretty girls draped themselves on top of tanks – rather different from the low-key reception in France where one witnessed the rather sinister roadside scenes of young women forced to submit to the razor: the shaven head was their badge of shame for having slept with a German.

The capture of Brussels on 3 September was rather overshadowed by the news received by Monty, three days before, that he was to lose command of the Allied Land Forces. We always knew that this was likely at some stage of the campaign, at the point where American Forces outnumbered those of the British. Pressures were mounting inside the United States in an election year for a home-grown commander. This would have been acceptable if there had been an experienced senior American available. But, sadly, Eisenhower lacked experience of high command in war and had not the personality to control his unruly lieutenants, who were allowed to go their own way. It was this lack of professionalism that really rankled with the battle-wise Montgomery who could see so clearly the way ahead. For Eisenhower, nice chap though he was, was an amateur at the game. Thus a pall came to be cast over the British command, which was to last on and off for the rest of the extended campaign.

The *débâcle* at Arnhem was largely the result of misunderstandings between Eisenhower and Montgomery. There were cogent reasons why Montgomery had his sights on the northern route into Germany whilst he was still Land Forces Commander.

But now he only had half-hearted support from SHAEF (Eisenhower's HQ) for this thrust aimed at the Ruhr, which was to carry us on to Berlin. Eisenhower procrastinated. At one moment he was backing a northern thrust and the next, having spoken to American commanders, he was backing a thrust in the south towards the Saar.

The rationale of the northern attack was that, firstly, it outflanked the Siegfried line, a consideration of some importance. Secondly, it was within range of our home-based airborne forces and avoided the heavy flak likely to be encountered at a Rhine crossing point nearer the Ruhr, such as Wesel. Thirdly, it was the least likely crossing place and therefore promised the element of surprise. Another bonus for the Arnhem route across the Rhine was that it would bottle up the stubborn German forces defending the vital ports of the Low Countries, Antwerp and the Scheldt Estuary.

It must be said, however, that the speed of our recent advance, rather than the need for ports, created this atmosphere of 'driving on' and 'bouncing' the Rhine bridges before any German recovery might take place. The immediate target was the Ruhr, Germany's principal industrial base, which, once denied the enemy, must lead to rapid collapse. As Monty himself recalled, 'My instructions were that the drive northwards to secure the river crossing would be made with the utmost rapidity and violence, and without regards to events on the flanks.'[1]

Various factors delayed the start of operation Market Garden. There was our own bridgehead over the Meuse-Escaut canal which had to be properly secured, for we had now turned north; there was the indecision of Eisenhower who seemed to be favouring a 'broad-front' policy, and the vitally important weather factor which remained adverse. Good weather was crucial, for our advances north across this waterlogged country meant crossing numerous canals over which only one road was feasible. Therefore an 'airborne carpet' consisting of two American and one British airborne divisions was to be dropped to capture all the important bridges including those at Veghel over the Wilhelmina Canal, Grave over the River Maas or Meuse, Nijmegen over the River Waal, and at Arnhem over the River Neder Rijn. Not until all these obstacles had been crossed would we be over the Rhine and into the heartland of Germany. Even critics like General Bradley, commanding the American 12th Army Group, considered this to be a breathtakingly daring plan.

Operation Market Garden was finally set for 17 September, and we LOs prepared for a difficult assignment, for this one-road axis of advance was going to cause terrific congestion and jams. With difficulty we managed to reach Nijmegen. But travelling by jeep up this road on 21 September I bumped into a terrific *mêlée* of men and vehicles at Veghel. German Panzers had counter-attacked, for there were cross-tracks along which they could infiltrate. It was impossible to get off the narrow road as deep dykes lay on either side. In fact the dykes and ditches criss-crossed this patchwork of sunken *polders* so that lateral movement was hardly feasible. Sporadic firing was taking place and there in front of me was a Tiger tank, luckily facing the other way. I could almost have touched it! It was a complete mix-up of German and British fighting vehicles and American paratroopers. It seemed to be safer on foot, but carrying a mapboard was rather conspicuous. But at such close quarters was this entanglement that very little firing by either side was possible! Eventually the Germans cut the road and I and my driver were stranded on the wrong side, cut off from home. Together with a fellow LO from Monty's headquarters, whom I soon bumped into, we spent the night in a very basic Dutch hostelry on the side of the road, sleeping on hard benches. It was the only night I had failed to deliver my usual message to Monty and I was more concerned about that than anything else. The road was closed for three days, but somehow we managed to squeeze through on the following morning and gave Monty an account of these developments. To what extent this disruption of our spinal route influenced his decision I do not know but on 25 September Monty decided to call the operation off, for even Polish Airborne reinforcements were not enough to save 1st Airborne Division now isolated west of Arnhem. As many as could escaped, ferried by night across two rivers.

The Arnhem operation has become notorious as 'a bridge too far'. Was Monty to blame? Who can tell? There were so many factors involved. British Airborne Forces, led by General 'Boy' Browning, were desperate to get into action, so many proposed operations having been cancelled that their morale was beginning to suffer. All I do know is that standing at the Nijmegen Bridge shortly after its capture, I talked with a Dutchman. And he told me, 'If *only* you had come a week before. All the Germans had gone!'

The autumn was now closing in, the Allied line bogged down on all fronts. As Supreme Commander, but also Land Forces Commander, Eisenhower had no strategic plan. His Army Commanders, including Monty, scenting indecision, went ahead, 'doing their own thing' without co-ordination or control. There was to be an equal advance all along the 400-mile front stretching from the North Sea to Switzerland. There was no concentration of force or massive thrust as envisaged by Monty which would bring the war to a rapid conclusion, possibly before Christmas, 1944.

Tac HQ was established in an unprepossessing hamlet called Zonhoven in Flemish Belgium. A heavy depression settled on Tac HQ. Meaningful conduct of the war seemed to have collapsed. Monty was eating his heart out in a small villa by the side of the road, burnt up with frustration. For the first time in the campaign we were living in buildings. As in days of old we had retired to 'winter quarters'. There was nothing to do, nothing to report; there was even time for a few days' leave. Colonel Joe Ewart, who was deputy to Bill Williams (Intelligence Chief at Main HQ) entertained us with his stories and a fascinating map of the enemy dispositions set out in his caravan. We were not to know it then, but his role was to feed *Ultra* messages into the CinC. By December winter truly had us in its grip. The weather was atrocious – snow, frost and fog. Suddenly, out of the blue, the Germans attacked in the American sector to our south. It appeared to be a serious effort at the American's weakest point, in the Ardennes. But we could get very little information from the American front. At this point the atmosphere changed completely, the gloom disappeared. Things were happening. We were in business again!

40

THE ARDENNES

'WAKE ME UP AT HALF PAST FIVE!'

The Ardennes offensive could not have come at a more unfortunate time for the Allies, already suffering from the setback at Arnhem. Coming as it did at the turn of the year 1944 and running into January, 1945, it seriously weakened the British and American negotiating position at the Crimean Conference at Yalta, which was to take place early in the following month. Conversely the rapid Soviet advance in the East had strengthened the Russian hand. This is how it seemed to us at the time:-

'Apart from the fact that the Germans have attacked, we have very little information at Tac HQ. The situation is far from clear. Montgomery decides to send two of his LOs, Dick Harden and myself, accompanied by Tom Bigland[1] to investigate. The attack is evidently directed at First American Army. We set out on the morning of 19 December in frost and fog for General Hodges' HQ which is located in the Ardennes at the old watering place of Spa. It feels oddly quiet and deserted. We arrive at First Army HQ, located in an hotel, and find it abandoned. A hurried evacuation has evidently taken place. We walk in. The tables in the dining room are laid for Christmas festivities. The offices are deserted. Papers are lying about. Telephones are still in place. It is as though we had come upon the *Mary Celeste* floating abandoned upon an open sea. The truth begins to dawn. The German attack is more serious than we had thought, for the evacuation of the headquarters shows every sign of a panic move. We can find no American troops nor civilian helpers to explain the mystery. Running through the offices, equipped with the usual paraphanalia, we collect some classified papers to prove that we have actually visited the place in case we are met with disbelief on our return.

'Through oddly deserted countryside we make our way to General Hodges' Rear HQ where we find him. He is considerably shaken and can give no coherent account of what has happened. Nor is he in touch with General Bradley's 12th Army Group under whose command he comes. Communiciations seemed to have completely broken down.[2]

'Then begins the long journey homewards with the best speed we can muster in the wintry conditions. Tom Bigland meantime sets off to find Bradley's Twelfth US Army Group at Luxembourg.

'Montgomery is clearly alarmed at my story. The flank of his 21st Army Group is now exposed. For the first time in the campaign I am instructed to travel overnight to find General Hodges where we left him at Chaudfontaine and give him an urgent and important message. Whatever time I return I am to wake up the Field Marshal and tell him what has happened. On no other occasion can I remember Monty wishing to be disturbed in the middle of the night, even at the height of the Alamein battle.'

As we subsequently discovered, what had happened was this. Von Rundstedt, in a vicious counter-attack, had used two Panzer Armies to smash through the First US Army on a wide front between the towns of Malmédy and Echternach in the Ardennes mountains. His unhindered advance now threatened the River Meuse crossings between Liège and Namur. If he could quickly seize the bridges intact, he would have a straight run through the rear areas of Ninth US Army and 21 Army Group, and thus seize the key port of Antwerp. This would be fatal to the Allied Campaign in Europe.

Monty briefed me as follows. 'Tell Hodges he must block the Meuse bridges!' I was to demand of General Hodges that he should take every precaution, immediately, to hold the river crossings, and I was to inform him of the movements of 21st Army Group to meet this threat. I asked Monty how I was to give him these orders, when he was not under his command. 'Just tell him!' he said. 'The Liège crossings in particular must be defended at *all* costs. He *must* block the bridges by any means. Call up L of C troops. Use any obstacles he can find, including farm carts! He must hold the bridges all day tomorrow [20 December], and make sure that officers supervise each operation. You can tell him so from me!' Finally I was to tell General Hodges that by dawn on the 20th there would be ninety SAS jeeps and officer patrols from PHANTOM to cover the river crossings as recce. Also at dawn 30 British Corps would sidestep into the Louvain – St Trond – Hasselt area to the north of the River Meuse, to block the route to Antwerp. 'Wake me up at half-past five if you're back!' he called after me.

I could see that my mission was going to be an extremely delicate one, even if I could find General Hodges and his elusive HQ in the middle of the night. My last instruction was that I must arrange a meeting between Monty and Hodges the next day. 'If possible bring him back here tonight!' My report on this visit still survives.

Top Secret
Liaison visit to General Hodges 19/20 Dec '44
(extract)

'Leaving Tac Army Group by jeep at midnight the journey to First US Army HQ, then south of the river near LIÈGE, took two hours. Heavy fog and numerous checkpoints made going slow. Flying bombs were falling in LIÈGE.

'At CHAUDFONTAINE where General HODGES had his Headquarters, the fog had cleared and the buildings were quite easy to recognize. The officers' sleeping quarters were across the TESDRE stream. An MP Corporal showed the way to the Chief of Staff's bedroom. General KEANE was sitting on his bed in his pyjamas telephoning with a blanket wrapped round his shoulders. He verified Field Marshal MONTGOMERY's handwriting on the letter. During a lull he put his hand over the receiver, he said "How is Freddie?"[3] and waited for the answer. After this he seemed happier. General HODGES was asleep in bed, with his ADC in the adjoining room. When he was awakened he sat up in bed with a blanket wrapped round him and read the letter. Having finished, he handed it to his Chief of Staff who was standing at the foot of the bed. There was some talk about consulting "Brad" and "Ike".

Then General HODGES re-read the letter. Reactions were slow. It was now 2.30 in the morning.'

Fortunately I had been introduced to General Hodges the day before, so he knew my face. This was lucky, as German parachutists had been dropped in American uniform. There were wild stories of assassination missions and the American Zone was riddled with trigger-happy checkpoints.

'When asked about the battle situation General HODGES or his Chief of Staff said that there were three gaps in the American defences where the situation was extremely fluid. As regards further enemy penetration, he said that there was an unconfirmed report that a small amount of armour crossed the road at HOUFFALIZE after dark that night.

'On the important question of the MEUSE crossings General HODGES had nothing to say. He implied that it was of no great consequence and had or would be looked after. When pressed, General KEANE stated LIÈGE, HUY and NAMUR crossings would not be seriously threatened within the next 24 hours. It was evident that the Army Commander was completely out of touch. His Chief of Staff was more completely informed but cagey or out of date. Neither of them seemed to be aware of the urgency of the situation and all that it might imply to the Allied foothold in Europe.'

Passing through numerous checkpoints I set off on my return journey and reached Tac HQ at 6 a.m. Monty was awake and sitting up in bed drinking a cup of tea. He was not altogether surprised at my story. I had arranged his meeting with General Hodges for later that day. There was no time to be lost. He wanted a full battle situation on the American front before the meeting. For this purpose five Liaison officers (two of whom were the American LOs) departed from the Ardennes immediately to cover the area of the breakthrough. It was not until 10.30 a.m. that Eisenhower placed First and Ninth US Armies under Monty's command, so now my mission was explained. I cannot remember much about that day, having been without sleep for the previous 24 hours, except that we went hell for leather through the snow and slush of the mountain roads, the five jeeps fanning out in different directions. As a precaution against the cold we were dressed in our newly issued 'tank suits' and were not too clearly recognizable as coming from the British Army of the North. We had many an awkward encounter with our American friends who, not surprisingly, were intensely suspicious about our identity. Even more so at the American divisional HQ who were not used to Montgomery's LOs swanning about the battlefield. Many of them were unaware that they were now under his command. But once they realized the position they took it in good part.

I cannot be certain whether it was this day or the day after that two of our British LOs penetrated to the isolated Bastogne. The journey was creepy – no American soldiers about and deserted snow-bound roads. On arrival at the American Airborne division HQ, located in a large château, the General seemed surprised, and said, 'Hullo, where have you come from? I thought I was cut off!'

Later there took place a memorable meeting in the forecourt of First US Army HQ. Both Hodges and Simpson (Ninth US Army) were present at Monty's request. The LOs had returned from their various journeys, the stench of baked mud clinging to the battered jeeps. We were all in a huddle round the bonnet of a staff car on which maps were spread. Montgomery's first words were to his own Liaison Officers. He failed to ask the American Commanders to brief him on the battle situation. Instead he asked his British and American Liaison Officers to do so, who of course had taken very good care to have visited the key divisional commanders. 'What's the form?' asked Monty in his characteristic metallic voice, and we told him. As the picture began to unfold it was a very sombre one. Our American friends, reeling from the blow of Von Rundstedt's offensive with their armies split and scattered, looked severely discomforted. It was a slight uncalled for on that day, for, as Monty later admitted, it was the fighting spirit of the American soldier that won the day.

Apart from his moments of tactlessness, this was the kind of situation which showed Monty in his element. He was now commanding most of Bradley's 12th (US) Army Group. Patton was in the south, still heading for Bastogne. Monty had soon created reserves out of bits and pieces of the American Armies which he withdrew from the line for counter-attack purposes. Hodges and Simpson were greatly relieved to be under the command of someone who knew exactly what he was doing and he got a good reception from the American soldiery. General Simpson, commanding Ninth US Army, wrote to his namesake General 'Simbo' Simpson at the War Office in London, 'You see from the start when I was under the command of "the Marshal" [Monty] I got clear and definite orders what I had to do. From Bradley and my own people I never got any orders that make it clear to me what I have got to do.'[4]

Monty was cock-a-hoop for he was now back in command of a large chunk of the Allied land forces.

Extraordinary to relate, Eisenhower, as actual Land Forces Commander, had issued no orders or directives between 28 October and 16 December when the attack began. Even now, after three nights and four days of the fighting, Monty, as 21st Army Group Commander, had received no order or even request.[5]

It is only now, after an interval of half a century, that I begin to realize the part I was playing in my mad dashes across country in that indescribable winter of 1944, and in particular the significance of my journey from the deserted town Spa to our Zonhoven headquarters. For to me there had always been a mystery as to how it came about that Monty could pass 'orders' to General Hodges when the latter was not under his command. I had assumed that all this was tied up in a conversation between Monty and Ike, but no such exchange had taken place.

Not a bit of it! As the history books tell us command did not change nor was it agreed it should change until 10.30 a.m. on 20 December. I am indebted to Nigel Hamilton for his detailed research into the sequence of events at Eisenhower's headquarters, still in Paris. Here another drama was being played out which had in it the seeds of certain imponderable events to come.[6]

Monty and Ike were like people from separate planets, so different had been their ambience. Perhaps I am exaggerating. Eisenhower *did* see Monty's point of view but he was continually being overruled, against his better judgement, by his own field commanders, and 'the folks back home'. However, in the following story the facts speak for themselves.

Eisenhower's headquarters at an hotel in Paris were as remote from the landbattle as could be. The possibility of Eisenhower, both Supreme Commander and Land Forces Commander, even meeting his two Army Group Commanders, Bradley and Montgomery, over that distance and in that winter weather was pretty remote.

At Eisenhower's SHAEF headquarters among the American, and British, senior staff officers there was a built-in prejudice against the cocky British Commander who always knew best and let the world know about it. Bedell Smith, Eisenhower's American Chief of Staff, was not the easiest of characters. Tedder, Ike's Deputy, was frankly hostile to the 21st Army Group Commander, even though they had worked closely together in the Middle East. The two other senior British officers at SHAEF however, Strong (Intelligence) and Whiteley (Operations), held a more neutral view.[7]

Not only was Eisenhower out of touch at this time, but, owing to the panic over the supposed German assassination gangs dressed in American uniform, Eisenhower was 'locked up' in his room at the Trianon Hotel at Versailles, 'with the windows closed, curtains drawn and shutters latched,' according to Air Vice Marshal Robb, then also on his staff.[8]

By this time (the night of 19/20th) Generals Whiteley and Strong were becoming so alarmed at the deteriorating situation in the Ardennes that they decided to wake General Bedell Smith in the early hours and press the need for Monty to take over command of the stranded First and Ninth US Armies. Bedell Smith therefore rang Bradley to get his reaction to this proposal.

> 'Bradley objected strongly . . . so much so that Bedell Smith became ashamed at having suggested it, and rounded on the two hapless British officers with whom it had originated, calling them "sons of bitches" and "Limey bastards" in one of the fits of rough American temper for which he was well known.'[9]

Strong and Whiteley were promptly sacked on the spot at 3.00 a.m. in the morning and would be returned to the UK the next day. This was at a time when the American front had been shattered, leaving a huge hole through which German armour was advancing.

At General Strong's last intelligence briefing early next morning Bedell Smith was glum, but approached the two British officers as they made their way to Eisenhower's office and virtually apologized. He was, he said, going to put forward *their* idea as his *own*. Better coming from an American!

It was not until mid-morning on the 20th that Monty received a telephone call from Eisenhower. It was a very bad line, but he got the gist of the message which was to assume command of the northern salient.

It seemed that Monty had jumped the gun when he had asked me to take his orders to Hodges at Chaudfontaine the night before. At that stage he had no authority over First and Ninth US Armies, nor could he confidently anticipate it. He had no authority to demand the presence of Hodges at Tac HQ in the middle of the night: 'Bring him back here if you can!' Nor could he really order Hodges and Simpson to meet him at Chaudfontaine the following day. But he was betting on what he thought was a certainty. There was no one else who could pull the chestnuts out of the fire but he! It was an emergency and this was emergency action based on his instinct as a field commander.

'Georgie' Patton with his Third US Army was meantime rampaging about the south. Denied his promised route into Germany through the Saar, he had been redirected by Bradley on to Bastogne at the southern edge of Von Rundstedt's salient. He was deriding Monty as 'a tired little fart!' for simply holding the northern line and letting the Panzers run up against it.[10] But Monty was in the business of creating reserves, not only ready for a counter-attack against the Panzer Armies but for the next operation, Veritable.

The breakthrough in the Ardennes was a blow to American esteem and shattered the morale of the commanders directly involved, Bradley, Hodges and Simpson. But lest this appear as sour grapes let it be said that the British Army had suffered far worse defeats during the course of the war and lived to tell the tale. The British by now were just that much more experienced.

Like a stone thrown into a pool the ripples from the Ardennes episode have travelled wider and wider. The end of the war, it is believed, was delayed by several months. This in turn held up our advance to the eastern European occupied countries and allowed the Iron Curtain to fall prematurely upon these hapless peoples. Thus opened half a century of Cold War the consequences of which we are only beginning to understand today. And if there is a moral to be drawn from what I have written it is this. Brilliant military commanders do not come on the cheap. You have to pay the price. In this case in soured relations with our principal ally. Nor do faithful allies come on the cheap. You have to pay the price. In that case, in the bigger dominating the smaller. And this, it may be said, was a political price which we are still paying off today.

41

ARDENNES AFTERMATH

'YOU'RE FINISHED – ABSOLUTELY FINISHED!'

Tracing, on the map, the events of the past few weeks, it can be clearly seen how, after the first few days, Rundstedt swung the main weight of his Panzer offensive to the north-west, towards the allied base at Antwerp. The brunt of his attack was taken by General Hodges' First Army, now under the command of Monty, with British 30 Corps on Hodges' right, down as far as Dinant. British armoured and jeep patrols had already secured the Meuse bridges, as promised, before command actually changed. All these moves had to be made with the utmost speed.

Just before Christmas Brigadier Roscoe Harvey had taken his battered British 29th Armoured Brigade to the rear areas near Brussels to be re-equipped with new tanks. While these changes were taking place the Brigadier very sensibly departed into the hinterland for a few days' woodcock shooting. Much to his chagrin, no sooner had he arrived at the scene of the chase than he was urgently recalled by General 'Pip' Roberts, his immediate boss, commanding 11th Armoured Division. Told that there was a German incursion in the south and that he must proceed forthwith to the Ardennes with his tanks, he expostulated, 'But I haven't got any bloody tanks – they've all been handed in!' Having once realized that this was not a practical joke but was for real, he was then told to take back the old ones, those that were still 'runners', and proceed at once to Dinant, the most westerly bridge over the River Meuse in the American Sector, to block the passage of at least two Panzer armies! To the south he was to expect the British 6th Armoured Division who would hope to join hands with Bradley's Americans across the great divide. Such were the crisis moves that Christmas of 1944![1]

Immediately after the change of command we were occupied in escorting Monty to his new American divisions. Quite like the old days at Alamein! But this time we were in grander style than the old open Humber. One such journey to the American front meant going through the city of Liège which I had been through before and thought I could find the way. Needless to say I led Monty's convoy into a cul-de-sac and had the embarrassing task of turning all the vehicles round and pointing them in the opposite direction! Monty turned not a hair. He was very good about that kind of thing. Fortunately the convoy was not a big one, consisting of Monty's black Rolls and two jeeps, which surprised the Americans.

By the time the German bulge had been squeezed back into position it was getting on for mid-January, 1945. It was estimated that the Germans had lost some 120,000 men in the battle, together with 600 tanks and assault guns. We had won the battle, but it was clear that we had by no means won the war. Von Rundstedt captured 25,000 American soldiers and destroyed over 300 American tanks.[2]

By the end of January the German offensive had petered out and Montgomery was gearing up for a major push across the Rhine in the north involving the British in Veritable and the Americans in Grenade as the codewords were named. This had Eisenhower's full backing, although Bradley, as ever, was reluctant to relinquish his hold on American troops. The object was to clear all the ground up to the River Rhine in preparation for a crossing of this last major obstacle before entering Germany. The battle was to begin on 8 February and became known as the Battle of the Reichwald, as the Germans held the forest of that name in strength. Just before the start we moved Tac HQ from Zonhoven to the little town of Geldrop just inside Holland but the distance still necessitated a lift by Auster to meet our jeeps at Nijmegen. Dick Harden[3] and I took off on 9 February, piloted by our own Flight Lieutenant McQueen.

Two days later, on 11 February, Monty sent the following signal to the DMO, General 'Simbo' Simpson, in London.

> 'On 9 February an Auster was carrying Dick Harden and Carol Mather up to the forward area and was attacked by a FW 190 over GRAVE. McQueen, the pilot, was killed at once. Carol received four bullets – arm, bottom, leg and kidney.
>
> 'Dick was sitting next to McQueen and he seized the stick and managed in some amazing way to land the machine by crashing it into a field, where it came to rest in a ditch with very little damage. Dick cut his head open on landing and has five stitches in the forehead; he is a bit shaken.

'Carol has had an operation and one kidney has been removed. His left forearm is badly shattered and there is a possibility that some of the nerve has been shot away; if this proves to be so then he might not have the full use of his left arm. In any case he will be over two months in hospital, and then a long period of convalescence will follow.'[4]

After such a passage of time it is curious to think that mine was the body to which all these things happened. But it was not quite as bad as it sounds and the details are not quite accurate.

It was in retrospect a most extraordinary experience, perhaps even stranger than that, as I will go on to relate. We were flying over the north of Holland at about 1000 feet to avoid hostile attack. Dick Harden was next to the pilot and I was in the seat immediately behind, back to back.

Suddenly out of the blue we were attacked. We never saw the plane but cannon shells apparently hit us, followed by the puffs of ack-ack bursts denoting unwelcome 'friendly fire' as well. At first we did not realize what had happened as we were still flying on an even course. But the pilot was slumped over the controls, shot dead. We were thus on our own. Neither Dick nor I had any experience of flying, but the slender craft was still sailing on regardless. Dick with difficulty tried to seize the joy-stick and manipulate it, but poor McQueen's body did not make things easy. However, he managed to coax the machine towards the ground and we glided low over a wood, unrealistically inviting being seen from above. My only contribution was to apply the brakes, for the handle operating the flaps was above my head. As we were about to crash I crawled towards the tail. Whether these two movements had any effect I do not know, but the next moment the aircraft stalled, pancaked through an opening in the wood and crashed. But the crash was into a shallow swamp which we entered with a splash!

Struggling out of our stricken craft we managed to wade ashore. We were not certain whether we were in Germany or Holland. McQueen's body we could not move so we set off across some fields to get help.[5] Dick's head was badly cut on landing, but my wounds were invisible as we were wearing our heavy tank suits. All I knew was that I was badly winded and one arm would not work. We came to a road and to our relief saw British vehicles. We flagged down a jeep and Dick told the driver to take us to the nearest MI Room. Here we were invited to take our place in the queue with the usual sick parade – a sobering experience after our high-profile disaster!

My memory thereafter was a bit hazy. A surgical operation at the Casualty Clearing Station ... the cries and moans of the German wounded from the Reichwald battle were all round me in the makeshift ward in which I lay ... the nice New Zealand surgeon who visited me next morning holding up a jam jar in which floated my kidney and his muttering, 'A perfect specimen. Quite untouched. A pity we took it out!'

A few days later, at a hospital near Eindhoven, Monty was standing by my bedside and quizzing the army doctor in a bracing sort of way, 'Tell me doctor', he demanded, 'how many holes in him?' and the doctor's reply, 'Counting the shrapnel – thirteen.' 'Thirteen, thirteen! Excellent, excellent!' was my Master's response, and he disappeared again. Evacuation by air to the UK, landing at Down Ampney. Ampney! Romantic name where I almost started my war. Then a long drive in an ambulance to a hospital in Hertfordshire, during which the driver lost his way.

Strange to relate, from the moment we were hit to the moment we crash-landed I did not experience the expected terror of such a disaster, nor was I aware of any pain. Although I was conscious all the time I became completely detached from the affair. An interested spectator, but no longer a participant. It was as if I was looking down on the events which concerned my body but I was not really part of it. I was literally hovering above the scene, a fascinated onlooker.

But lest this be thought an hallucination let me say that this connects with something that happened to me a long time ago and since forgotten. During my schooldays at Harrow I had this disorientating sensation of being disembodied.

It went on for several years, on and off, and sometimes lasted for days on end. It was a feeling of being quite separate, outside my own body with only a distant interest in it. I never told anyone. I would have felt a fool and I had no words to explain it. At that age it was a frightening experience and I dreaded the visitation of this 'thing'. It was not as if the soul had detached itself from the body, for that is the nearest analogy I can think of, for over the whole period my detached body and myself remained earthbound, but I was hovering always slightly above the scene. However, as adolescence grew to manhood the phenomenon thankfully passed away, and if ever I thought of it again I put it down to growing pains.

But was not my experience in the aircraft exactly similar, a hovering above the scene of action, disinterested but observant? Or was it even a hovering between life and death? A fail-safe signal received from

Above! It would be nice to think so, except for one thing. It happened again, and this did not involve an injury. This third occasion is not part of this story, but suffice it to say it was one of the great tests of my life. And there I was – once again on auto-pilot!

I was allowed out of hospital for the first time on VE Day. I made my way to London and stood in front of the Palace with the delirious, cheering crowds. The Royal Party appeared on the balcony again and again. But what was I going to do now? A whole way of life had come to an end. Peace? What did it mean? What point was there in life any more? During my adult life I had no other experience but war. The alarms and excursions, the camaraderie, even the boredom of it was familiar and worthwhile.

In July I was fit enough to return to Monty's headquarters at Östenwalde, near Osnabruck in Germany. He had now become Military Governor of the British Occupied Zone. Trying to salvage something from the wreck of war-torn Europe was an absorbing task, which I have described elsewhere.[6] My liaison trips throughout Western Europe kept me fully occupied for the rest of that year and into the next. But the nagging question remained. What am I going to do now? I could not entertain the thought of demobilization and settling down to a 9 to 5 job at an office desk. I decided to stay on. I enlisted Monty's help in getting me through the Medical Board, which I had already failed once. Monty as usual was short and to the point. He looked at me and said, 'You're finished! Absolutely finished! Quite finished!'

I was somewhat taken aback. This, from a normally considerate man. But in a way it was quite in character. If he thought one was trying to pull a fast one he was ruthless in slapping one down. And fixing the medical board, with the new responsibilities he was about to undertake, was perhaps one over the odds. At any rate he was to become CIGS at the War Office in London and my time was up. I was to return to my regiment, the Welsh Guards, with the expectation of being invalided out. Considering that I had hardly been with them for the greater part of the war, they were very kind to me. They organized a new Medical Board, which I passed, and then it was only a matter of time before I obtained a Regular Commission. The wheel of fortune had turned again.

Part of the attraction of staying on was that my regiment had been posted to Palestine, to keep the peace between Arab and Jew, under the League of Nations (later United Nations) Mandate. I could not wait to get back to this alluring hinterland, largely unchanged since biblical days. In itself this was an epic period, but I must resist the temptation to continue.

While in Palestine I had been scheming to get back to the mysterious Libyan desert and had managed to persuade the powers that be to equip a small expedition, which I was to lead, to explore the southern Libyan passes, and on to the Tibesti mountains, the legendary land of Prester John. By March of 1948 all was set for departure and I had secured two months' leave when, consequent upon the ending of the British Mandate in Palestine, the Arab-Israeli war broke out and cut us off from Egypt!

EPILOGUE
'WHEN THE GRASS STOPS GROWING'

'Never since the heroic days of Greece has the world had such a sweet, just, boyish master. It will be a black day for the human race when scientific blackguards, conspirators, churls, and fanatics manage to supplant him.'
George Santayana on British Rule in 'The Weather in his Soul', from his *Soliloquies in England.*

Britain was the sole survivor of all the European Powers engaged with Hitler's Reich. We survived for six years, often alone, sometimes fighting against two enemies on three different fronts.

Before the war Britain had world-wide commitments to support its mercantilist system and sustain the mother country, a major contribution to the peace of the world. The post-war régime swept all this away. We can lament with George Santayana the passing of this era and the coming of the 'fanatics', which he foretells with rare prophetic vision.

Within six months of VE Day the western allied armies in Europe had virtually dissolved or been rendered incapable of action through early demobilization or needs elsewhere. In Eastern Europe the Russian Armies still faced us in full strength.

Some words come back to me from a former era, which I found recorded in a wartime notebook. It was following the Retreat from Moscow. A figure, cloaked and battle-stained, stumbles into a French camp where a former comrade demands, 'Who are you?'

The fugitive replies, 'I am the rearguard of the grand army. I have fired the last musket shot on the bridge of Kovno. I have thrown the last of the arms into the Niemen, and have come hither through the woods. I am Marshal Ney.'[1]

Did we throw our victory away? Even in recent years, have we not thrown our arms away in face of an increasingly volatile world situation? These are big questions, but as relevant today as they were fifty years ago.

My expedition to Libya had, by force of events, to be abandoned. Now I had to think of other ways of making use of my windfall leave of absence. This came about in a fortuitous way. I had become friends with the Transjordanian Arab Legion, sometimes knows as 'Glubb's Girls' through their long-skirted cloaks which were part of the uniform. Glubb Pasha was their legendary leader, assisted at that time by Lash Bey, his second-in-command, these oriental titles being an agreeable relic of colonial days.

This was the last of my desert journeys, to ride by camel along Lawrence's route to Aqaba, made famous by the Arab Revolt against the Turks. Lash Bey readily agreed to supply me with Arab Legion camels and guides, and, thus equipped, I set out from the oasis of Azrak on a stormy day in March.

No need now to go into the details of this journey. But I must record that the bedouin tribes whom we met were very hospitable and endless delays ensued on account of elaborate feasts among the bat-winged tents, for they were all out on the spring grazing. Later, whenever we came across a patch of vegetation our little caravan came to a halt to allow our beasts to graze. This could go on for hours on end. Although I had accepted the bedouin ways I was still at heart a westerner. I knew I had a boat to catch home, leaving Haifa on a certain date, and if I failed to catch it there would be trouble ahead, for I would have exceeded my generous leave. Metaphorically I was 'looking at my watch', a condition unknown in these boundless wastes. Thus, during one of these interminable halts I called to my guides, '*Mar-ha-ba*! (Hail!). When are we going to move on?' and the reply came back, '*Ham-dil-illa*! (By the grace of God!). When the grass stops growing!'

NOTES

INTRODUCTION

(p. xi)

1. The Yukon gold rush started in 1898. In 1939, the year of my visit, there were still some old-timers from that era prospecting and earning a precarious living. There was a lot of unexplored and unprospected country out there, and I planned to return the following year, with an American boy of my age I had met, who was going to borrow his father's seaplane! We would hop from 'pond to pond' panning out the creeks. Unfortunately the war intervened.

CHAPTER 1

(pp. 3–8)

1. Field Marshal Mannerheim had been a former officer in the Imperial Army when Finland was part of Russia, and so knew the Russian soldier.
2. Most of the quotations, not otherwise identified, come from the regimental records of the Scots Guards. Marked SG.
3. Sergeant H. Wake (alias Captain H. Wake 60th Rifles KRRC). Now Sir Hereward Wake, Bt, MC, DL. Individual quotations taken from his diary are marked HW. From the author's diary marked CM.
4. Freddie Spencer Chapman was the hero of the ascent of Chomolhari (24,000 ft) in 1937. Subsequently the author of *Watkins' Last Expedition* and *The Jungle is Neutral*, Chatto and Windus, 1949.

5. Lieut-Colonel J.S. Coats MC (late Coldstream Guards).
6. Lieut-Colonel Commanding Scots Guards, Colonel E.W.S. Balfour. Major General Commanding Brigade of Guards, Lieut-General Sir B.N. Sergison Brooke (known as 'Boy Brooke').

CHAPTER 2

(pp 9–18)

1. As Wake points out, Ironside was CIGS at the War Office. He took a prominent part in the Cabinet discussions on Finland. It was he who urged that ski troops were essential in winter months until the spring thaw in May when ordinary infantry could be used. His own experiences in leading the British Expeditionary Force to Archangel in 1918 were influential.
2. WO 166/4100 PRO.

CHAPTER 3

(pp 19–24)

1. *Great Morning*, Osbert Sitwell, London, 1948.
2. Recollections of Colonel R.E.K. Leatham, DSO, Edited by C. Thursby-Pelham and J.D.N. Retallack.
3. Ibid.
4. 4th Baron Delamere; his father was one of the founders of Kenya Colony.
5. Captain Francis L. Egerton, MC, later to be adjutant of the 3rd Bn.
6. Leatham, op. cit.

CHAPTER 4

(pp 27–32)

1. My great-great-great-great uncle, Captain John Macdonell, had been ADC and Military Secretary to Bonnie Prince Charlie at the battle of Culloden. Wounded, he later fled to Holland. Two other great uncles were present on that day.

CHAPTER 5

(pp 33–38)

1. The *Men at Arms* series by Evelyn Waugh.
2. Mick, soubriquet for Irish Guards.
3. *Joy Street*, wartime Letters between Mirren Bradford and Lieutenant John Lewis. Edited by Michael T. Wise, Little Brown & Co, 1995.
4. WO 218/170 'B' Bn Layforce War Diary, formerly known as No. 8 Commando.
5. Ibid.

CHAPTER 6

(pp 41–43)

1. WO 218/169 PRO.
2. HMS *Aphis*, (Lt-Commander Jock Campbell RN Ret). A Royal Navy Gunboat on the China Station used to keep the peace on the Yangtze River. She and her sister ship HMS *Ladybird* had sailed over from the China Sea to join the Mediterranean Fleet. Being river gunboats they had an extremely shallow draught, but breadth of beam prevented excessive rolling. The absence of much metal beneath the waterline proved to be a useful protection against depth charges and dive-bombing.
3. Walter Cowan had persuaded his old shipmate Admiral Sir Roger Keyes, then Chief of Combined Operations, to let him be attached to a commando (No. 8). He was captured whilst on the perimeter in Tobruk, became a PoW and much to his disgust was repatriated, as being too old for active service, a year later. Not content with this, on his return, he took part in the Anzio landings and then attached himself to Lietenant Commander Morgan-Giles (SNO Vis) in charge of naval and raiding operations in the Yugoslav islands.
4. Admiral Cowan in a letter to Lord Glanusk, Commanding Officer Welsh Guards Training Bn, Sandown Park, June, 1941.

CHAPTER 7

(pp 44–48)

1. The highlight of Commando operations in the Middle East was to be Lt-Colonel Geoffrey Keyes's raid on Rommel's HQ at Beda Littoria, for which he was awarded a posthumous VC. He was the son of Admiral Keyes.
2. Lieutenant Lord Jellicoe. Now the Rt Hon Earl Jellicoe, KBE, DSO, MC, PC, FRS. Son of Admiral Jellicoe, the First World War Scapa Flow hero.
3. Jackson, *History of the Second World War, Vol. II. The Mediterranean and Middle East.*
4. Told to me by Rear Admiral Morgan-Giles DSO, OBE, GM, then serving in Tobruk as assistant to SNOIS (Senior Naval Officer Inshore Station).
5. Jackson, op. cit. The American Lease-lend Act was passed on 11 March, 1941, and from this point onwards military equipment began to flow in increasing quantities. Its first main impact was felt with the supply of Stuart Tanks (Honeys) in time for the winter battle in the desert of 1942. But it is worth noting that the output at first was very small. During March, 1941, only fourteen tanks were produced in the whole of the United States.
6. Just before our first attempt we had been staying at the headquarters of Colonel Burg's G(R) mission to the Senussi. This was located in a number of disused cisterns just behind the western perimeter where it met the sea. He and John Haseldon, a former cotton merchant in Cairo, who was shortly to take part in the raid on Rommel's HQ, ran a number of Arab agents on short-term missions into enemy locations, for the information of the Tobforce commander. Our intention had been to use one of these spies, named Abdulla as a guide, but after endless negotiations he failed us. However, John Haseldon, a fluent Arabic speaker, agreed to make a simultaneous attack on the enemy aerodrome of El Adem, just beyond the southern perimeter, but, as we have seen, the plan was aborted. But Haseldon had other ideas. He planned for a long journey into Senussi territory, then in enemy hands, to preach revolt against their masters, the Italians. The Senussi, although they hated the Italians, were not very warlike people, living independently and not in tribal groups, so such efforts were not well rewarded.

CHAPTER 8

(pp 49–53)

1. Lord Sudeley, 6th Baron, whose ancestor was responsible for choosing Barry to design the new Houses of Parliament in 1835. Sadly, he died on passage to the UK.
2. Philip Dunne, a descendant of John Donne, the Elizabethan poet, was a former Member of Parliament, a Captain in the Royal Horse Guards, and now a Commando. It was with him in mind that Waugh wrote in *Officers and Gentlemen*, of his character Ivor Claire: 'Guy remembered Claire as he first saw him in the Roman spring in the afternoon sunlight amid the embosoming cypresses of the Borghese Gardens, putting his horse faultlessly over the jumps, concentrated as a man in prayer. Ivor Claire, Guy thought, was the fine flower of them all. He was quintessential England, the man Hitler has not taken into account.' Waugh then leads his fictitious character, Claire, into a discreditable adventure in Crete, which has no connection with the real life model.
3. Lord Milton, later 9th Earl Fitzwilliam who died tragically in an air crash after the war.
4. Lord Stavordale (Fox-Strangways), descendent of the 18th century politician Charles James Fox and heir to 7th Earl of Ilchester, and historic Holland House (shortly to be destroyed by enemy action).
5. WO 201/731 PRO.
6. *The Diaries of Evelyn Waugh*, Weidenfeld and Nicolson, 1976.
7. WO 201/731 PRO.
8. Ibid.
9. Ibid.
10. The one exception was the far-sighted, intense but brilliant Jock Lewis.

CHAPTER 9

(pp 57–61)

1. *There is a Spirit in Europe, A Memoir of Frank Thompson*, Victor Gollancz, London, 1947.
2. Ibid.
3. Frank Thompson met an untimely and tragic death while serving with the British Military Mission to the Bulgarian Partisans in 1944. The Mission had been surrounded and some killed by

Bulgarian Government troops, who at that time supported the Axis powers. Frank and other partisans were captured. They stood a mock-trial in the village of Litakovo and were summarily shot on 6 June, 1944.

CHAPTER 10

(pp 62–67)

1. Barrie Pitt, The *Crucible of War*, Jonathan Cape, 1980.
2. Several expressions had been borrowed from the South African War. The Vortrekkers and later the Boers adopted the leaguer for their wagon trains at night. The word Commando signified a Boer raiding party.
3. Brigadier 'Jock' Campbell commanded 7th Support Group, part of 7th Armoured Division. For these actions he was awarded the Victoria Cross. About the same time (February, 1942) he was appointed to command 7th Armoured Division, but was sadly killed in an accidental car crash. 'Jock columns', roving colums of all arms, were named after him.

CHAPTER 11

(pp 68–73)

1. D. Frazer Norton, *History of the 26th. Battalion*, Historical Publications Branch, Dept of Internal Affairs, Wellington, N.Z.
2. Barrie Pitt, op. cit.
3. Ibid.

CHAPTER 13

(pp 82–89)

1. The Long Range Desert Group was established by R.A. Bagnold, a resident of Cairo before the war. Promoted Colonel, he had Wavell's blessing to raise this unusual unit. His weekend trips into the desert were to study the geophysics of desert landscape. As a Fellow of the Royal Society he was well qualified to write a book on the subject. The real value of these trips was not apparent until the war broke out, when his experiences of desert navigation (the

Bagnold Sun Compass) and desert travel (sand mats and channels) became invaluable. (see also Ch. 17, Note 1)
2. David Russell had also been a member of the 5th Bn, Scots Guards – the ski battalion.
3. We knew it then as Fuka. Its correct name was Sidi el Haneish.

CHAPTER 15

(pp 98–104)

1. There was a theory that the Stukas were led by Rommel's pilot, whom we had fortuitously allowed to escape, that one of the aircraft waggled its wings as it passed over us as a kind of 'thank-you' gesture. I must admit that I only heard this story years later. It did not occur to us at the time. In any case Hitler had accused our raiding parties of committing nameless atrocities in consequence of which he ordered that we were to be exterminated if caught. Fortunately Rommel ignored these orders as he believed, like us, that this was 'a gentlemen's war'.
2. This chapter is based on an account entitled 'A Journey Through the Qattara Depression', which I wrote for the *Royal Geographical Society Journal* published in March, 1944.

CHAPTER 17

(pp 120–129)

1. The late Sir Laurens van der Post told me that, according to the theory of the Abbé Breuille (who had made a study of rock paintings), the men who created the Gilf paintings, those at Lascaux, those engraved on the rocks in Spain, and that of the Bushmen, all had a common ancestor. It is said that those caves were visited by the Hungarian Count Laszlo de Almásy during his desert expeditions from Cairo in the 1930's, probably accompanied by the Egyptian Prince Kemal el Din. We saw nothing of Almásy on his later alleged spying visits to the Nile Delta from Rommel's HQ during the war. Although I am told that Almásy did indeed raid an LRDG petrol dump near the oasis of Dakhla and later dropped two spies on the Nile who were later captured. A highly fictionalized book entitled *The English Patient* has been written about the activities of this man. It has recently been made into a film.

CHAPTER 18

(pp 130–139)

1. Julian Berry was an officer in the Royal Horse Guards. He told me this story forty-five years after these events!
2. Geoffrey Gordon-Creed later won fame as the man who blew up the Asopos Viaduct, the main line to Athens, which was cut for four months during the German occupation of Greece. For this he was awarded the DSO. (He had been recommended for a V.C.)
3. See Fitzroy Maclean's account in *Eastern Approaches*, Jonathan Cape, 1949.

CHAPTER 19

(pp 140–152)

1. Later Air Vice Marshal L. Pike.
2. Sergeant Almonds (later Major) survived. He was taken PoW. He was a big tall Coldstreamer and, objecting to an Italian officer's attitude, he struck him and knocked him down. He was lucky to get away with it and to escape to allied lines after the Armistice. He rejoined the SAS in NW Europe and was commissioned by Montgomery in the field.

CHAPTER 20

(pp 153–161)

1. David Lloyd-Owen DSO, MC, OBE, later Major-General commanding Near East Land Forces.

CHAPTER 21

(pp 165–168)

1. Nigel Hamilton, *Monty, the Making of a General*, Hamish Hamilton, 1981.

CHAPTER 22

(pp 169–174)

1. De Guingand, *Operation Victory*, Hodder and Stoughton, 1947.
2. Air Officer Commanding Desert Airforce, later Air Marshal Sir Arthur Coningham, a New Zealander.
3. Later Lt General Sir Francis de Guingand, Chief of Staff at 21st Army Group in NW Europe.
4. Later Lt General Sir Brian Robertson, who was the son of the First World War Field Marshal, 'Wully' Robertson.
5. Brigadier E.T. Williams, like Robertson, occupied the same role in NW Europe.

CHAPTER 23

(pp 175–184)

1. De Guingand, op. cit.
2. It must be admitted that the South Africans had taken a terrible pasting in previous desert campaigns, and their manpower was not unlimited.
3. Douglas Darling, RB, was Lumsden's regular GSO II Staff Officer. With a distinguished record he was later to become a Major General. Bill Mather (later Sir William), recovering from wounds, was attached in a supernumerary capacity.

CHAPTER 24

(pp 185–190)

1. Geoffrey Keating, the Rifle Brigade, was a very amusing fellow who was Monty's Public Relations Officer with the Press.
2. 'The Wire' figured prominently in the initial stages of the desert war. A barbed wire fence marked the boundary between Egypt and Italian-occupied Libya. A Treaty allowed British Troops to be stationed in Egypt for purposes of defence. Soon after the war broke out the Italian army crossed the wire and invaded Egyptian territory. All that we were initially able to provide was a light screen of armoured cars belonging to the renowned 11th Hussars.

An Amusing story was told to me by their former quartermaster, Major Addis, who was present at that historic time, as I remember his words, 'We had just gone up to the "wire" where our squadron was involved in rather a nasty scrap. We had one or two killed and badly wounded. So our squadron commander got us together after it was all over and addressed us thus.

"Now lads, you've had your bit of fun. Now we've got to get down to a bit of proper soldiering!"'

This piece of *sang-froid* made the troops laugh and saved the day!

3. It may be wondered why we stuck to the main road and did not use the wide open desert. The coast road had now become the main axis of advance, but it was hardly wide enough for two vehicles to pass. The surface was sometimes tarmac, sometimes sand bound with salt. On either side there was danger of mines, and the recent flooding had caused boggy patches, so the road itself, cleared of mines, was the best route.

CHAPTER 25

(pp 191–196)

1. An allusion to the Cedars of Lebanon. Wishful thinking on my part to imagine any snow there in November.
2. Monty's expression 'my reliable sources' may be thought to refer to Ultra. But Ultra was not the only source of intelligence available. As Sir David Hunt, then GSI(a) at GHQ Cairo, has pointed out to me, Ultra was indeed high level strategic intelligence decrypts. 'Y' intercepts of battlefield enemy signal traffic, or tactical intelligence, was equally useful and speedier in delivery. Photo-recce and prisoner interrogation, by then trustworthy techniques, also played their part in producing the whole intelligence picture.

   The chocolate given to Freyberg was the Suchard which John and I had looted from the enemy dump a day or two before, up till that time unknown in the desert.
3. These controversial comments which have lost their sting after the lapse of 50 years were uttered in private, it must be said. Such dismissive remarks were characteristic of the man. Senior officers who he thought inadequate were often described as 'deadbeats'. Gatehouse was, a little unfairly, called 'a steady old fowl'. Others earned the title of 'a good plain cook', whilst the accolade of 'the cat's whiskers' was reserved for few.

4. Later Field Marshal Lord Harding GCB, CBE, DSO, MC, Chief of the Imperial and General Staff.

CHAPTER 26

(pp 199–203)

1. It is likely that the SAS were in possession of Martuba airfield before Lumsden's men arrived.
2. Pat Hore-Ruthven was the son of the 1st Earl of Gowrie VC, Governor of South Australia.

   Vivian Street (later Major-General) CMG, OBE, DSO, MC, at that time was in the Rifle Brigade.

   Wilfred Thesiger was later to become the famous explorer, was to cross the Empty Quarter in southern Arabia and is the author of several books on Arabian travel. He had a narrow escape while lying up later near El Fascia. An enemy patrol nosed into the hiding place where they lay. Thesiger was convinced that this was the same patrol referred to in Rommel's Diaries (edited by B.H. Liddell Hart):

   'On 23 December [1942] we set off on a beautiful sunny morning to inspect the country south of our front. First we drove along the Via Balbia and then, with two Italian armoured cars as escort, through the fantastically fissured Wadi Zem-Zem towards El Fascia. Soon we began to find tracks of British vehicles, probably made by some of Stirling's people who had been round here on the job of harassing our supply lines. The tracks were comparatively new and we kept a sharp look out to see if we could catch a 'Tommy'. Near to El Fascia I suddenly spotted a lone vehicle. We gave chase but found its crew were Italian. Troops from my Kampfstaffel were also in the area. They had surprised some British commandos the day before and captured maps marked with British store dumps and strong points. Now they were combing the district, also hoping to stumble on a 'Tommy'.'

3. I recounted this story to David 50 years later, while he was in hospital in his final days. To do him justice he enjoyed the story, but added ruefully, 'That was a bit hard!'

CHAPTER 28

(pp 209–213)

1. This was the notorious British deserter, by then employed by the enemy as a spy. His parentage was half British and half Swiss. After the war he was rounded up and almost certainly shot. He appeared to later prisoners in my own clothes, this time posing as an SAS officer.

CHAPTER 29

(pp 214–221)

1. *Joy of Youth, Letters of Patrick Hore-Ruthven*, Peter Davies, 1950.
2. As told by Vivian Street (later to become Major General). The full account was published by *Blackwood's Magazine* (No 1577) in March, 1947.

CHAPTER 30

(pp 223–228)

1. Eric Newby, Author of *Love and War in the Apennines*.
2. Captain A. Hubbard, the Rifle Brigade, was my escape companion throughout Italy.
3. These army boots, which were to carry me down Italy, were subsequently worn on King's Guard at Buckingham Palace.

CHAPTER 33

(pp 243–248)

1. In fact, by filtering it through one's gasmask, it effectively removed the red die!
2. Lt-Commander Hugh Hodgkinson had seen many naval actions as a captain of destroyers, particularly with HMS *Hotspur* off Crete. One of his tenets was that 'the officers must be tougher than the men'. After the war became headmaster of Milton Abbey, one of the country's most successful private schools.
3. The vindication of Monty's point about dealing with the most

important thing and ignoring the rest is shown in this letter from General Simpson, commanding Ninth US Army, to his English namesake, General 'Simbo' Simpson, at the War Office in London. This describes a visit made my Monty to Simpson's HQ during the Ardennes battle.

'He came in and said, "Bill, how are things going with you?"

'And I told him all my problems.

'He had a look through them and said, "There are only three of these problems that matter: this one, this one and this one. The answer to those three are: so and so, and so and so, and so and so." He said, "Let the others go to hell." I did what he told me and the others just disappeared.'

Nigel Hamilton, *Monty the Field Marshal*, Hamish Hamilton, 1986. Quoting an interview with General Sir Frank Simpson.

CHAPTER 34

(pp 251–256)

1. Some 65,000 Allied Servicemen were lost during the Normandy campaign.
2. *Testament of Youth* by Vera Brittain.

CHAPTER 35

(pp 257–262)

1. See *Aftermath of War – Everyone Must Go Home*, by the author, Brasseys, London, 1992.

CHAPTER 36

(pp 263–268)

1. Louis or 'Fuzzy' Sanderson was a gallant officer from the Kings Own Scottish Borderers (KSOB), who served Montgomery as ADC in pre-war Palestine, and again in France at the time of Dunkirk. He won his MC at Termoli in Italy. The nickname 'Fuzzy' was on account of his curly black hair. He served Montgomery as GSO 2 (Liaison) throughout the N.W. Europe Campaign. Part of my account of De Gaulle's visit came from 'Fuzzy', as he told it to me

at the time. His own account, from memory, is contained in his memoir, *Variety is the Spice of Life*, Lt. Col. L.G.S. Sanderson, Minerva Press, 1995.
2. The booking was made by one of De Gaulle's staff, but it turned out to be for a conference the following day not involving the General.
3. Commander C. Maud, RN.
4. King George VI visited Montgomery's headquarters about ten days after we first landed.
5. The reason that she had not been aware of who the visitors were was that Monty ordered all the shutters on that side of the house to be kept closed. Pétain, of course, was considered by us to have been a great collaborator.
6. The newspaper correspondents who accompanied HM the King were responsible for a major lapse in security in giving away the position of the château where the C-in-C had his HQ. As a result the German reaction was immediate. They shelled the camp and one soldier was killed and two wounded. The next day they mistakenly bombed the Château de Creully in the village of that name, completely destroying it. In it had been established the BBC!

CHAPTER 37

(pp 269–272)

1. This independent armoured Brigade (6 Guards Tank) was equipped with Infantry 'I' tanks, in this case Churchills.
2. This story about the water carts was told to me by a former Chief Engineer Officer at the time of our visit to Normandy for the 40th Anniversary of D-Day in 1984.

CHAPTER 38

(pp 273–278)

1. *Normandy to the Baltic*, Montgomery, 1946.

CHAPTER 39

(pp 279–283)

1. *Normandy to the Baltic*, Montgomery, 1946.

CHAPTER 40

(pp 284–291)

1. Lt-Colonel Tom Bigland was Liaison Officer between Bradley (12th Army Group) and Montgomery (21st Army Group). He was based at Bradley's HQ.
2. What had happened was that a Panzer Army had passed very close to First Army HQ at Spa, narrowly missing this and a huge fuel dump nearby. Communications had been shattered as the Americans were now using landlines for telephonic communication and there seemed to be no wireless back-up.
3. 'Freddie' refers to Major-General de Guingand, Chief of Staff at 21st Army Group.
4. Nigel Hamilton, quoting General Sir Frank Simpson at the War Office.
5. Ibid.
6. Eisenhower's HQ in Paris was at the Trianon Palace Hotel at Versailles.
7. Tedder had been Air C in C Middle East, at the time of Alamein, with Coningham's Desert Airforce under command.
8. Quoted by Nigel Hamilton. Pogue interview with Air Chief Marshal Sir James Robb on 3 February, 1947.
9. Ibid.
10. Ibid.

CHAPTER 41

(pp 292–297)

1. As told to me by the late Brigadier Roscoe Harvey just before he died in 1996.
2. Nigel Hamilton, op. cir.
3. Major Richard Harden RTR was later to become an Ulster Unionist Member of Parliament. His achievement, as a non-pilot,

in steering the aircraft to the ground was truly remarkable.
4. Hamilton, *Monty The Field Marshal*. It is noted in this reference that the FW190 German fighter was smaller, lighter and better gunned that the Spitfire. We always thought it was a Messerschmitt 109!
5. Flight Lieutenant McQueen's death was a great loss. He was slightly older than us and of a scholarly disposition. He shared the same mess and became a close friend.
6. *Aftermath of War*, by the author, Brassey's, 1992.

EPILOGUE

(pp 298–299)

1. I found this quotation in my campaign notebook, and so far have been unable to trace its author. Marshal Ney (1769–1815), one of Napoleon's Generals, was the son of a cooper. During his service he was made successively Duke of Elchingen, Prince of the Moskowa, and Marshal of France. His conduct of the retreat of the rearguard from Moscow earned him immortality, but it did not save him from a firing squad, as a result of a change of loyalty in his final days.

INDEX

Abbassia, 160
Abyssinia, 167
Adair, General Sir Allan, 274
Agedabia, 69, 133, 201
Aiguillettes, Les, 14
Ain el Gazala, 41, 45, 72, 194, 195, 196, 199, 200
Aircraft:
   Auster, 277, 279, 293
   Bombay, 99, 101
   CR42s, 143, 145, 146
   FW190, 293
   Heinkel, 91
   JU87, 42
   JU88, 42
   Junkers, 91
   Lodestar, 196
   Lysander, 196
   Macchi, 145, 148
   Messerschmitt (109), 91, 97, 145, 177
   Savoia, 79, 42
   Spitfire, 177
   Stuka, 42, 45, 47, 91, 92, 94, 96, 97, 100
Alamein, El, 81, 83, 84, 85, 97, 98, 107, 108, 109, 131, 132, 137, 158, 160, 168, 169, 171, 175, 178, 186, 196, 216, 246, 252, 261, 270, 271, 274, 285, 293
Alam Halfa, 179
Alaska, xii
Albergo Tobruk, 45, 195
Aldershot, 5
Alexander, General, 109, 173
Alexander, Michael, 107, 108, 186

Alexandria, 41, 44, 47, 49, 83, 107, 131, 169, 173, 181, 187, 200
Algeria, 174
Allenby, General, 75, 76
Allied Land Forces, 280, 288
Almonds, Sergeant, 127, 128, 130, 142
Alps, Italian, 13
Alston, Gordon, 131, 144, 145, 159, 200
Americans, 195, 246, 254, 271, 273, 276, 277, 278, 280, 281, 283, 290, 293
Ampney Park, 18
Ankara, 76
Antelat, 70
Antwerp, 280, 284, 286
Apennines, 224, 226, 233
Aqaba, 299
Aquila, L', 232
Arabs Gulf, 80
Arctic, 7
Arctic Ocean, 159
Ardennes, 283, 284, 285, 290, 291
Army
   British, 34, 287
   2nd (British), 251
   Eighth, 57, 62, 72, 83, 87, 169, 172, 173, 187, 199, 200, 239
   1st (US), 284, 285, 286, 287, 290, 291
   3rd (US), 290
   9th (US), 285, 287, 288, 290
   Red (USSR), 2
Army Groups

   12th (US) 281, 285, 288
   21st (BR), 246, 285, 288, 289
Arnhem, 279, 280, 281, 282, 284
Arran, Isle of, 30, 33, 34
Astor, Gavin, 36, 52, 251
Aswan, 160
Asyut, 110, 111
Athens, 239
Auchinleck, General, 87, 193
Australia/Australians, 40, 47, 177, 179, 182
Azimuth (card), 58
Azrak, 299

Baalbek, 82
Backhouse, Jasper, 72
Baghdad, 75
Bagnold, 82
Baguish-Siwa Telegraph Line, 100
Bailey, Chris, 87, 133, 138, 140, 141, 145, 151
Baku, 10
Balfour, Colonel E.W.S., 17
Baltic, Sea, 2
Baltic States, 2
Barbarossa, Operation, 48
Barce, 109, 132, 149, 153
Bari, 211, 212, 215, 240
Barkworth, Lt, 52
Barrel Hill, 182
Barrowclough, Brigadier, 68
Bastogne, 287, 288, 290
Battalions
   1st KOSB, 167
   2nd Middlesex, 167

2nd Queens, 167
5th Scots Guards, 5–17, 132
15th (Aust), 180
119e Des Chasseurs de Haute Montaigne, 13, 14
Battle of Britain, 29
Battleaxe, Operation, 40
Bayeux, 248, 264, 265, 266, 269, 271
BBC, 159, 225, 253, 254, 275
Beirut, 132
Bekaa Valley, 82
Belgium/Belgian, 2, 20, 138, 279, 282
Benghazi, 69, 107, 108, 109, 114, 123, 131, 132, 133, 136, 137, 139, 142, 143, 145, 151, 156, 159, 199, 201
Berka, 137, 145
Berlin, 11, 247, 280
Berry, Lt Julian, 36, 52, 131, 132
Biferno, River, 236, 237
Bigland, Colonel Tom, 284, 285
Bimbashis, 130, 132, 160
Bimbashi Stubbs, 132, 159, 160
Bir el Chleta, 69 (Bir – arabic – 'well')
Bir el Garrari, 153
Bir Hacheim, 72
Bir Zalten, 201
Birdcage Walk, 19
Birmingham, 16
Bizerta, 195
Black Sea, 10
Blay, 273, 274
Blitzkreig, 19
Bocage, 271, 273
Bois de Cerisy, 266
Bolton, Brigadier Linden, 67
Bonnie Prince Charlie, 27
Bordon Camp, 4, 5, 7
Bracken, Bill, 6
Bradley, General, 281, 288, 289, 290, 291, 293
Brévan, 14
Brigades
  2 Armoured, 71
  4 Armoured, 60, 64, 66, 70
  7 Armoured, 63, 66
  9 Armoured, 181, 183, 188, 189
  22 Armoured, 63, 66
  29 Armoured, 292
  20 Australian, 180
  6 Guards Tank, 271
  22 Guards, 52
  9th Infantry, 166
  4th Light Armoured, 190, 192, 194
  New Zealand Infantry, 68
  Polish, 132
  15 Scottish, 271
  1 South African, 70
  5 South African, 69
  SS Brigade, 51
Briggs, General, 176, 183
Brighton, 245, 248
British Arctic Air Route Expedition, 6
British Empire, xii, 5, 298
British Expeditionary Force (BEF), 11, 17, 19, 21, 40
Brocklehurst, Major Sir Philip, 53
Brodick, 30, 33
Broomfield House, 245
Brother Gregory, 228
Brown, Lt M., 52
Browning, General 'Boy', 282
Brussels, 271, 277, 280, 292
Buchanan, (Desmond) 'Kelpie', 27, 52
Buq Buq, 190, 192
Burg el Arab, 169, 172
Burma, 63, 251
Burnham-on-Crouch, 28, 29
Buseima (oasis), 133

Caen, 254, 271, 273, 274, 276
Cairo, 37, 49, 51, 57, 63, 71, 74, 75, 85, 86, 88, 98, 99, 103, 107, 108, 109, 120, 121, 127, 139, 146, 157, 159, 160, 169, 171, 173, 187, 196, 200, 210
Calvocoressi, Captain Ion, 67
Cambridge, xi, xii, 166
Cambridge University, 166
  OTC Cavalry Squadron, 166
Campbell, Captain RN, 41, 42
Campbell, Brigadier Jock, VC, 66
Campobasso, 233
Canadians, 271, 277, 278
Cape Town, 34
Capuzzo, El, 193
Carver, Betty, 165, 166
  Dick, 165
  John, 165
Castel Guelfo, 218, 240
Castel Nuovo, 227
Caucasus, 10, 15, 75
Caumont, 276
Cavalry, 64
Cecil Hotel, Alexandria, 49, 107
Cerredolo, 226, 240
Chamonix, 7, 11, 12, 13, 15
Chamberlain, Prime Minister, 2
Chapman, F. Spencer, 6
Chasseurs Alpins, 7, 11, 12, 111
Chatham, 166
Chaudfontaine, 284, 286, 290
Cherbourg, 254, 271, 272
Cheshire, 239
Chicago, xii
Chieti, 215, 216, 217, 218, 232, 239
China, 41, 53, 227
Churchill, Randolph, 28, 31, 35, 37, 108, 251
  Winston, xi, 17, 40, 174, 196, 267, 273
C.I.G.S., 51, 274
Clarke, Sir Rupert, 4
Claridge's Hotel, 244
Coats, Lt-Col Jimmy, 6, 7, 8
Colchester, 19
Colditz, 108, 215, 243
Collins, Lt Ian, 36, 52, 251
Colville, Sir John (Jock), 17
Commando
  No. 3, 51
  No. 7, 37, 51
  No. 8, 28, 34, 35, 37, 40, 49, 50, 51, 58, 83, 119, 122, 131, 133,
  No. 11, 37, 51
  ME, 51
Coningham, A.V.M. 'Maori', 173, 189, 195, 245
Continental Hotel, 107
Copts, 58, 59
Corps
  13, 70, 181
  30, 172, 254, 286, 292
  Afrika Korps, 46, 64, 69, 170, 185
  10 Armoured (Corps de Chasse), 175, 183, 184, 189, 194

317

Royal Army Medical, 6
Royal Army Service, 160, 202
Cowan, Admiral Sir Walter, 43
Cresta Run, 6
Crete, 35, 40, 51, 87, 109
Cruelly, 258
Cripps, John, 9, 11, 12, 14, 15, 17, 18
Croce (Italian Interpreter), 216
Cruellet, 258, 273
Cruewell, General, 69
Crusader, Operation, 62
Culloden, 27
Cumper, Bill, 132, 141, 142, 143, 145
Cunningham, Admiral, 45
Cussabat, 204, 211
Cyprus, 87, 133
Cyprus Mule Company, 87
Cyrenacia, 40, 133
Czechoslovakia, xi

Daba, El, 84, 187, 188
Dahkla Oasis, 114, 115
Daly, Lt-Col Dermot, 28, 36, 37, 49, 52, 53, 57, 58, 70, 71, 72, 83, 251
Dalziel, 93, 147
Dardanelles, 10
Darling, Douglas, 184, 192
Davos, 7
Davy, Brigadier, 63
Dawnay, Lt-Col Kit, 274, 275
D-Day, 109, 172, 243, 247, 253
Dead Sea, 80
De Douval, Madame and L'Abbé, 260, 261, 266, 268
De Gaulle, General, 261, 263, 264, 265, 266, 267
Deir el Antonyus, 59
Delamere, Tom, 21, 22, 24
Derna, 149, 158, 160, 171, 199
Desert Air Force, 173
Desert Rats, 193, 274
Dieppe Raid, 161
Dillon, Brian, 160
Dimopoulos, Evie/Jenny, 107
Dinant, 292
Divisions
   1st Airborne, 282
   American Airborne, 288

1 Armoured, 71, 176, 183
2nd Armoured, 243
6 Armoured, 292
7 Armoured, 60, 62, 69, 133, 189, 193, 194, 274
10 Armoured, 176, 184, 189
11 Armoured, 292
9 Australian, 44, 170
Guards Armoured, 243, 245, 276
51 Highland, 176, 183
2 New Zealand, 170, 176
Polish Armoured, 274
Down Ampney, 295
Drongin,Cpl, 122, 123, 124, 127, 128, 130, 143, 145, 151, 152
Duke of York's Headquarters, 29
Dunkirk, 17, 20, 27
Dunne, Captain Philip, 36, 49, 52
Duveen, Arthur, 145, 147

Easonsmith, Jake, 153, 154
Echternach, 285
Egerton, Francis, 23
Egypt, 40, 51, 69, 74, 87, 111, 1121, 171, 186, 229, 261, 297
Egyptian Post, 99, 111
Egyptian State Railway, 50
Eight Bells Pass, 81, 114, 117, 121, 122
Eindhoven, 295
Eisenhower, 245, 261, 273, 280, 281, 282, 287, 288, 289, 290, 293
El Adem, 194
El Agheila, 69, 186, 193, 100, 201
El Fascia, 202
Elmhirst, Tommy, 195
Elwes, Simon, 23, 71
Escarpment Rendezvous, 82, 85, 97
Esher, 21
Ethiopia, 167
Evans, Arthur, 20
Everest Expedition, 6
Evetts, General, 37
Ewart, Colonel Joe, 282

Falaise Pocket, 276
Farida, Queen, 71
Farouk, King, 71

Ferguson, Lt-Col Bernard, 77
Finland, 2, 3, 4, 10, 13, 15, 16
Finnish Expedition, 28
Finnish Minister, 4
Firenzuola, 227
Fitzclarence, Eddie, 35
Fontanellato, 217, 218, 240
Fordham, Basil, 27
France/French, 2, 20, 85, 111, 116, 125, 161, 220, 251, 252, 253, 254, 267, 276, 280
Franks, Brian, 202
Frary, Maurice, 270
Fraser (Clan), 30
Free French, 72, 85, 108
   Harent, 85
   Haron, 125, 160
   Klein, 85
   Le Grand, 85
   Lesec, 145, 160
   Martin, 85, 111, 120, 121, 134, 135, 145, 160
   Zirnhold, 85
French Canal Company, 37
French Equatorial Africa, 83
French Foreign Legion, 151
Frenchman's Halt, 117
Freyberg, General, 170, 176, 181, 182, 183, 189, 190, 192
Fuka, 88, 153, 158, 183, 186, 188

Gallivare, 17
Gambut, 195
Gatehouse, Brig Gen Alec, 64, 66, 69, 70, 176, 185, 189
Gavin, David, 11, 14
Gavin, J.M.L., 6
Geldrop, 293
Geneifa Camp, 37, 50
Genoa, Gulf of, 224
George V Dock, 16
German Reich, 4
German-Soviet Pact, 2
Gezira, 107, 109
GHQ Middle East, 49, 50, 51, 52, 109, 127, 171, 200
Gilf Kebir, 80, 114, 116, 117, 118, 120, 121, 122, 123, 124, 131, 155
Gillard, Frank, 275
Glanusk, Lt-Col Bill, 23, 24
Glasgow, 16, 202
Glubb Pasha, 299

Goat Fell, 33
Goodwood, Operation, 276
Gordon-Creed, Geoffrey, 132
Goschen, Major Johnny, 5
Gosport, 251
Gott, 'Strafer', 66
Gran Sasso D'Italia, 232
Grant, George, 72, 82
Grave, 281, 293
Great Bitter Lakes, 37, 109, 114, 130
Great Sand Sea (Grand Erg), 59, 80, 135, 153, 154, 155, 156, 157, 159
Greece, 40, 57, 109, 156, 240, 298
Greenland, 6
Greenock, 30
Grenade, Operation, 293
Griffith-Jones, Mervyn, 36, 52
Gastaad, 165
Guards
  Brigade of, 7, 21
  Brigade of, Major General, 7
  Coldstream, 27, 36, 52, 93
  Grenadier, 23, 27, 36, 47, 52
  Irish, 28, 50, 52, 132
  Life, 36, 52
  Royal Dragoon, 76
  Royal Horse (Blues), 30, 36, 52
  Scots, 5, 6, 7, 28, 52, 87, 122
  2nd Scotss, 85
  5th Scots, 5–17
  Welsh, 7, 9, 19, 23, 28, 46, 50, 52, 170, 243, 296
Guingand, Brigadier Freddy de, 173, 176, 192, 193
Gulf of Sirte, 69
Gurdon, Robin, 86
Gurowski, R.D.M., 10

Haifa, 299
Hale, L-Cpl, 50
Halfaya Pass, 192
Halfway House, 200
Hamilton, Nigel, 289
Harden, Dick, 284, 293, 294
Harding, General John, 71, 193
Harrow, 61, 295
Harvey, John, 4, 7
Harvey, Brigadier Roscoe, 292
Harwich, 21

Haseldon, John, 109, 132, 154, 161
Hasselt, 286
Hastings, Major Lewis, 159
Hastings, Stephen, 84, 85, 95, 96, 98, 107, 108, 132, 134, 135, 136, 137, 139, 144, 145, 158, 159, 160
Haute Savoie, 7, 15
Hawari, 133
Hawawiri, 133
Haw-Haw, Lord, 11, 13
Heliopolis, 99
Henderson, (Johnny), JRH., 239, 274, 275
Henry (Rhodesian officer), 154
Herbison, 'Herbie', 72
Herodotus, 114
Hitler, Adolf, xi, 2, 273, 298
Hodges, General, 284, 285, 286, 287, 288, 289, 290, 291, 292
Hodgkinson, 'Hughie', 244
Hodgkinson, Reggie, 244
Holland, 293, 294
Holy Land, 75
Homs, 202, 203, 210
Hong Kong, 30
Hooper, Geoffry, 64
Hopton, Eric, 4, 9, 11, 14
Hore-Ruthven, Pat, 202, 214
Horne, Alistair, 279
Horrocks, General, 181
Houffalize, 287
Hough, Andy, 203, 210, 212, 215
'Hound', Major, 50
Howard's Cairn, 155, 156, 157
Howeitat Tribe, 75, 76
Hubbard, Archie, 224, 230, 231, 234, 235, 239
Hussars
  4th, 87
  7th, 60, 63
  8th, 65, 69
  10th, 185
  11th, 173, 189, 192, 193
Gloucester, 108
Huy, 287

Independent Companies, 31
India/Indian, 44
  Civil Service, xii
Infantry
  Base Depot, 52, 53

Durham Light, 52, 133
Somerset Light, 52
Inverailort House, 30
Inverary, 30
Iraq, 75
Ironside, General, 10
Isigny, 266
Islamic, 113
Ismailia, 37
Italy/Italians, 13, 37, 46, 113, 138, 141, 167, 189, 202, 203, 204, 205, 206, 210, 216, 217, 220, 223, 224, 226, 229, 230, 231, 236, 239, 246, 251, 261, 274

Jalo, 109, 132, 133, 135, 151, 154, 155, 159, 160
Japan, 247
Jarabub, 59, 62, 68, 80, 133, 154, 155
Jebel Akhdar, 69, 109, 136
Jebel Owenat, 114
Jellicoe, George, 7, 36, 44, 45, 46, 47, 49, 52, 84, 87, 88, 95, 96, 108, 138, 195, 251
Jerusalem, 75, 77
Jof, 133
John, Augustus, 165
John, Prester, 297
Jordan, 97
Jordan Valley, 80
Juliana Mole, 137
Jutland, Battle of, 43

Kabrit, 82, 83, 109, 110, 124, 160, 161
Karelian Isthmus, 2
Kasserine Pass, 277
Kealy, Capt Michael, 52, 133, 145, 147, 148, 149, 156, 157
Keane, General, 286, 287
Keating, Geoffrey, 185
Kemal El Din, Prince, 114
Kent, Brian, 7, 9
Kenya, 160
Kershaw, Sergeant, 147
Keyes, Lt-Col, Geoffrey, 131
Keyes, Sir Roger, 34
Kharga, 110, 111, 112, 113, 114, 118, 120, 122
King David Hotel, 75
Klondike, xii
Klosters, 7

Knight, Brodie, 7, 14
'Knightsbridge', 178
Koenig, General, 72
Kovno, 298
Kufra, 81, 83, 108, 109, 112, 113, 114, 115, 117, 118, 121, 122, 123, 124, 126, 127, 128, 129, 130, 131, 132, 133, 146, 150, 151, 153, 154, 155, 158, 159, 160, 200, 210
Kunetra Crossing, 100

Labrador, 6
Ladoga, Lake, 2
Lady Chatterley's Lover, 36
Lambie, Corporal, 93, 95, 97
Lancaster, John, 189, 196
Lance, Capt, 52
Langton, Tommy, 'Tubby', 36, 52, 131, 132, 154
Largs, 30
La Spezia, 224
Lash Bey, 299
Lawrence of Arabia, 76, 86, 299
Laycock, Lt-Col Bob, 30, 31, 35, 37, 51
Layforce, 37, 50, 107, 109
Leatham, Col Chicot, 19, 20, 23
Lebanon, 75
Leese, General Oliver, 177, 179
Le Havre, 15
Leptis Magna, 202, 203
Levant, 83, 173
Lewis, Jock, 24, 28, 29, 36, 52, 82
Liaison Officers, 184, 192, 244, 245, 247, 264, 269, 270, 277, 279, 281, 284, 287, 288
Libya/Libyan Desert, 80, 203, 297, 299
Liège, 285, 286, 287, 293
Lily, Corporal, 93, 94, 95
Lindsay, Martin, 6
Lion D'Or, Bayeux, 265, 266
Liphook, 5, 8, 248
Litani River, 51
Lloyd, Colonel 'Gaffer', 46
Lloyd-Owen, David, 154, 156, 157
Lochailort, 30, 31
Loch Fyne, 122

Lock & Co, 30
Lombardy, Plain of, 217, 224
London, 13, 21, 51, 71, 243, 244
Long Range Desert Group (LRDG), 53, 81, 82, 90, 99, 109, 114, 126, 128, 129, 130, 132, 149, 150, 153, 155, 156, 157, 171
Louvain, 286
Lovat, Lt-Col Shimi, 30, 31
Lovat Scouts, 30
Lumsden, General, 175, 177, 183, 184, 189, 192, 194
Luxembourg, 285

Maas, River, 281
Maclean, Fitzroy, 108, 139
Maiella, 233
Malmédy, 285
Malta, 194
Manila Rounds, 2
Mannerheim, Field Marshal, 2, 3
Marada, 159
Market Garden, Operation, 281
Martuba, 194, 200
Matcek, General, 274
Mather, Bill, 165, 175, 184, 192
Mayfield, Major Brian, 5
Mayne, Paddy, 87, 88, 91, 131, 134, 136, 151, 157, 189, 201, 210, 215
Mediterranean Sea, 41, 80, 113, 133, 175, 177, 210, 214
Melot, Bob, 138, 141, 145, 151
Mena Camp, 104
Mena House Hotel, 57, 104
Mersa Matruh, 41, 42, 84, 188, 189, 245
Meuse, River, 285, 286, 287, 292
Meuse-Escaut Canal, 281
Middle East, 82, 109, 268, 289
Milton, Peter, 36, 50, 52
Minox camera, 30
Misurata, 201, 203
Miteirya Ridge, 178, 186
'Mo' (Souffragi), 110
Molotov, 2, 4
Mont Blanc, 11, 13
Montgomery, General B.L.

new Eighth Army Commander, 87
Family connections, and appearance, 165
his wife's death, 166
Commanding 9th Infantry Brigade, Portsmouth, 166
manoeuvres, Salisbury Plain, 167
Address, Eve of Alamein, 169–170
his effect on morale, 171
his system of command, 173
refuses to be hustled by Churchill, 174
creates a 'Corps de Chasse', 175
armour fails to break out – a crisis conference, 176–177
his routine during battle, 178
relations with Gen Pienaar, 179
switches axis of attack, 179
a form of relaxation, 181
his regard for Freyberg, 182
anger with Lumsden, 184
captures Gen Von Thoma, 185–187
Monty in the advance, 192
his view on Desert Rats, 193
bets on end of war, 195
resists Churchill's bullying tactics, 196
'place for mad people in war', 200–201
Monty's HQ in Italy, 289
I am invited to rejoin Monty, 244
domestic matters at Broomfield House, 245
'Eve of Invasion' address, 246
unwelcome visitors, 263
arrival of De Gaulle, 265
Monty's technique – refinements in, 270–271
the 'looting' incident, 273–274
acquires a dog, 275
vindication of strategy, 275–276
rigidity in US system, 277
use of LO's, 278

320

loses command of Land
  Forces, 280
Operation 'Market Garden',
  281
stagnation after Arnhem,
  282
Ardennes Offensive, 284
pre-empts Eisenhower,
  285–286
LO's sent off fact-finding,
  287–288
crisis in command set-up,
  289–291
two LO's crash, 293–294
a hospital visit, 295
post-war HQ at Östenwalde, 296
Moorehead, Alan, 275
Morgan-Giles, Cmdr. RN, 47
Morshead, General, 45, 46, 170
Moscow, 298
Mount Sinai, 58
Msus, 134, 136
Msus Stakes, 72
Mulberry Harbours, 272
Murmasnk, 10, 17
Mussolini, 171, 229, 253
McGowan, Billy, 36
McQueen, Flt. Lt., 293, 294

Namur, 285, 287
Naples, 226, 227
Narvik, 17
Neder Rijn, River, 281
Ness, Pat, 47
Newby, Eric, 223
New Zealand/ers, 40, 47, 83, 153, 171, 182, 188, 194, 295
Ney, Marshal, 299
Niemen, River, 299
Nijmegen, 281, 282, 293
Nile/Nile Delta, 59, 74, 83, 103, 104, 109, 110, 112, 113, 120, 121, 160, 173, 203
Nile, Battle of the, 43
Normandy, 168, 251, 255, 256, 263, 266, 274, 275, 277, 278, 279
North Sea, 282
North Wales, 17
Norway, 10, 17, 21, 31, 111
Norwegian Campaign, 17
Nuremburg War Crimes
  Trials, 36

Odgers, Major Paul, 270
Olivey, Captain, 150, 151, 153, 154
Omar Khayyam, 57
Ombashi/Bimbashi, 132
Orne, River, 276
Ortona, 245
O'Shaugnessy, Major, 45
Osnabruck, 296
Östenwalde, 296
Oxford
  Union, xi
  Rowing Blue, 36, 132

Palestine/Palestinians, 74, 75, 108, 135, 171, 296, 297
Palmyra, 76
Pantellaria, 52
Panzer Divisions, 63, 66, 169, 182, 273, 281, 285, 290, 291, 292
  15th, 193
  21st, 193
Paris, 13, 111, 273, 277, 289
Parma, 217, 223
Pas de Calais, 255, 272
Patton, General, 277, 290
Pearson-Gregory, John, 47
Pedder, Colonel, 51
Pescara, River, 215, 233, 240
Pétain, Marshal, 267
Petsamo, 10, 17
Phantoms (GHQ Liaison
  Squadron), 53, 57, 64, 286
'Piccadilly' (Codeword), 178
Pickering, 243, 244
Pienaar, General Dan, 70, 178, 179
Pike, Lorry, 87, 145
Pisa, 223
Pitt, Barrie, 63, 68
Pleydell, Malcolm, 85, 86, 136
Pluto Fuel Pipeline, 272
Poland/Polish, xi, 2, 44, 274, 282
Poland, Capt Patsy, RN, 48
Portsdown Hill, 246
Portsmouth, 166, 244, 245, 248, 251
Poston, John, 173, 175, 188, 189, 192, 193, 201, 247, 248, 253, 258, 265, 273
Prisk, Eddie, 270

Qara, 98, 100, 101, 102

Qattara Depression, 80, 83, 85, 97, 98, 99, 101, 102, 103, 108, 131
Qattara Spring, 84, 85, 98, 100, 102
Quebec Barracks, 5

Raeburn, Major Digby, 14
Ramsay, Admiral, 245
Raumsley, Derek, 87
Red Cross, 216, 218, 219, 230
Red Sea Hills, 58, 59
Reichwald, Battle of the, 293, 295
Regiments
  Alpini, 218
  Armoured Car, 76
  Household Cavalry, 34, 131
  18 (KEO) Indian Cavalry, 46, 47
  12th Lancers, 194
  Queens Bays, 47
  60th Rifles, 132
  Rifle Brigade, 202, 203
  Royal Tank, 64
  3 Royal Tank, 69
  5 Royal Tank, 69
  4th South African
    Armoured Cars, 189
  Scottish Horse (Yeomanry), 36
REME, 108, 114, 117, 118, 119, 120, 123, 128, 135
Rhine, River, 280, 281, 293
Rhodesia/Rhodesian, 150, 151, 154
Rhodes, 37
Ribbentrop, 2, 4
Ribiana, Sand Sea, 133
Riley, Quinton, 6
Ritchie, General, 71
Robb, Air Vice Marshal, 289
Roberts, Lord, 43
Roberts, General, 292
Robertson, General Brian, 173
Rockets
  V1, 272
  V2, 272
Roman Way Camp, 19, 20
Rome, 240, 253
Rommel, Field Marshal, 62, 69, 71, 95, 109, 131, 161, 170, 172, 173, 183, 185, 186, 201, 245

Royal Air Force/RAF, 40, 87, 134, 137, 141, 142, 145, 176, 199, 217, 220, 277
Royal Engineers, 45, 133
Royal Marines, 34, 35, 51, 109
Royal Military Academy, 3, 4, 5, 6, 7, 19
Royal Navy, 40, 43, 45, 156
Rualla Tribe, 75
Ruhr, 280
Rundstedt, General Von, 285, 288, 290, 292, 293
Russell, David, 7, 9, 87, 97, 132, 154
Russell, Colonel Leo, 252, 265, 270, 273
Russia/Russians, 16, 48, 139, 262, 284, 298
Russian Orthodox Church, 20
Ryder, Capt, 9

Saanen Möser, 165
Saar, The, 280, 290
Sadler, Michael, 90
Salisbury Plain, 166, 167, 168, 246
San Benedetto, 227
Sanderson, 'Fuzzy', 264, 265, 266
Sandown Park, 21, 22, 24, 71
Sangro, River, 233
San Stephano, 232
Santa Maria, 227
Santayana, George, 298
Sappho, 120
S.A.S. ('L' Detachment), 6, 34, 36, 53, 81, 83, 108, 127, 156, 159, 170, 171, 199, 200, 215, 243, 286
S.B.S., 107, 108, 109, 130, 156
Scandinavia, 2, 15, 33
Scheldt, River, 280
School of Musketry, Hythe, 31
Scotland, 15, 27, 33
Scott, J.M., 6
Scratchley, Sandy, 87, 98, 99, 101, 108, 111, 112, 113, 114, 115, 116, 117, 120, 121, 126, 127, 128, 130, 144, 145, 151, 157, 159, 160
Seine, River, 273, 277
Senussi Tribe, 59, 113, 133, 137, 149, 204

Shark Squadron, 189
Shepheard's Hotel, Cairo, 50, 53, 199, 200
Ships, HM
  Aba, 45
  Aphis, 41, 42, 43, 44, 45
  Auckland, 45
  Baretry, 16
  Ben-My-Chree, 15
  Chakla, 45
  Cossack, 244
  Costa Rica, 40
  Coventry, 160
  Dainty, 45
  Diamond, 40
  Ducks (Dukws) (landing craft), 255, 256, 257
  Eureka, 45, 47, 48
  Fiona, 45
  Glencairn, 40
  Glenroy, 34, 37
  Grimsby, 45
  Karapara, 45
  Ladybird, 45
  Landing Ship Tank (LST), 251, 255
  Medway, 41
  Pass of Balamaha, 45
  Pennland, 45
  Rhino Ferry, 255
  Rodney, 253
  Sikh, 161
  Slamat, 40
  Ulster Prince, 10, 40
  Victory, 251, 253
  Vita, 45
  Waterhen, 45
  Wryneck, 40
  Zulu, 161
Ships (Axis) Louisano, 182
  Italian Submarine, 209–213
Sicily, 221
Sidi (title)
  Abd el Rahman, 183
  Azeiz, 193
  Baguish, 41, 188
  Barrani, 86, 190
  Bishr, 107
  Haneish, 188
  Ibeid, 183
  Omar, 69
  Rezegh, 62, 66, 67, 68, 69
Siegfried Line, 2, 280
Silk Route, 53
Silvertop, David, 64
Simpson, General Frank

'Simbo', 288, 293
Simpson, Lt. Gen. William H., 288, 291
Sinai Desert, 74, 83
Sinclair's (Photographic), 30
Singapore, 109
Siwa Oasis, 80, 99, 155
Skew, Quartermaster Sergeant, 117, 128, 135, 151
Smith, General Sir Arthur, 52
Smith, General Bedell, 288, 290
'Smithy', 258
Smuts, General, 261
Smythe, Professor, 147
Solent, 251, 253
Sollum, 190, 192, 194
South Africa/ns, 47, 178
Southampton, 10, 15, 16
Southwick House, 168, 245, 246
Soviet Union, 2
Spa (Belgium Watering Place), 284, 289
Spain, 220
Spanish War, 5
Special Service Volunteers, 52
Spencer, Major John, 243
Spithead, 251, 256
Stalin, 2
Stavordale, Harry, 50
Stirling, David
  the Ski Battalion, 6
  No. 8 Commando, 28
  his climbing skills, 33
  voyage round Cape, 34
  subsequent sickness, 38
  confrontation with a cab-horse, 49
  disenchantment with military, 50
  due 'repatriation', 52
  tries to recruit me, 53
  a new idea born, 82
  his leadership technique, 84
  raiding behind the lines, 85–86
  the mass attack, 87–91
  its aftermath, 95–96
  preparation for raid on Benghazi, 108
  Stirling's 'ideal man', 122
  his insistence on speed, 127–128
  casualty on the Trigh el Abd, 136
  compulsive leadership, 138

322

his change of plan, 139
facing disaster, 140–143
victim of strafing, 146
his confidence and
   cheerfulness, 151
goes missing, 158
his return, 160
relationship with Army
   Commander, 169,
   200–201
his new scheme, 191
a dinner at Shepheard's
   Hotel, 199
his breezy attitude towards
   survival, 202
he comes to grief – a
   visionary leader, 215
languishes in Colditz, 243
Stirling, Peter, 109
St Gervais-les-Bains-le-Fayet,
   11, 15
Strauss, Cyril, 132
Street, Vivian, 202, 214, 215
Strickland, General, 195
Strong, General, 289, 290
St Trond, 286
Studland Bay, 244
Sudan, 83, 121, 133, 158, 171
Sudan Defence Force/SDF,
   109, 122, 123, 130, 132,
   151, 154, 155, 159, 160
Sudan Political, xii
Sudeley, Major 'Bones', 49
Sud-Tyrol, 226
Suez/Suez Canal/Gulf of
   Suez, 34, 35, 37, 58, 74,
   75, 82, 130
Supercharge, Operation, 183, 187
Sweden/Swedes, 2, 10, 16, 17
Switzerland, 114, 165, 217,
   220, 282
Syria, 51, 75, 76, 82, 191, 202

Taiserbo Oasis, 133
Talakh, 133
Tanks
   Churchill, 271
   Cromwell, 271
   Flail (Scorpion), 172
   Honeys (Stuart), 65, 67,
      108, 132, 190
   Sherman, 271
   Tiger, 281
Tarhuna, 209
Tebus, 133
Tedder, Air Marshal, 245, 273,
   289

Teheran, 75
Tel el Aqqaqir, 183
Termoli, 216, 266
Tesdre, stream, 286
Thesiger, Wilfrid, 202
Thoma, General Von, 185,
   186, 187, 188, 245
Thompson, Frank, 58, 72, 82
Thompson's Post, 182
Thornton, Richard, 61
Thursby-Pelham, Christopher,
   20
Tibesti Mountains, 297
Tibet, 13
Tidworth, 167
Timpson, Alastair, 4, 7, 153
'Tinker', LRDG Navigator, 86
Tobruk, 40, 41, 44, 45, 47, 48,
   49, 52, 62, 63, 65, 66, 69,
   83, 87, 109, 132, 138, 150,
   154, 156, 160, 170, 182,
   194, 195, 196, 199, 216
Tocra, 109
Tollab, 133
Tolstoy, Leo, 62
Torch Landings, 174
Trans-Jordanian Arab Legion,
   299
Trianon Hotel, 289
Trig (Arabic 'Track')
   Cappuzzo, 65
   El Abd, 69, 134, 135, 154
Tripoli, 109, 199, 201, 202,
   207, 210
Tripolitania, 62, 195, 203,
   211, 214, 215, 224
Tunis, 195
Turkey/Turkish, 74, 76, 77, 247
Turkish-Syrian Frontier, 75
Tutton, Corporal, 115, 117, 120,
   124, 125, 126, 128, 151

U-Boat, xii
Ultra, 273, 282
Union Club, 107
Usher, Capt Frank, 28, 34, 52,
   251
USSR, 4
Uweinat, 128

VE-Day, 296, 298
Veghel, 281
Veritable, Operation, 291, 293
Versailles, 289
Via Tiburtina, 233
Vichy French, 51, 75
Villers Bocage, 266, 274

Waal, River, 281
Wadi, (arabic 'Valley')
   Gamra, 133, 137, 138, 145,
      147, 148, 149, 150, 151,
      159
   el Gattara, 141, 143, 144
   Halfa, 160
   Natrun, 83
   Sura, 123, 125, 126, 127, 128
Walster, 202, 204
Ward, QMS 'Daddy', 36, 119,
   124, 128, 138, 140
War Office, 31, 51, 274, 288,
   296
Warren, Trumball, 258, 259
Watkins, Gino, 6
Waugh, Evelyn, 35, 37, 50,
   251
Wavell, General, 40, 51, 53,
   140
Wesel, 280
Western Desert, 51, 64, 85,
   137, 245
Western Desert
   Force/Desforce, 40
Western Front, 2, 12
Wey, River, 24
Whistler, Laurence, 175
Whistler, Rex, 23, 245, 276
Whiteley, General, 289, 290
White's Club, 9
Wigram, E.H.L., 6
Wilder, Nick, 132, 153
Wilhelmina Canal, 281
Wilkinson's, swordmakers, 30
Williams, Bill, 173, 282
Wimberley, General, 176
Windsor-Lewis, Col. Jim, 243
'Winter War', The, 2
Woking, 24
Wyndam Aerial, 57, 184

Yalta, 284
Yeomanry, 64, 132, 154
   Middlesex, 202
   Notts, 188
   Scottish Horse, 36
Yugoslavs, 212, 213, 240
Yukon, xii

Zafarana, 59
Zawia (arabic 'school'), 144
Zerzura Oasis, 114, 123
Zieghen, 133
Zonhoven, 282, 289, 293
Zouias, 133
Zuruk, 133